Popular Fronts

# Popular Fronts

## CHICAGO AND AFRICAN-AMERICAN
## CULTURAL POLITICS, 1935–46

## Bill V. Mullen

University of Illinois Press • Urbana and Chicago

Frontispiece: "A History of the Negro Press" (1940, mural) by Charles White.
Reprinted courtesy of the Estate of Charles White. White's award-winning mural
was featured at the 1940 Exhibition of the Art of the American Negro assembled
by the American Negro Exposition in Chicago.

Library of Congress Cataloging-in-Publication Data
Mullen, Bill V., 1959–
Popular fronts : Chicago and African-American cultural politics, 1935–46 / Bill V. Mullen.
p.    cm.
Includes bibliographical references (p.    ) and index.
ISBN 0-252-02440-0 (acid-free paper)
ISBN 0-252-06748-7 (pbk. : acid-free paper)
1. American literature—Illinois—Chicago—History and criticism.
2. American literature—Afro-American authors—History and criticism.
3. American literature—20th century—History and criticism.
4. Afro-Americans—Illinois—Chicago—Intellectual life.
5. Afro-Americans—Illinois—Chicago—Social conditions.
6. Chicago (Ill.)—Intellectual life—20th century.
7. Afro-Americans in literature.
I. Title.
PS285.C47M85    1999
810.9'896077311—ddc21    98-19740
CIP

*For Liz and Max*

# Contents

# Acknowledgments

Bronzeville has a big heart. Many of its people became in the course of my research tutors, colleagues, and friends and opened doors for discoveries that otherwise would have been impossible.

Foremost among those who helped is Dr. Margaret Taylor Goss Burroughs, Chicago's "griot," who frequently became my eyes, ears, and, at times, voice in the creation of this book. Dr. Burroughs's meticulous records and remarkable recall of facts, people, and places were matched only by her generosity in helping me find new truths about a world she both inhabited and created. Her assistance in contacting the artist Elizabeth Catlett and the Estate of Charles White allowed the generous appearance of their artwork in this book. Susan Cayton Woodson was likewise a terrific spirit and knower. With her I met the eminent painter William Carter and learned important information about Fern Gayden, Horace Cayton, and other Chicago artists. Michael Flug, head archivist of the Vivian C. Harsh Collection of the Carter Woodson Library, was a straight-up and tireless guide to the papers of William McBride, Ben Burns, and the "Negro in Illinois" project and a penetrating interpreter of South Side history. Also extremely helpful and supportive of this project were Linda Evans and Archibald Motley Jr. of the Chicago Historical Society, who gave access to and context for the Claude Barnett Papers, a remarkable collection still not done full justice by scholars of black cultural history.

Many other veterans of Chicago's black cultural front provided important help through interviews and written responses to author queries: Gwendolyn Brooks answered letters directly and with concision; Ben Burns was a careful and feisty source of information about the old *Chicago Defender;* Herb Nipson provided important insight into the early days of *Ebony* magazine and the South Side Community Art Center; Ishmael Flory brought forward in living color the days of his own, and his colleagues', Chicago radicalism; Barbara Browning Cordell was magnanimous in providing personal memorabilia and artifacts from the collection of her mother, Alice Browning; Margaret Walker tantalized with spellbinding stories of her early Chicago years. I am also indebted to the Special Collections at the University of Illinois at Chicago, home of the papers of John Walley, and the Kent State University Periodicals Rooms staff, who patiently and ably helped me through eleven years of *Chicago Defender* microfilm.

A number of people have also read drafts of this book, or pieces of it, along the way, each one doing extraordinarily generous service to help make it better. Mark Naison both stoked my fires and threw a much-needed wet blanket over excesses in prose and tangents to my story early on. His ruthless critical eye was equaled only by his enthusiasm and encouragement to finish the task. Bill Maxwell offered sage advice at various stages of the manuscript, showing fabulous attention to important detail and an excellent grasp of what this book wanted to be, and could be. Jim Miller likewise brilliantly rode herd in all the right places, pushing ideas in important directions and never letting the book's racial politics off the hook. Barbara Foley ferreted out moments of linguistic (or political) bad faith while constantly honing my judgments. David Roediger's formal and informal remarks on the proposal and introduction enhanced the book's final draft in important ways. At a very early stage in the research, Alan Wald offered words of encouragement that helped make a single MLA essay on *Negro Story* magazine the genesis of a much larger ambition and idea. Closer to home, Homer Warren provided provocative questions and queries on the book's early portions. Phil Brady's careful reading of the chapter on Gwendolyn Brooks confirmed his greatness as a critical muse. He and Linda Strom also offered deeply felt and deeply appreciated personal support during the writing of this book between and around our friendly games and capers.

The University of Illinois Press also earns my deepest thanks for continuing to play ball with my ideas. I am especially grateful to Karen Hewitt for recognizing the book's potential and urging me to get after the writing, and to Richard Wentworth for the courage to continue bringing radical literature and history to the rest of us who need it. Important institutional support came from the Youngstown State University Research Council, which provided funding for several research trips to Chicago, and the Research Professorship Committee, which awarded one invaluable quarter free for the writing of early parts of this book. My thanks to them and to Peter Kasvinsky for his show of good faith and support. The YSU Media Center was expert in reproducing artwork for publication here. Finally, my deep thanks and appreciation to my Chicago "family" during the research for this book: Fred, Susan, Rico, and Mari Gardaphe, who made space for a tired and heavy head after long days at the library.

Lastly, in celebration of Liz Petrasovic, my best friend and best critic, and of Max, who had better read this as soon as he is able: if this book can capture and reflect their own precocious brilliance and love, it and I will be lucky.

I am grateful to Gwendolyn Brooks for permission to quote from "the old-marrieds," "southeast corner," "patent leather," "the end of the day," "when I die," "the progress," "Queen of the Blues," "Ballad of Pearl May Lee," and "The Sundays of Satin-Legs Smith"; to Ben Burns for permission to quote from correspondence with me and from *Nitty-Gritty;* to the Collection of Dave and Reba Williams for permission to reproduce "Poverty and Fatigue" by William Smith and "Mother and Child" by Elizabeth Catlett; to the Estate of Charles White for permission to reproduce "A History of the Negro Press" and "There Were No Crops This Year"; to the *Chicago Daily Defender* for permission to reproduce "Negro Troops Slaughtered at Savannah" and "Remembering Sikeston, Mo."; and to Elizabeth Catlett/VAGA for permission to reproduce "Negro Mother and Child" and "Mother and Child." Portions of chapter 4 previously appeared as "Popular Fronts: *Negro Story* Magazine and the African-American Literary Response to World War II," *African American Review* (Spring 1996): 5–15.

Popular Fronts

# Introduction

*Now, in this critical war time period, we have our own plans for defense;*
*a plan in defense of culture.*
　　—Dr. Margaret Taylor Goss Burroughs, from a speech written on behalf
　　　of artists of the South Side Community Art Center on the occasion of
　　　its dedication, May 8, 1941

*Discontent is widespread in Bronzeville. . . . That the resentments and*
*discontent do not explode more often is partially due to the existence of a*
*class system within the Negro community.*
　　—St. Clair Drake and Horace R. Cayton, *Black Metropolis*, 1945

"Paul Robeson and Our Cultural Front." So read the headline for the September 12, 1942, *Chicago Defender* editorial on the occasion of Robeson's opening night performance as Othello in Cambridge, Massachusetts. The opening was a crowning moment for Robeson, a fixture in the pages of the *Defender* since his 1939 return to the United States from self-imposed exile to Europe. On the heels of quite different accomplishments—the former's concert hall operas and benefit performances for organized labor, the latter's knockout of Nazi opponent Max Schmeling—Robeson and Joe Louis had become two of the most visible faces and names in the country's leading black newspaper.

As was its wont, the *Defender* saw the Robeson performance symbolically, as a reminder to readers of the larger context of black wartime struggles. It sought to conjure the persistent memory of A. Philip Randolph, whose threatened March on Washington Movement in the spring of 1941 had been the first major national black political strike of the war. Summoning liberals, radicals, and trade unionists together for what threatened to be an all-black march on the nation's capital, Randolph had been credited with forcing Roosevelt to create the Fair Employment Practices Commission to investigate hiring discrimination in wartime industries, and to pass political order 8802 attempting—with very mixed success—to outlaw such practices. The *Defender* editorial was a tour de force attempt to conjoin America's most prominent black radical, Shakespeare's defiant Moor, black America's most credible civil rights advocate, and FDR into a rousing political mosaic:

> Paul Robeson's magnificent Othello in Cambridge, Mass. is a victory for Negro America on the cultural front that can be compared to that great political Order 8802 of President Roosevelt....
>
> Our fight for democracy and full participation in the war effort is on the economic, political and cultural fronts.
>
> Each of these fields is dominated by powerful financial groups who see more profits in the division of peoples along lines of race, creed, color and nationality than they see in national unity. In fact they are seeking to use the prejudices they have brought into being against us as weapons to break unity....
>
> Everywhere we must seek to make a breach in these walls of segregation. The fight on the cultural front is one of the most important.
>
> No one can measure the influence of or evil, of jim-crowism and lynching that "Birth of a Nation" and "Gone With the Wind" have had. We would indeed be a naive people if we did not see in the production of such infamous caricatures of Negroes and distortions of American history the aims to create contempt and hatred of Negroes and incidentally of democracy.
>
> Robeson's Othello puts the stage on the side of progress and democracy. It is a weapon of culture in the fight for equality of opportunity, just as Order 8802 and the Fair Employment Practices committee are weapons of an economic and political character in the same fight.
>
> Our offensive has to be all along these lines if we are to win the war. The battle of ideas is a deadly serious fight. Our Negro artists in every realm of art must recognize this fact.
>
> Hail and more power to Robeson! Let Othello come to Broadway. The Negro artist must get into the struggle for freedom and democracy. Othello is an excellent start against slander, contumely and prejudice in art.[1]

The *Defender* editorial's central trope of a "cultural front" could have in 1942 conjured up a welter of images and ideas as complex as its ideological synthesis. The expression, as Michael Denning has shown, dated at least to 1932, when it was used as the title of a column in the mimeographed *Baltimore John Reed Club Bulletin*.[2] By 1938, it was the title of a column in the Popular Front glossy photo-magazine *Direction,* and a phrase used increasingly by Leftists to connote their insistence on culture as one arm, or front, of a widening campaign for social, political, and racial equality.[3] Indeed this insistence had been central to the Communist Party's shift from its Third

Period policy to the Popular Front. Responding to the international crises of global depression and fascism, the Comintern's 1935 Seventh World Congress had replaced its call for a proletariat-led global revolution with a call for a "Broad People's Front" coalition of liberals, radicals, trade unionists, farmers, socialists, blacks and whites, anti-colonialists and colonized. In an effort to unify this broad constituency, the party simultaneously inaugurated a campaign to promote what it came to call "people's" culture. As Lawrence Schwartz has argued, the Popular Front opening signified that the party "came to accept the notion that there was such a thing as a people's democratic culture; it actually sought to create such a culture as part of the struggle."[4] This turn had inspired the party's 1935 creation of the American Writers' Congress. On June 4, 1937, American Communist Party General Secretary Earl Browder, speaking at the opening of the Second National American Writers' Congress, urged constituents "to defend culture, to unite culture with the strivings of the people to preserve and extend our democratic heritage."[5]

Yet for its black South Side readership in 1942 the *Defender* editorial's call for a "cultural front" would more likely have hearkened memories of the 1936 National Negro Congress attacks against the U.S. culture industry for its negative and stereotypical images of blacks, radicals, and other racial minorities. In that year Chicago had hosted the first NNC, an independent body formed by black and white Communists, liberals, and other radicals in part in response to the CP's 1935 shift to a broad "united front." On February 14, 1936, 817 delegates from 28 states attended the congress representing 585 organizations, including 83 unions and 71 "fraternal" organizations. The opening session drew five thousand people to the broadest coalition of black groups ever assembled. Seven political demands guided the congress: for rights to black jobs at decent wages and the right to join trade unions; relief and security for needy families; aid to Negro farmers; the fight against lynching; the right of youth for education and jobs; equality for women; to oppose war and fascism.[6] These political goals coincided with the congress's stated support for the advancement of black "culture and cultural workers," particularly in the fight against demeaning and stereotypical images in the public arts.[7] In the words of James Ford, the party's 1932 and 1936 vice presidential candidate and a keynote speaker there, the congress meant to undertake the fight against the "retardation of the cultural life of the Negro people by reactionary politics and inferiority doctrines."[8] In 1938, after the opening of what the CP called its "Democratic Front," a further broadening of its Popular Front, Ford reiterated and revised this formulation in keeping with both the spirit of Browder's charge to cultural workers and the specific aims of the 1936 congress. "In general," he wrote, "we must bring about the recognition of the fact that the cultural tradition of the American Negro is basically of the same pattern as the tradition of American democracy in general."[9]

The 1936 National Negro Congress officially inaugurated what the Communist Party U.S.A. hoped would become a "Negro People's Front," an auxiliary to the Popular Front meant to promote a synthesis of communism and black cultural and political work.[10] The *Defender*'s enunciation of "our cultural front" in its 1942 editorial was a reminder of that aspiration six years later, and an emphatic revision. Absent any reference to organized radicalism or the Communist Party, the newspaper editorial claimed for itself the symbols, terminology, and tone of a united front class- and race-based radicalism that had permeated black Chicago since the National Negro Congress. Its dexterous conflation of politics and culture, as well as its call for ideological affiliation between liberals, radicals, and cultural workers, also marked it as a quintessentially Popular Front/Negro People's Front document, despite the "official" termination of that period of policy in Communist history three years earlier. Indeed 1939 was frequently evoked in the newspaper's pages *not* as the year of the Stalin-Hitler pact that signaled the "official" end of the party's Popular Front period, but of *Gone With the Wind.* Supported by the Chicago organized Left, including the Communist Party, the newspaper had created and led boycotts of the film in Chicago theaters when it opened, and reported throughout the war years of attempts by blacks across the country to limit its theatrical release. From 1939 to 1945, the film in fact became in the newspaper's pages a *synecdoche for the world war itself:* a sign of both political and cultural "imperialism" abroad and a more ominous enemy within U.S. borders—namely the alliance between white capital ("powerful financial groups") in Hollywood, and the culture industry.

I begin with this anecdote because it helps to foreground the themes most central to this book. First, the *Defender* editorial challenges and complicates critical accounts of African-American history and U.S. radicalism that view the Popular Front period in American history as cause or antecedent to a collapse in relations between African Americans and American communism. Previous studies by Wilson Record, Harold Cruse, Irving Howe and Lewis Coser, for example, have generally pointed to the Popular Front and the 1939 Stalin-Hitler pact as terminal moments of black-Left alliance that awakened African Americans to the duplicity, manipulation, and totalitarianism of American communism and radicalism.[11] These accounts have relied on cold war models of both Soviet and American communism, and generally deployed dramatic accounts of black anti-Communist severance—the bitter if ambiguous testimonials and writings of Ralph Ellison and Richard Wright, for example—to buttress their claims. With few exceptions, most notably Mark Naison's *Communists in Harlem during the Depression,* Robin D. G. Kelley's *Hammer and Hoe,* and Michael Denning's *The Cultural Front,*[12] historians of the Popular Front have also treated it with patronizing dismissal for its ironic capitulations to mainstream capitalism, and measured their arguments by exclusive focus on white culture.[13] As a result, none have taken under close study the ambitions of the U.S. interracial Left to foster a separate, companion "front" for African Americans: the Negro People's Front. In so doing they have failed to realize what Naison calls the "deep-rooted appeal of Popular Front cultural policies, particularly those relating to the black experience."[14] Indeed, as the *Defender* editorial suggests, and as this book will undertake to show, the Popular Front "survived" notably and indelibly beyond its tenure as official Communist Party policy as a nascent model and inspiration for cultural insurrection created and led by African Americans.

Secondly, and in conjunction, Chicago's selection as a site of this project provides an important occasion for revision of twentieth-century black cultural history generally. The astonishing explosion in black Chicago's cultural scene between 1935 and the end of World War II has been documented in important critical studies by Robert Bone, Carla Cappetti, and Craig Hansen Werner.[15] Yet each has evaded the possibility of widespread radical influence, choosing more conventional and overt marks of its inspiration—like the Chicago School of Sociology, or canonical figures of study like Richard Wright—as their focus. Like traditional scholarship on the U.S. Left, these cultural histories are modestly or severely inflected by an anxious relationship to U.S. radicalism that obscures or delimits their ability to perceive moments enunciated by texts like the *Defender* editorial. As the preceding preliminary sketch of 1930s Chicago history quickly brings into focus, during the Depression and after the city was an important, perhaps even the preeminent site of African-American activism, exchange, and affiliation with the organized Left in America in mid-century. Expanding upon and deepening this preliminary sketch in subsequent chapters, this book will argue that what has been more famously labeled Chicago's cultural "renaissance" of the 1935 to 1950 period is better understood as the fruit of an extraordinary rapprochement between African-American and white members of the U.S. Left around debate and struggle for a new "American Negro" culture.[16] Put another way, I will argue that Chicago's late 1930s and 1940s "renaissance" was one of black and interracial cultural radicalism best described and understood as a revised if belated realization of the Communist Party's 1936 aspiration for a Negro People's Front.

Indeed, the 1936 opening of Chicago's black "cultural front" represented both a culmination and new beginning for African-American engagement of and revision within the U.S. Left. Chicago's cultural "renaissance" and the CPUSA's Popular Front/Negro People's Front, this book will show, were events that were historically mutually constitutive and in many ways unthinkable in separation. From the 1919 founding of the Communist Party USA in Chicago until the 1936 National Negro Congress, Chicago's African-American South Side population was continuously what Harvey Klehr calls a "shining exception" among black American communities in the degree and kind of its response to the presence of American Communism.[17] As early as World War I, South Side African-American radicals imagined Marxism as a tool with which to construct an indigenous local black protest. Joseph Bibb, A. C. McNeal, and William C. Linton, editors of Chicago's militant newspaper *The Whip*, for example, incorporated Marxist-Leninist readings into their Free Thought Society and forums on the South Side in the early 1920s. The society was the genesis of Chicago's chapter of the Marxian African Blood Brotherhood, which attracted a young Harry Haywood into membership in 1922 and later permanently into American Communism.[18] *The Whip* editors deployed their forum discussions in the first significant postwar black economic protest movement on the South Side, the "Don't Buy Where You Can't Work Movement" and "Spend Your Money Where You Can Work" campaigns, whose boycotts and pickets created more than two thousand jobs in Black Belt stores.[19]

*The Whip* forums were among the first in a series of political developments on the South Side in which Marxian politics infused black-led protest or interracial radicalism. In 1925, responding to the widespread appeal of Garveyism to South Side Chicagoans and Harlemites, the Communist Party formed the American Negro Labor Congress, led mainly by former African Blood Brotherhood members whose goal was to build interraciality in the labor movement.[20] In Chicago, the ANLC reflected recognition by the party of the city's fast-growing black industrial labor population created by the Great Migration, and foreshadowed the 1936 congress's stress on coalitionist politics to foster black participation in organized American radicalism. In 1930, in conjunction with a Comintern resolution against "Negrophobia" prompted in part by low black party membership,[21] the CP sponsored the auxiliary League of Struggle for Negro Rights and held in Chicago the founding convention of the National Unemployed Councils. In retrospect, these were crucial chapters in black Chicago and the white-dominated Communist Party's reconsideration and reconstitution of each other. Both represented the gradual moving away from the party's so-called Black Belt Thesis formulated at the opening of its Third Period in 1928, which stressed the right of self-determination for southern blacks.[22] The Unemployed Councils in particular adopted issues and strategies already being undertaken by non-Communist black agencies on the South Side such as the Chicago chapters of the NAACP and Urban Leagues: rent eviction, job discrimination and layoffs, meager public relief, unfair treatment by social service agencies, high rents, and police brutality.[23] The response of South Side Chicagoans to this turn in party emphasis was dramatic and immediate. Blacks soon comprised as much as 21 percent of the leadership and 25 percent of the membership of Chicago's Unemployed Councils and Workers Committees.[24] By the end of 1931, Chicago blacks made up more than half of the one thousand black party membership nationwide.[25] In 1932, African-American James Ford, who had entered the Communist Party through Chicago's ANLC in 1926, helped the Chicago Communist Party attract twelve thousand votes—nearly six times as many as in 1928—for its Communist Party presidential candidate William Z. Foster.[26] Seventeen percent of Foster's votes, over a thousand voters, came from the South Side's all-black second and third wards.[27]

The two-to-one ratio of black Communist votes to black Communist Party members in 1932 is one example of the covert and creative appropriation by Chicago blacks of a Communist presence. Yet the most lasting and foretelling moment of black remaking of Chicago Communism was Bronzeville's response to the 1931 Scottsboro Boys case. On the South Side the burden of the publicity campaign on behalf of the nine Alabama boys accused of raping two white women fell mostly to the League of Struggle for Negro Rights and the new United Front Scottsboro Committee.[28] The "United Front" appellation was intended to foreground interracial solidarity and to invite blacks from all social and economic backgrounds into the Scottsboro protest. The result was a dramatic widening of party popularity and support. Communists were for the first time given opportunities to speak in black South Side churches and black newspapers suddenly lent open support to the International Labor Defense—the party's legal support for the Scottsboro Boys—and the League of Struggle for Negro Rights. Several "united front conferences" allowed the party for the first time to attract blacks from outside its auxiliaries; at one Chicago meeting 285 delegates attended, including representatives from eighteen black churches and sixteen clubs and lodges.[29] In their seminal sociological study of Chicago's South Side, Horace Cayton and St. Clair Drake summed up the early Depression and Scottsboro years relationship of the party and Black Metropolis as follows:

> the Negro masses . . . were not Marxian Socialists dreaming of a Socialist society—they were hungry, frustrated, angry people looking for a program of action. And the Reds had a plan. So Negroes joined the parades, attended the picnics, and fought bailiffs and policemen. As they did so they found white men marching and fighting beside them. Together they carried the signs, BLACK AND WHITE UNITE. . . . Thousands of Negro preachers and doctors and lawyers, as well as quiet housewives, gave their money and verbal support to the struggle for freeing the Scottsboro Boys and for releasing Angelo Herndon. . . . Every time a black Communist appeared on the platform, or his picture appeared in a newspaper, Negroes were proud; and no stories of "atheistic Reds" or "alien Communists" could nullify the fact that here were people who accepted Negroes as complete equals and asked other white men to do so. Some of the preachers opposed the Reds publicly, but remarked privately, "If the Reds can feed the people, let 'em." Politicians dutifully denounced them, but privately admired their spunk.[30]

Chicago's United Front Scottsboro Committee has long faded from public view. Yet its name and success make clear how its interracial cross-class example inspired both the CP's policy of a broad "Popular Front" after 1935 and the possibility of a companion Negro People's Front. Indeed this book will contend that the Popular Front/Negro People's Front in Chicago might best be understood as a climactic "black" moment in the history of U.S. radicalism when African-American political culture actively and willingly engaged, revised, reformed, and deployed "Communism" in a manner generally consistent with official party policy, yet primarily derived from and utilized in relation to the "objective conditions" of life in Black Metropolis. As Robin Kelley has noted of Alabama Communists in this same period, policy and ideas traditionally emanating from Moscow or New York were applied liberally and creatively by both party members and other black and white radicals to existing local problems and conditions in ways that left both remarkably changed.[31]

For example, the leadership and the constituency of the National Negro Congress in Chicago that officially launched Chicago's black Popular Front was a model of both the Communist Party's new inclusivity, and the host city's changing demographics. By 1936 Chicago's South Side comprised the second largest black population in America after Harlem, nearly 250,000 people.[32] While ten of the seventy-five members of the NNC Executive Committee were party members,[33] included among the delegates were black and white Communists, Republicans, union officials, rank-and-file, Democrats, socialists, churchmen, artists, writers, professionals, and businessmen. This broad coalitionism bespoke the manner in which the shift in Communist Party policy from a "revolutionary struggle" to a "People's Front" reflected and responded to many of the emerging strands of South Side Chicago political culture of the mid-1930s. These included the upsurge of black participation in Democratic party electoral politics initiated nationally by Roosevelt's 1932 and 1936 presidential campaigns and locally by the upstart 1934 election of South Side Congressman Arthur Mitchell over Republican hero Oscar DePriest. The significant presence of organized labor at the congress marked the success with which CIO recruiting drives had attracted new interest and new members among Chicago's industrializing black workforce as well as the continuing affiliation of the CIO to earlier radical black incarnations like the League of Struggle for Negro Rights. Of the nearly 70 percent of Bronzeville comprising its poor and working classes during the Depression, the majority of its men were stockyard, steel, and factory workers, while nearly half of its working women were employed as domestics.[34] In addition, the Popular Front/Negro People's Front's appeal to middle-class and upper-class blacks was especially redolent on Chicago's South Side, where a growing black entrepreneurial and professional class sought to attain the literal and cultural capital to become a "player" in democratic capitalism and its culture. *Ironically, the Communist-inspired Popular Front represented for many South Siders at least a symbolic version of this aspiration.* The 1936 National Negro Congress aptly foretold this; its program stressed mainstream political and economic issues like decent wages, education, unemployment insurance, and aid to Negro farmers; included discussion of the needs of black small businessmen, advocated the organization of black consumer and producer cooperation, and even included a "church session" adopting a resolution for black churches to "work out an adequate technique comprehending social and economic problems affecting our group and working with non-Christian groups whose economic and social ideas are of value to the solution of our economic and social problems."[35]

The American Communist Party's 1935 shift in policy toward an expanded "cultural front" with special emphasis on black culture likewise reflected and coincided with an ongoing revision among African-American artists and intellectuals leading a national reconsideration of a black aesthetic and political program. By 1935, Richard Wright, Langston Hughes, and Arna Bontemps,

the three most prominent Chicago-affiliated African-American intellectuals
of their generation, had already firmly committed to a leftward shift in their
writing and political work. In addition, a number of younger, aspiring Chicago-based artists, writers, cultural workers, and intellectuals coming of age
during the Depression were beginning to fashion a political and cultural front
independent of the Communist Party but often symbiotic with its popular
front objectives and aspirations. These included Margaret Burroughs, Fern
Gayden, Alice Browning, Ted Ward, Gwendolyn Brooks, Horace Cayton, St.
Clair Drake, Willard Motley, Charles White, Margaret Walker, Bernard Goss,
and Frank Marshall Davis. By 1936, these figures were sowing the seeds of
Chicago's "cultural front," one that would give birth to a distinctive black
radicalism that relied on an improvisatory spirit of local collaboration, "democratic" radicalism, class struggle, and race-based "progressivism." Between
1936 and the end of World War II, their influence would be felt in and through
the institutions and products that comprised Chicago's black cultural renaissance: Claude Barnett's Associated Negro Press, the first African-American
news agency; the *Chicago Defender,* the leading black newspaper of the period; *Negro Story* magazine, the first magazine devoted to publishing short
stories by and about black Americans. In literature, Wright's short story collection *Uncle Tom's Children* and his novel *Native Son;* Margaret Walker's
poetry collection *For My People;* Gwendolyn Brooks's *A Street in Bronzeville;*
Frank Marshall Davis's poetry collections *A Black Man's Verse, I Am the
American Negro,* and *47th Street;* and Willard Motley's novel *Knock on Any
Door* were all produced between 1935 and 1948. In sociology the well-documented "Negro in Illinois" project of the Illinois Federal Writers' Project, one
of the country's largest and most radical,[36] provided before its 1941 expira-
tion the material for Cayton and Drake's monumental South Side study *Black
Metropolis;* Richard Wright's *Twelve Million Black Voices;* Arna Bontemps and
proletarian novelist Jack Conroy's *They Seek a City.* In the visual arts the Marxian painter Charles White in 1937 became one of the first black painters to
study at the prestigious School of the Art Institute of Chicago. White was also,
along with fellow radicals Margaret Burroughs and Bernard Goss, instrumen-
tal in developing and promoting the South Side Community Art Center, the
WPA-supported center whose 1941 opening culminated one of the largest
Federal Art Projects in the country.

These same cultural workers and cultural institutions also cultivated an
independent brand of radicalism that contested party authority when it
didn't fit their perceived purposes. The Communist Party's retrenchment on
racial equality during the war years—its encouragement of black workers to

support a "no-strike pledge" for example—only intensified the committment of black radicals to carry forward their own fight or "front." Frank Marshall Davis recalls the party's downplaying of racism during wartime in respect for national unity as "an attitude similar in effect to that of conservatives who tried to shoosh anybody who might rock the boat."[37] Describing himself as a "freethinker," Davis writes that he "never uncritically accepted party positions anyway," though he routinely worked with party members and organizations—like American Youth for Democracy—whose spirit of racial equality and inclusiveness he found welcoming. Davis's response is typical of Chicago's black cultural workers, who increasingly as the war progressed assumed a "radical" mantle that included Communist thinking, influence, and affiliation yet that considered itself more politically vanguard, particularly in the fight against racism, than even those supportive "avowed Reds."[38] This was reflected in black Chicago's wartime cultural work, which selectively emulated and revised leadership strategies from the organized Left, merged Communist with black nationalist programs and ideologies, and looked to foster autonomous cultural centers and institutions for progressive interracial work that would create a "new Negro" culture. Indeed, *especially* during the war years Chicago's race radicals created the outlines of a modern African-American mass culture synthesizing ever-changing Popular Front conceptions of "proletcult." In chapter 5, for example, I demonstrate how black radical and progressive writers challenged and reconstituted the marketplace and literary conventions of the short story as a means of remaking the black cultural front. As they did in painting and journalism, black radicals selectively intervened at strategic points that they felt could best foster the birth of a progressive black culture. At its best, this work constituted among the most aesthetically and politically complex black art of the century, challenging the commonly shared assumption that Popular Front art universally succumbed to an ameliorated populist aesthetics or a mawkish sentimentality.[39]

Yet a second important current bearing on Chicago's Negro People's Front is signaled in the pluralization of this book's title. The shift toward "united" interracial and cross-class affiliation among and between whites and blacks during this period also exacerbated increasing black self-consciousness of inequities in Bronzeville's class structure within an already rigid caste and class formation in the United States. This black class differentiation—a crucial subject of Gunnar Myrdal's 1944 *An American Dilemma* and a conceptual center of St. Clair Drake and Horace Cayton's 1945 *Black Metropolis*—was surfaced by widening economic gaps in a period of growing black capitalism and an adjacent explosion of self-reflective "images" of black life. Between 1927 and 1937 black-owned businesses in the retail, wholesale, and service sectors increased by nearly 80 percent in Chicago.[40] Joblessness meanwhile remained high and poverty widespread: more than 50 percent of Bronzeville blacks were on relief in 1934; of those working the majority were in unskilled, manual labor or domestic servitude positions.[41] The resulting increase in class stratification was represented most notably in the growing power and popularity of an expanding, energized black popular press that during the war earned its greatest circulation increases and profits, diversified its advertising and marketing strategies to meet the needs of an expanding black consumer economy, and branched out into nascent media technologies like radio. Ofttimes assimilationist images and organizing strategies of black middle-class life produced by these media were at once complementary to and in conflict with an outpouring of negative or revolutionary images of black poor and working-class life provided by the media themselves, sociological data compiled by academics and WPA researchers, and by both black- and white-produced literature about "the Negro." These competing images of black self-description encapsulated many of the tensions and traumas of socialization attendant to black Chicago's ongoing migration and settlement. Often taking the form of anxieties about "getting ahead" or staying "respectable" in a Depression-ravaged clime, these concerns played out largely in the form of selective social attachment to churches, social clubs, fraternities, and sororities: nearly 95 percent of South Side blacks attended some form of church in the 1930s, while during 1937 almost eight hundred social clubs totaling between ten and eleven thousand members on the South Side reported their activities in the *Chicago Defender*.[42] The complex but important correlation of church and social club membership to social status or "standing" in turn contributed to an increasing sense of cultural stratification (into "high" and "low" or mass culture), and reflected new social forms of conspicuous consumption and an insatiable desire for "upward mobility."

In *Black Metropolis*, St. Clair Drake and Horace Cayton refer to these phenomena under the appropriately diffusive term "fronting."[43] Noting the emergence in the late 1930s and early 1940s of a nouveau riche black entrepreneurial and professional class, the growth to nearly one-third of a tenuously defined "middle class," and the aspirations of a majority described as "strainers" and "strivers" after middle-class status, Cayton and Drake argued that competition for both real and cultural capital drove much of the day-to-day political longing and racial discourse for many in Chicago's South

Side.[44] Indeed Frank Marshall Davis described the challenge and opportunity of Depression and wartime Bronzeville this way: "In Chicago we could dream of some day escaping by climbing over or burrowing under the high walls of the ghetto."[45] Davis's metaphor of enclosure transcended by upward mobility or sub-version contains in microcosm many of the tensions implicit to Chicago's Negro People's Front. Stoked simultaneously by a wave of black capitalist growth and the most accessible and pliable version of Marxian radicalism ever put before it, black Chicago's cultural politics between 1935 and 1946 sustained a precarious tension between climbing and burrowing, between gold-digging and the "grave-digging" work of Marxist-influenced political change and reform. Not surprisingly, these tensions produced not a fixed but a fluid and dynamic black cultural politics toward oftentimes self-conflicting ends. Chicago cultural sites to be studied here like the *Chicago Defender,* the South Side Community Art Center, and *Negro Story* magazine were marked by the participation of Communists, socialists, or fellow travelers who hewed to Marxian or radical politics well into the war years while funded and ultimately controlled by a new breed of "cultural worker" summoned by Popular Front/Negro People's Front radicalism from the black bourgeoisie. Hence a final turn on my title: popular fronts also refers to the routine practice of black and white radicals of disguising, masquerading, or renaming Communist, socialist, or other radical political terms, ideas, and figures under a popular *front*—like a newspaper ad or comic strip, for example—in order to avoid federal political repression sharpening significantly during the war[46] and to appease or compromise with a growing black patronage class whose reputations, social standing, and economic resources seemed imperiled by the forging of revolutionary or even aggressively reformist cultural politics.

These conflicting tendencies resolved themselves in part in the complex relationship of Chicago's radical African-American artists and cultural workers to the postwar period. Here, *Popular Fronts* will both say "yes" and "no" to orthodoxy. The final chapter of this study will demonstrate a tension between rootedness and "exile" for radical black intellectuals and cultural workers caught in the political backlash of Negro People's Front culture wars. In flight from what both Richard Wright and Horace Cayton have called a "no man's land" in reference to the blighted areas of Chicago's South Side, black intellectuals with leftist roots found that "no man's land" to be everywhere once forced to contend not only with McCarthyite repression but the fatal seductions of success and the increasing postwar hegemony (and anti-Communism) of black political culture. In the case of writers to be studied here—

Richard Wright, Horace Cayton, Chester Himes; and to a lesser extent
Gwendolyn Brooks, Willard Motley, and Frank Marshall Davis; and more
peripherally still painters like Elizabeth Catlett, Margaret Burroughs, and
Charles White—tensions between Marxian or radical commitment and personal achievement were often manifest in tortured self-assessment of their
relationship to a new postwar category: the black bourgeoisie intellectual. This
figure, forged in the fire of Negro People's Front celebrity and achievement,
became at best a politically vulnerable figure in the aftermath of the Negro
People's Front, at worst an expatriate from progressive cultural commitment.
And while McCarthyism bears a singular burden for their ostracization or
marginalization, the plight of Chicago's racial radicals can also be understood
as belated versions of Davis's dream of escape from the ghetto: over the wall
into, say, Paris, Hawaii, or Mexico; or underground, at times simultaneously,
into covert political rebellion or *internal* flight. Ultimately, the postwar evacuation, silencing, or muting of Chicago's radical black intellectuals and cultural workers may be read as the culminating moment of the Negro People's
Front period's contradictions, a moment when revolutionary political commitment and *embourgeoisement* could be understood and appreciated for
providing the same thing: a ticket out of "Bronzeville."

*Popular Fronts* is organized into seven discrete chapters and a postscript. Each
is meant to represent a geographical, cultural, and political point on a map
of Negro People's Front Chicago. Cumulatively, the points are meant to con-
vey both the local specificity and the physical and intellectual proximity of
figures, ideas, and events on the South Side between 1935 and the end of World
War II.

Chapter 1, on Richard Wright, challenges American cultural historians to
rethink both Wright's critical reputation generally and his role in Chicago's
cultural and political "renaissance" described in this book. Wright's eminence
in American letters and as a radical American writer has traditionally both
illuminated and obscured important subtleties of black Chicago's political and
cultural formations in the years up to and after his departure from Chicago
in 1937. While he is appropriately credited with helping to build and inspire a
Left-inflected black political culture in Chicago, his own ambivalence toward
the Communist Party turn toward a Popular Front, and his consuming celebrity during and after the war, I argue, have prevented critics from understanding how his career was unique among black intellectuals of this period,
both in his notorious disaffection with Communism and in its symbolism of

tensions and ambiguities in the black cultural front. This chapter thus reads Wright's critical reputation in and through Chicago's own Negro People's Front in these years in order to demonstrate the limitations of ascribing him too much significance as a representative "Chicago" writer and to explain why, and how, he has overshadowed other black institutions, figures, and events there in the late 1930s and early 1940s. It argues that reclaiming a complete history of twentieth-century black culture and African-American radicalism requires reading both against and around Wright's critical legacy.

Chapter 2, on the *Chicago Defender,* argues for the centrality of that newspaper to the creation of black Chicago's "cultural front." The 1940 death of autocratic *Defender* founder and publisher Robert S. Abbott, the chapter claims, allowed his successor John Sengstacke to reimagine the *Defender* and the black press generally as a progressive national political and cultural alliance. Sengstacke moved to replace Abbott's gaudy entrepreneurialism and sensationalist journalistic practices with black cooperative economics and Popular Front-style political coalitionism that included sympathetic coverage of radicals and Communists and their increasing participation as writers and editors for the newspaper. During the war the paper's increasing circulation and political influence also foretold the political and economic direction of Bronzeville, especially the increasing power of its growing middle class. The paper's complex political "radicalism" is reflected in its shifting, often contradictory editorial line in response to events like the 1943 Detroit riots and the end of the war. Ultimately, this chapter contends, the newspaper was the most powerful and influential symbol of Chicago's creative engagement with and appropriation of Negro People's Front-style cultural politics.

Chapter 3 tells the important and under-reported story of the South Side Community Art Center, Chicago's Federal Art Project landmark and the hub of much of its most progressive and improvisatory cultural work. Dedicated in 1941 on the heels of the monumental Chicago Negro Art Exposition, the center was the breeding ground for some of Chicago's most important black cultural workers and interracial alliances: Gwendolyn Brooks, Margaret Burroughs, Charles White, Bernard Goss, and Fern Gayden worked shoulder to shoulder there with white radicals and progressives Morris Topchevsky, Jack Conroy, Peter Pollack, and John Walley, among others, to make the center a flashpoint for experiments in painting, sculpture, writing, and performance. Yet lingering tension and conflicts between its black bourgeoisie patronage and its bohemian Left rank and file over the center's community mission and cultural direction also helped contribute to its splintering and diminution of energies in the postwar period. While still active today, the center reached its peak

of local and national influence and importance during the Negro People's
Front for its risk-taking as an avatar of black vanguard cultural production.

Chapter 4 reclaims *Negro Story* magazine as an important piece of Chicago's radical renaissance. Though it published for only two years, between 1944 and 1946, the bimonthly magazine coalesced much of black Chicago's earlier literary radicalism and helped foreground the short story as a genre for black radical voicing. Coeditors Alice C. Browning, wife to Chicago *Defender* publicity man Charles, and her friend Fern Gayden, a veteran of Richard Wright's South Side Writers' Group, brought entrepreneurial savvy and a distinctively Negro People's Front-style editorial politics to the first magazine devoted to short fiction by and about African Americans. The chapter demonstrates how the magazine borrowed and emulated the strategies of its counterparts in the radical little black and white press of the 1930s, maintaining its emphasis on "proletarian" literature yet stressing racialized wartime experiences, particularly of black women. Supported by black and white radicals like Richard Wright, Frank Marshall Davis, and Jack Conroy, the magazine jump-started the literary careers of a number of prominent postwar writers, including Gwendolyn Brooks, Ralph Ellison, and Chester Himes. The chapter also demonstrates that a "united front" politics cohered the disparate writers and stories under a mask of political neutrality necessitated by wartime surveillance of the black press.

Shifting the emphasis to the cultural politics of genre, chapter 5 describes how the short story became in the hands of African-American writers of the 1930s and early 1940s a tool for altering the trajectory of black culture, especially black periodical culture. Using Cary Nelson's Bakhtinian analysis of the transformation of poetry and poetic reception in the early years of the century, the chapter argues that short stories published in Chicago or by Chicago writers advanced a radical or reformist politics that helped to push American literary and political discourse on race, class, and gender left and the short story stage center in the mid-century reformation of black political culture. Here *Negro Story* is again invoked as an avatar of black entrepreneurial radicalism. The magazine provided space for the most politically daring work of, among others, Ralph Ellison, Langston Hughes, and Chester Himes. Of equal significance, the magazine provided space for literary amateurs and laborers to establish themselves as affiliated cultural workers in the cultural front. The magazine's disappearance from public view, the chapter concludes, is a sign of critical amnesia about progressive cultural work done by African Americans of mid-century lost in the shadows of canonical figures like Wright and more celebrated genres like the novel.

Chapter 6 offers a close reading of Gwendolyn Brooks's 1945 first book of poems, *A Street in Bronzeville,* as a prism refracting the Negro People's Front in dazzlingly original ways. Brooks especially brings to Chicago's radical renaissance an unsystematic feminist skepticism that she turns on both the purveyors of African-American radicalism in Chicago and elsewhere and on the calibrated and self-conscious class structure of Bronzeville. Brooks's much remarked use of irony, it is argued here, is in the service of a progressive politics and poetics forged in the radical ambience of the South Side Community Art Center, where she conceived and wrote early drafts of the book's poems, and through acquaintance with poetic contemporaries like Margaret Walker. *A Street in Bronzeville* is also read as an intertextual response to previous works of male literary radicalism—Wright's *Native Son,* for example—found wanting by the poet for their myopic avoidance of black women's lives, much less their political consciousness. Ultimately *A Street in Bronzeville* and Brooks herself are read into a "radical" literary tradition into which her nuanced and subtle poetic mask, as well as her lifelong public persona, have resisted assimilation.

Chapter 7 examines the sudden and widespread postwar diaspora out of Chicago or underground of its leading race rebels both black and white. The coming cold war, the appearance of McCarthyism, and the increasing economic and political power of Chicago's black middle class and anti-Communists, it is argued, conspired to force the silencing or evacuation from the city of its most progressive individuals and to permanently "liberalize" its leading institutions. Contributing to the waning of black radicalism were the internecine struggles both within the institutional Left (including the Communist Party) and black radical circles. Absent the common goal of the defeat of fascism both at home and abroad and in the face of diminishing political tolerance, Chicago's "united front" cultural politics quickly splintered into both political and personal squabbles over the direction of postwar African-American culture. By 1946, this chapter argues, the general *embourgeoisement* of black Chicago's political culture was foretellable in the editorial shifts of the *Chicago Defender,* the reduction in importance and energy of the South Side Community Art Center, the disappearance of *Negro Story,* and the tailing off of political and cultural work by Chicago's Negro People's Front's organizers and contributors. For these individuals, exile, expatriatism, personal gain, and survival of the cold war became short-term strategies for riding out the backlash against public notoriety and political committment.

Finally, in my postscript, I describe the complex legacy of Chicago's Negro People's Front for race radicals and enterpreneurs of our time.

# 1    Chicago and the Politics of Reputation: Richard Wright's Long Black Shadow

*Honestly, I'm beginning to feel almost respectable! I thought I was radical, but the public is catching up with me, taking everything I give 'em. I got to think hard about that next book.*
—Richard Wright in a letter to Claude Barnett, Feb. 5, 1941

Picture two parades. Parade number one: It is May Day 1936, the annual day of celebration of international workers' solidarity. On the South Side of Chicago the local unit of the Communist Party marches through the streets in unison, singing the "Internationale." In the gutter along the parade route, a twenty-eight-year-old Communist, Richard Wright, sits and watches his unit pass. Moments before, he has been physically removed from the parade by two white comrades who have charged him with "Trotskyite" tendencies. Now he follows the parade on foot before veering off to Grant Park to sit on a bench where, he writes, he can faintly hear a song "floating out over the sunlit air":

> *Arise, you pris'ners of starvation!*
> I remembered the stories I had written, the stories in which I had assigned a role of honor and glory to the Communist party and I was glad that they were down in black and white, were finished. For I knew in my heart that I would never be able to write that way again, would never be able to feel with that simple sharpness about life, would never again express such passionate hope, would never again make so total a commitment of faith.
> *Arise, you wretched of the earth . . .*
> The days of my past, of my youth, were receding from me like a rolling tide, leaving me alone upon high, dry ground, leaving me with a quieter and deeper consciousness.
> *For justice thunders condemnation . . .*
> My thoughts seemed to be coming from somewhere within me, as by a power of their own: It's going to take a long and bloody time, a lot of stumbling and a lot of falling, before they find the right road.[1]

Parade number two: It is August 13, 1938, the day of the annual "Bud Billiken Day" parade in Chicago, named for the mascot of the children's page of the *Chicago Defender*. Thousands of children and their families have come out to see floats, marching bands, and heavyweight champion Joe Louis, and to devour ice cream, candy, and orangeade at the picnic grounds of Washington Park where the parade route ends. Watching the procession pass are black and white luminaries of 1938: Robert S. Abbott, editor and publisher of the *Defender;* Illinois Governor Henry Horner; Chicago Mayor Edward J. Kelly; Illinois Congressman Arthur W. Mitchell; and Chicago's aldermen, its postmaster, and the city's two ranking black police officials. Also among the spectators is a young researcher working under the direction of sociologists Horace Cayton and Lloyd Warner on the Cayton-Warner Research Project, a WPA-supported study of Chicago's South Side. In *Black Metropolis,* the book much of the WPA research would become, Cayton and coauthor St. Clair Drake recount the researcher's description of the parade:

> Among nearly two hundred floats was one representing the Young Communist League. It bore the slogans BLACK AND WHITE UNITE and FREE THE SCOTTSBORO BOYS. On it rode a group of Negro and white youngsters. . . . a wave of applause followed the float along the whole route. Old women shouted, "Yes, free the boys!" People commented: "Them's the Communists. They don't believe in no differences. All's alike to them." Here and there a 100 percent Negro-American would begin to denounce "the Reds," and a little knot would gather around him to argue. A few skeptics sneered: "Them trashy white women on that car don't mean the Negro no good." And some of the teen-age boys whistled and shouted "Hello, honey" at the white girls on the float. In general, however, Bronzeville demonstrated that it approved of whatever the Communists stood for in its mind.[2]

Parade number one, the closing scene of Wright's two-part 1944 *Atlantic Monthly* series "I Tried to Be a Communist" and part two of his autobiography, *American Hunger,* has become a landmark moment in critical understanding of the author's life. According to Wright, it marked his first decisive disaffection with communism, a significant moment in the political life of the most celebrated black Communist author in American history. It has also come to represent the end of the "Chicago" phase of his intellectual and literary career. Though he returned frequently off and on to the city, it wasn't long after the parade (though exactly how long, we will see momentarily, isn't clear) that he left Chicago for New York, then later Paris. The parade is also a singularly powerful moment in his autobiography—the climax of his "youth" in his own dramatic rendering. Finally, the parade scene has become, like Wright himself, representative of a version of black cultural history in which black Americans struggle to find artistic and political voice in relationship to the dictatorial and brutalizing tendencies of the white Left—particularly the Communist Party.[3]

For these reasons, the first parade overshadows the second in accounts of Wright, Chicago, and African-American relations to the Left during the period of the late 1930s. Yet the second parade account may also be used to interrogate the first. For starters, the confluence of elderly women, police officers, and elected officials politely applauding a Communist float in a newspaper-sponsored parade for children suggests a much more varied and complex reaction and relationship to "the Reds" on Chicago's South Side than Wright's account might allow. The second parade route, lined with black working-class and petit-bourgeoisie, sexist males and high-tone women, latent nationalists and pubescent boys—all of whom see the YCL float as representing whatever was "in its mind"—suggests imaginative levels of affiliation, fraternity, and spiritual comradeship Wright's powerful symbolic account of black/Communist schism two years earlier would seem to foreclose. Indeed Cayton and Drake use the parade anecdote as evidence of the success of the Communist Party's "united front" against fascism in Bronzeville during the Popular Front period. Between 1938 and the outbreak of the Second World War, they note, South Side Communists played an increasingly active part in Bronzeville's Left wing that included even Catholic lay leadership.[4] This late 1930s CP popularity reflected a persistent black political memory of party support for black civil rights dating to the Scottsboro case of 1931. Between that event and the numerous Communist-led interracial struggles of the mid-1930s, black support for the *idea* of the party had by 1938, this anecdote suggests, transcended even the baser question of whether or not one called oneself a "Communist"—precisely the strategy party leaders had hoped might result from the opening of its Popular Front and Negro People's Front in 1936.

In addition to providing two vastly different accounts of communism and its relationship to black America, these parades more generally suggest two different ways of interpreting history: as private symbol or public event, psychological drama or social text. These tensions are implicit to attempts to understand Richard Wright and the city of Chicago. The sheer literary force of the May Day Parade account is a reminder of how one of Wright's legacies to African-American cultural history is his successful appropriation *of* the city for the creation of a personal and political myth. Craig Hansen

Werner has argued, for example, that if we "align our perspective with that of Bigger Thomas," protagonist of Wright's most acclaimed novel *Native Son,* writing produced by Wright and Chicago writers of the 1930s and 1940s reveals an "increasing awareness of the city not as promised land but as an unreal wasteland that destroys blacks in particularly vicious ways."[5] Werner suggests that the Chicago of *Native Son,* from the "Wright" angle of vision, becomes, as in parade number one, a powerful symbol of the way modernity's competing "discourses" like Marxism alienate or ruin black intellectual and creative autonomy.[6]

Werner's analysis begs the question of why critics concerned with understanding the political and cultural geography of a city as large and varied as Chicago—or a discourse as complex as Marxism—should peer through the glasses of a fictional character. It also leaves unspoken the dangers of conflating authors with characters, characters with places, places with writers. Yet such a critical conflation has also often been the fate of accounts of Chicago and Richard Wright. Robert Bone, in an important essay devoted to the topic, concluded that Wright was the "towering figure" in a Chicago "renaissance" in literature and politics between 1935 and 1950. Yet Bone's characterization of Wright's relationship to the renaissance and the renaissance itself is shot through with critical conundrums. For example, Bone dates the renaissance's beginnings not with Wright but with Arna Bontemps's arrival in Chicago in 1935 and his work on the Illinois Writers Project. He cites a litany of literary and sociological works produced during the 1935 to 1950 period but fails to show how Wright directly influenced them. He wonders openly how a geographical renaissance can be attributed to a writer who was *absent* from its scene for thirteen of the fifteen years of its duration. Finally, arguing Wright's importance as a "social protest" novelist, Bone undermines his claims for Wright's "influence" on the Chicago scene by claiming that "No sooner had ...Wright supplied them [Chicago writers] with a model than their literary efforts were interrupted by the war."[7]

Carla Cappetti and Margaret Walker have also identified a "Chicago school" or "Wright school" in Chicago during and after the time of his life there, 1927–37.[8] No other single figure is so closely associated with or credited with making a single place in African-American culture. Yet none of these accounts have raised an important question bearing on Wright's Chicago reputation. Namely: how are we to weigh Wright's interpretation of Chicago and his political experiences there when accounts of Wright's relations to and departure from the South Side Communist Party and the city are murky at best? Addison Gayle, for example, notes in his biography of Wright that "two years after he had arrived in New York, he wrote his friend Joe Brown of his decision to leave Chicago. He did not offer his difficulties with the Party as a rationale for leaving. The trip had been germinating in his mind for some time."[9] He also notes that *American Hunger*, the final third of Wright's autobiography, presents a chronology of events that is "confusing." Wright, Gayle writes, "seems to coalesce episodes from his Chicago and New York experiences" in the book, particularly experiences that embittered him to the Communist Party.[10] Similarly, Wright biographer Michel Fabre argues that, "Certain insults and public humiliations that he claims to have suffered in Chicago during the thirties seem actually to have taken place in New York during the forties."[11] Fabre also notes that in a 1959 letter to a newspaper editor Wright claimed he left Chicago for New York in 1936, when he didn't leave, according to Fabre, until Feb. 9, 1937.[12] Finally, the farther Wright moved from Chicago, the nearer he tried to place his break with communism to that disputed moment. Gayle again reports that Wright told a reporter in 1943 that he broke with the party in *1940*, a year he contributed numerous articles to the New York *Daily Worker*, signed an "Open Letter to President Roosevelt" protesting the Dies Committee published in the April *New Masses*, and returned to Chicago to conduct research on *Twelve Million Black Voices*.[13]

The congruent confusion—and obsession—in the Wright record about his "break" from Chicago and his ultimate fall-out with communism suggests that understanding of Wright and Chicago in particular, as well as of black/Left relations in that city in the late 1930s and early 1940s, is still in need of what Bone calls an illuminating "framework and nomenclature."[14] To find one, we might begin by asking what is the connection between Wright's misremembering or misidentification of Chicago with his "permanent" political change of heart, and the critical association of Wright with a "renaissance" described by critics like Bone and Cappetti in that city? One obvious answer is the recurring attempt to erase the impact of political radicalism. Neither Bone nor Werner nor Cappetti addresses communism or radicalism as a significant influence on Wright or Chicago's cultural scene after 1936, the year of Wright's *American Hunger* break, despite the fact that Wright didn't *publicly* break with the party until 1944. Indeed, Bone systematically evades the possibility of radical political influence on Chicago. Attempting to credit Wright with a wave of "social protest" writing in Chicago, he writes that, "The war boom had siphoned off the discontent of the 1930s, but the Wright school persisted as an anachronism";[15] a moment later, this "anachronism" is described as the "peak of social consciousness" in the black novel. Yet Bone's chapter title to describe this supposed "peak" is "The Revolt against Protest: 1940–1952."[16]

How is the "peak" of a literary movement also an anachronism? How can a protest literature be a protest against protest? How can a "renaissance" be so definitively attributed to a figure who doesn't take part in it? How can a time and place—Chicago in the late 1930s and early 1940s—be reduced to a scene in a novel? Finally, how can simple facts and dates, like a man's departure from Chicago, become so patently conflicted? Critical paradoxes of this sort depend on the conscious or unconscious erasure of ideas and history. Common to each of the above critical conundrums is a critical and ideological gap. It is both temporal—the years between the opening of the Popular Front/Negro People's Front and the end of World War II; and physical, namely exclusive from the Chicago scene of *dozens* of other, lesser-known writers, artists, institutions, and cultural workers beyond Wright. Cumulatively, these paradoxes suggest an omission of time, place, and events occasioned by a failure to engage with another critical possibility: that Chicago's "renaissance" so-named was created, led, and sustained by people *other* than Wright who broke neither with Chicago, nor American radicalism, when Wright did.

This book will contend in subsequent chapters precisely the latter. Here, it will argue that the critical gaps and historical inconsistencies in accounts of Chicago's South Side cultural and political scene of the late 1930s and 1940s are largely attributable to the successful erasure of the nature, influence, and practice of radical political thought and culture there. Fundamentally, it contends that the inchoate record of Richard Wright and African-American relations to the Left in Chicago in the late 1930s and early 1940s is best understood as emblematic of conflicts endemic to Wright's (and American cultural criticism's) own evasive relationship to the Popular Front and Negro People's Front. Indeed, Wright's life, politics, and reputation between 1935 and 1946 were shot through with a characteristic Popular Front ambivalence and ambiguity Barbara Foley has called "the felt contradiction between the demands of satisfying a liberal audience on the one hand and calling for the overthrow of liberal capitalism on the other."[17] Largely because of the commercial and critical success of *Native Son,* Wright was absorbed into "progressive" African-American culture during the Negro People's Front even as his own politics became calculatingly evasive and anti-Communist. Put another way, Wright became a symbol of the legitimation of a modern radical black cultural politics mushrooming in cities like Chicago during the war at the very moment he sought to escape forever the confines of his reputation as that symbol. Thus, against his will, Wright became something like the Negro People's Front literary avatar. After *Native Son* especially, Wright's life and work became tools in black Chicago's culture and political wars used both to legitimate black participation in democratic capitalism and to argue against the racist and classist exclusions of black Americans. Rather than leading a Chicago renaissance or literary revival then, Wright more accurately may be described as a sign and symbol of competing public discourses in the creation of Chicago's Negro People's Front cultural front. Wright's, and the critical tradition on Wright's, confusion about his relationship to the Left in this period can be read in part as a result of his attempts to *confuse or escape* his celebrity, which was one of the Negro People's Front's most pressing political stories. Indeed, this chapter will demonstrate how Wright's *public* anti-Communist drift during the war years was more inverse than parallel to the direction of his contemporary artists, writers, and cultural workers on the South Side of Chicago. This book will argue that the South Side's native political and cultural radicalism possibly crested in the very year—1944— Wright was renouncing his American radical allegiances forever. This chapter thus will offer a new reading or "unreading" of Richard Wright and Wright criticism as a necessary preamble to recover not only more accurate perspective on who Wright *was* in late 1930s and early 1940s Chicago, but a multitude of obscured figures, moments, and ideas in the city in its so-called Wright years.

Ambivalence and ambiguity in the record of Richard Wright's relationship to the Chicago Communist Party can be traced to 1935, the year of the international opening of the Popular Front. In that year the Communist-led American Writers' Congress declared the abolition of the John Reed Clubs and the new journal *Left Front*—to which Wright had been a contributor— and announced the establishment of the League of American Writers. Wright's entree into literary radicalism had come through the 1932 formation of the Reed Clubs in Chicago, where he was introduced to the likes of Nelson Algren, Abraham Chapman, and the painter Bernard Goss. In his 1944 "I Tried to Be a Communist" essay Wright claims that the 1935 destruction of the John Reed Clubs was a sign of the party's increasing hostility to the idea of nurturing writers—especially black writers. Yet Wright himself was an initial supporter of the Popular Front. He was one of only two black writers—Langston Hughes was the other—to sign a January 22, 1935, "Call for an American Writers' Congress" published in *New Masses* asking for the creation of a League of American Writers. The "Call" proclaimed that "A new Renaissance is upon the world; for each writer there is the opportunity to

proclaim both the way of life and the revolutionary way to attain it."[18] It also
attacked "white chauvinism," especially against blacks. Wright's retrospective account of his break with the CP in *American Hunger* conveniently erased
his support for the Popular Front opening. His anti-Communist turn thus
requires a more careful scrutiny than it has been given.

The Communist Party's call for a Popular Front and "people's culture"
signaled its recognition that, in northern urban areas like Chicago, coalitionist
politics and more fluid institutional boundaries could better attract a reform-
minded black constituency eager for participation in liberal democratic capitalism. Wright offered his retrospective ambivalence toward this turn in party
policy in his description of his removal from the WPA Federal Negro Theater in Chicago. Wright was transferred from the South Side Boys Club to
the Federal Negro Theater in Chicago in 1936 to work as publicity agent. In
*American Hunger* he recounts his loathing for the work he found the theater
producing, undistinguished plays on conventional themes—the Middle Ages,
for example, "recast . . . in terms of southern Negro life with overtones of
African backgrounds."[19] Wright's disdain for the commonplace Popular
Front strategy of remaking and reshaping "white" Western artifacts to a black
fit, a strategy that reached its peak in Orson Welles's spectacular Harlem
Shakespeare productions of the late 1930s, reveals a commitment to a Third
Period "communism" the Popular Front was deliberately meant to displace.
Attempting to "update" and modernize its Black Belt thesis centering on
black autonomy in the agrarian south, the party simultaneosly invited northern urban blacks to reimagine their own feudal roots in something like an
interracial red carnival embodied by Wellesian-style theater.

In 1936 Wright was not yet ready to make that move. Proudly, he passed
out copies to cast members of Paul Green's *Hymn to the Rising Sun,* a "grim,
poetical powerful one-acter dealing with chain gang conditions in the
South."[20] In *American Hunger* Wright claims he was shocked when a black
actor, a former southern migrant, declared he had never seen southern chain
gangs, called the play indecent, and pleaded with the Jewish director Wright
had himself brought in for a less embarrassing play "that will make the public
love us."[21] The tension in this exchange is emblematic of Wright's dilemma
during the Popular Front period. During the 1930s and early 1940s Wright
sought to document the black experience in a manner that reflected his personal trajectory from southern black boy to radical urban intellectual. Up
until the shift in party policy to the Popular Front, this goal coincided with
the movement's. Wright's avowed preference for Third Period "dramatic
realism" was undermined by the new party aesthetic that tended to subor-

dinate the "roots" of his own southern experience to the integration of black experience into a larger framework of Western culture. Yet Wright's account of the Federal Negro Theater, written after a series of much more hostile encounters with Popular Front and commercial American culture, also contains some exaggeration of that aesthetic's flaws. For example, Wright's equation of the production of the medieval play with black stereotypes of "clowns, mammies, razors, dice, watermelon and cotton fields" is at best implausible— no Federal Negro Theater project on record was ever so retrograde.[22] Wright's insistence that the black cast was "scared spitless" is also used to mark them as "children [who] would never grow up," an image fitting into a crudely conspiratorial portrait of unsuspecting rank-and-file blacks as lackeys under party hands.[23] Wright's account of this event, given retrospectively, is at best suspect and indicative of a selective political memory characteristic of his written recollections of the Popular Front era.

Arguably Wright's formation of the Chicago South Side Writers' Group in the same year of 1936 was another strike against the party line shift on culture after 1935. In an attempt to resurrect the spirit and structure of the disbanded John Reed Clubs, Wright called together a close circle of aspiring black writer friends to meet and discuss—cadre style—their work and its relationship to American culture at large. In April 1936 the playwright Ted Ward, Robert Davis, Edward Bland, Russell Marshall, Fern Gayden, Dorothy Sutton, the essayist Theodore Bland, Julius Weil, Barefield Gordon, Frank Marshall Davis, and shortly thereafter Margaret Walker formed the incipient group where Wright was to read several stories that would appear in *Uncle Tom's Children*. Out of the writer's group came its most important early manifesto "Blueprint for Negro Writing," published in *New Challenge* in 1937. Citing Lenin, Wright notes that oppressed minorities "often reflect the techniques of the bourgeoisie more brilliantly than some sections of the bourgeoisie themselves."[24] Wright saw this manifested for black Americans in the difference between their two primary sources of culture: the church and folklore. The latter includes folk music, spirituals, and the blues and is "unwritten and unrecognized"; the former is "for the sons and daughters of a rising Negro bourgeoisie, parasitic and mannered."[25] Much of "Blueprint" is taken up with this divide. Negro "nationalism" resides in both the folkloric and the black social institutions that are the exclusive channels for black identification. Negro writers must transcend this nationalism while keeping an eye to the status of blacks as proletarians in an American and global capitalist order. At the same time, they must recognize in black folk culture the "complex simplicity" that resides also in the works of Western classic authors like

Gorky. Ultimately, the black writer must construct a politics out of the usable remnants of this hybrid culture:

> The ideological unity of Negro writers and the alliance of that unity with all the progressive ideas of our day is the primary prerequisite for collective work. On the shoulders of white writers and Negro writers alike rest the responsibility of ending this mistrust and isolation.
>
> By placing cultural health above narrow sectional prejudices, liberal writers of all races can help to break the stony soil of aggrandizement out of which the stunted plants of Negro nationalism grow. And, simultaneously, Negro writers can help to weed out these choking growths of reactionary nationalism and replace them with hardier and sturdier types.[26]

Wright's program both echoes and significantly departs from aspects of the post-1935 Left. Its emphasis on a *cultural* program for social change echoes the Popular Front conversion to a broad-based and fluid front well beyond inner party circles. Similarly, its appeal to interracial alliances echoes both the Left's increasing internationalism and its attempts to move beyond separatism marked by earlier Third Period pronouncements on the "Negro question." By calling for a coalition of liberals and radicals Wright also seemed in-step with the party's new ethos.

Yet Wright clearly gives no quarter in the essay to black or northern mass and popular culture. The church, Negro middle class, and petit bourgeois are conjoined as symptoms of cultural and political malaise, a no man's land poised between the "authenticity" of the black folk and the intellectual fluency of Western literary giants. Yet it was precisely in this "no man's land" that the Popular Front/Negro People's Front would attempt to take root and where Chicago's black culture wars would largely be fought up through the 1940s. In northern urban centers like Chicago, black churches, social organizations, unions, women's clubs, media outlets, fraternities, and small businesses all became targeted centers for the proliferation of BLACK AND WHITE—UNITE AND FIGHT slogans. It was in part for this reason that the party had inaugurated the Negro People's Front in Chicago by creating the National Negro Congress.[27] And as Wright would also have known, the congress was not the only political force in 1936 seeking to expand and consolidate its South Side constituency. What Horace Cayton and St. Clair Drake call the city's "safe leaders"—middle- and upper-middle-class churchgoers and businessmen—countered the formation of the NNC that year with their own Council of Negro Organizations. The council intended not only to block the congress but to seize control of all of Chicago's social organizations. By the late 1930s, it listed as its affiliates fifty-seven organizations representing more than one hundred thousand people. Only nineteen were civic organizations; ten were social clubs, six fraternities and sororities, ten were church groups, six were labor unions, and five were technical and professional societies.[28] By 1938 the council was itself "organizing demonstrations in the proletarian style,"[29] demonstrating for better housing conditions, black school board members, and black-owned businesses. From 1938 until the outbreak of the war, the council had become, along with the NAACP, a "respectable" venue for black protests against discrimination and for black employment in industry.[30] The struggle for control of the soul of the South Side between the more vanguard, if ecumenical NNC and the reformist CNO symbolized a political divide in black Chicago loosely analogous to the cultural one Wright had identified between the folk and church: between Chicago's vast majority working-class and poor and its smaller, more efficiently organized and better-funded petit bourgeoisie. From his 1937 position of lingering Third Period militancy, Wright might well have been suspicious of *both* groups' attempts to remake Chicago political culture.

Wright left the city a little-known leftist writer when he headed for New York some time in 1937. Indicative of his marginal status, and perhaps also of Chicago's parochialism, the *Chicago Defender* ran no review of *Uncle Tom's Children* after its March 1938 publication. Yet the book was widely reviewed in both mainstream and Left media. Critical praise ran from *Time*'s patronizing applause that Wright might become the first "first-rate Negro novelist"[31] to Granville Hicks's *New Masses* proclamation that "the revolutionary movement had given birth to another first-rate writer."[32] In addition to the uniqueness of a black Communist writer winning critical praise and commercial popularity among both the white commercial press and its most radical white and black Left, however, publication of *Children* complicated Wright's life and reputation in other ways. For one, it made Wright a target of the newly formed Dies Committee. For another, it began what would become a running feud with black women and black anti-Communists. The most scathing attack on *Uncle Tom's Children* was Zora Neale Hurston's. In the *Saturday Review of Literature*, she attacked the melodrama in each of the four stories, targeting the "wish-fulfillment theme" of black male revenge and the narrow portraits of black women. She also worried the book's violence: "There is lavish killing here, perhaps enough to justify all male black readers."[33] Most damagingly for potentially conservative black Wright readers,

Hurston played the red card: "Mr. Wright's author's solution, is the solution of the PARTY—state responsibility for everything and individual responsibility for nothing, not even feeding one's self. And march!"[34]

Hurston's review was fueled both by resentment at Wright's earlier negative review of her own *Their Eyes Were Watching God* and ideological differences beyond the scope of this chapter over the value of the southern experience in African-American literature and culture. Yet it is also significant for demonstrating the symbolic critical burden Wright would bear in the early years of his popularity. Wright's obvious potential (or in Hurston's eyes, threat) to become the Great African-American Writer made him for better or ill a "race man" in black letters.[35] The designation carried with it the requirement of total dedication to the betterment of black Americans through firm commitment to "self-improvement," race pride, and accountability to virtually all constituents lumped under the politically vague euphemism of the "race." In short, the "race man" designation was an institutionalization of northern black middle-class norms meant to suggest a progressive gentility associated with the best of New Deal liberal culture. Hurston's review for the genteel *Saturday Review of Literature* implicitly deployed these standards to hang Wright. The violence, Marxism, and occasional gothic overheatedness of Wright's book hardly conformed to the figure of moderation suggested by the "race man" conception. Hurston's review also demonstrated that if Wright was going to market black radicalism, he was going to have to contend with hostile consumption by readers across a vast political spectrum in cities like Chicago. It was not the first—or last—time Wright would face the test of these standards, which were emboldened and spread by the increasing prosperity of the South Side community in the early war years. Indeed this prosperity coincided with and was ironically symbolized by Wright's own success after publication of *Uncle Tom's Children,* making him an even more easily appropriable sign and symbol of Chicago's deepening class and culture wars as his career moved forward.

The two largest advertisements on page six of the March 30, 1940, *Chicago Defender* were serendipitously set side by side. On the left was an in-house ad for Richard Wright's new novel *Native Son.* A blurb by Lucius C. Harper, editor of the newspaper, described the new Book of the Month Club selection as the "Best novel ever written by a Negro novelist." The ad included a "Native Son" coupon, which readers were encouraged to clip out and send to the *Defender,* along with $2.50, to receive their copy of the book. To the right of the ad was a recurring one in the *Defender's* 1940 pages for the new model Frigidaire six-cubic-foot refrigerator.[36]

The ad was the first mention of *Native Son* in the pages of the *Defender* since its publication. Its March 1 appearance had been overshadowed in Chicago by the death of *Defender* founder and publisher Robert S. Abbott, a story receiving serial front-page coverage for weeks afterward. Wright's debut in the paper's pages as a best-selling Negro literary superstar—the Frigidaire of 1940 African-American writing—completed the author's curious circle from nascent critic of American mass culture to one of its emerging icons. As many critics have noted, *Native Son* had borrowed heavily from newspapers and lifted references and techniques from movies, magazines, and popular music in part to damn the allure, particularly for poor urban blacks, of a viciously stereotyping consumer culture.[37] Yet by the time the March 29 *Defender* ad ran *Native Son* had already become the first African-American blockbuster, selling two hundred thousand copies and becoming a number one best-seller.[38] Nationally, the Left and mainstream press again competed for accolades toward the novel. Lewis Gannett in the *New York Herald Tribune* was one of dozens of critics to favorably compare it to 1939's literary sensation *The Grapes of Wrath; Time* magazine, echoing its left-handed patronization of *Uncle Tom's Children,* praised the story of "bad nigger" Bigger Thomas as a book "only a Negro could have written," adding that "until now no Negro has possessed either the talent or the daring to write it."[39] Malcolm Cowley in the *New Republic,* noting the book's roots in the proletarian novel of the 1930s, also compared it favorably to *Grapes of Wrath.* Meanwhile C. L. R. James, in a May 1940 review titled "Native Son and Revolution," cut straight to the heart for Marxist readers: "The book . . . is not only a literary but also a political event," he wrote. "The career of Bigger Thomas is a symbol and prototype of the Negro masses in the proletarian revolution."[40]

In Bigger Thomas's hometown, response to *Native Son* took a more parochial and complex form. While the *Defender* was quick to advertise and facilitate sales of the book, it broke its custom for new titles by black writers by not publishing a review. Instead, the first "reaction story" to the book was a five-inch item on page 7 of the May 25, 1940, edition titled "Says 'Native Son' Fails Its Purpose." The story reported that more than one hundred guests attending the second annual musical tea of the Youth Association for the Advancement of Colored People were treated to a "review" of *Native Son* by George R. Dorsey, "noted sociologist and teacher." Dorsey praised the novel's action and its accurate portrait of living conditions on the South Side of

Chicago, but complained that the book "failed to get the reader's sympathy for its leading characters." Dorsey also seconded a review by Lilian Johnson in the *Baltimore Afro-American,* a *Defender* competitor, claiming she "hit the nail on the head when she said that we need more writers like Richard Wright, but we do not need more novels like 'Native Son.'"[41]

Three weeks later, the *Defender* ran a longer story reporting that Dr. Julius Caesar Austin, pastor of the enormously influential South Side Pilgrim Baptist church, had dedicated the entirety of his June 9 sermon the previous week to Wright's new novel. Under the subheading "Attacks Native Son" the story reported that Austin, "apparently blazing from conflicting emotions set afire" by Wright's novel, ministered to the congregation of 2,500 thusly:

> Mr. Wright has written one of the most powerful novels I have ever read, and I praise God for the ability, imagination, mastery of language, beauty of rhetoric, diction displayed by the writer. . . . Had such a book been written when Harriet Beecher Stowe wrote *Uncle Tom's Cabin,* we would have remained in slavery, and *Native Son* is accepted and endorsed by this same society against which he endeavors to write because they see played up in it accusations against the Negro whose greatest desire for freedom and everything else is consummated in his association with white women. . . .
>
> If Corrigan, who flew the wrong way, can rise from poverty to power; if Lindbergh, who was called the flying fool, can become a messenger of goodwill and peace; if Frederick Douglas [*sic*] can rise from slavery to be America's greatest orator; if Toussaint L'Ouverture can become the hero of Haiti; Richard Allen become the founder of the A.M.E. church; Booker T. Washington the wizard of industrial education, and Robert Sengstacke Abbott, who walked the streets of Chicago in poverty can give the world its greatest race organ for human expression of freedom, it is possible for every Negro boy and girls [*sic*] to overcome the restrictions of race prejudices, and surmount obstacles, not by reason of advantages and in spite of handicaps and make a contribution.[42]

The Austin sermon keynoted "Chicago Defender Day" at Pilgrim Baptist, symbolizing the paper's alliance with the black church in the battle against social deterioration on the South Side. In the week following its in-house ad for *Native Son,* for example, the newspaper carried a page-one banner head, OPEN WAR ON KID GANGS, reporting that the city planned to hire youth workers to encourage unemployed Chicago adolescents to associate themselves with the South Side YMCA, YWCA, South Side Boys Club, South Side Settlement House, or Boy or Girl Scout Troops.[43] Three weeks later the newspaper would report, in a tone and style quite different from Wright's novel, on a gun war between boy toughs: "Sunday night two young hoodlums took time out from their regular routine of beating defenseless school students and robbing errand boys, and staged a shooting scrape between themselves at Forty-seventh street and Vincennes avenue"—a site just blocks from the home Wright had purchased for his family in February 1940 and not far from the mean streets of Bigger Thomas.[44]

The complex context created by the Austin, Dorsey, and *Defender* "sermons" and ads for *Native Son* bespeak myriad ways in which black South Side Chicago constructed a reaction to and identity for itself both beholden to and abhorrent of the implications of Wright's novel. Churches and newspapers of South Side Chicago 1940 from which a novelist like Wright would invariably draw his readership, for example, were anything but monological during the Popular Front. Though generally conservative, churches were also centers of free speech where bulletin boards were just as likely to list a meeting of a left-wing labor union or even of Communist organizations as a meeting of an American Legion post.[45] The *Defender* likewise preached a complex ideological line to readers, both promoting Communist support for black civil rights while providing boosts for the creation of black consumer groups like the Illinois Housewives Association.[46] *Native Son* provided a site where these Negro People's Front ideas and social currents could be played out, dramatized, and evaluated. At once combining proletarian realism, a Marxian analysis of American capitalism, and a brutal depiction of black urban poverty with Hollywood-style courtroom drama and page-turning melodrama generated by Wright's love for and emulation of American "true crime" detective stories, the novel and its commercial success adumbrated black aspiration and anxiety over tensions between gradualism and radicalism, cultural immersion and cultural revision, racial marginalization and racial legitimation, capitalist jouissance and capitalist despair.

Wright's and the novel's endless spin-off successes and notoriety in the immediate wake of its publication likewise suggested for Chicagoans the dizzying range of these possibilities. Immediately after its March publication Wright began his research into the book that would become *Twelve Million Black Voices;* signed a contract with John Houseman and Orson Welles for the stage production of *Native Son;* visited North Carolina to begin work with Paul Green on the stage adaptation of the novel; met with Jack Conroy and Nelson Algren to launch the Left magazine *New Anvil;* was elected vice-president of the Popular Front League of American Writers; was elected vice-president of the American Peace Mobilization, a Communist-sponsored group opposed to U.S. intervention in World War II, and saw Harper reissue *Uncle Tom's Children* with the addition of "Bright and Morning Star" and "The Ethics of Living Jim Crow." Wright's 1940 success was symbolically capped off by his selection as winner of the NAACP's Spingarn Award, which prompted Wright's February 1941 letter to Barnett on his newfound "respectability." The letter simultaneously demonstrates both Wright's amazement at just how popular the Negro "popular front" had become and how the most radical messages in his own work had pushed the black cultural front forward. The letter's subtextual anxiety about these same phenomena could only have deepened when, in the same month, rehearsals for the New York stage production of *Native Son* began. The play received generally glowing reviews with the exception of the anti-Communist Hearst press, catapulting Wright in front of an entirely new audience. Yet the play also reflected a tendency for his own adoring black fans to succumb to what Wright called elsewhere with disdain the "restlessness, the crazy fads, the inescapable loneliness . . . and the whole dismally lowered tone of American personality expression."[47] Much of the New York cast remained when the play moved to Chicago in the fall, most notably Canada Lee as Bigger. Al Monroe reviewed the play glowingly, noting its superiority to retrograde race dramas like "The Green Pastures."[48] Yet for black Chicago theater goers—particularly of the petit bourgeoisie—the play's deeper significance was as a cultural wagon to hitch their social star. In December 1941, the same month as the release of the Okeh Record album featuring "Joe Louis Blues" with music by Count Basie, lyrics by Wright, and vocals by Paul Robeson—arguably Wright's consummate Popular Front project—*Defender* entertainment pages were larded with accounts of the splash made not by *Native Son* the book or play but by its Chicago *cast* on the South Side night-life circuit. Charles Christian, host of the popular Plantation Cafe, hosted the entire cast during the first week of December, as did Ruby Henderson, president of Chicken Shack, Inc., the South Side's most successful fried chicken business, the following week; on Dec. 20 the *Defender* announced a Christmas party at the Pioneer Club with Canada Lee and the cast of the play, while the January 3, 1942, edition announced a private party at the "Edward Harrises" with Lee and the cast. By the end of 1943, Lee had become in *Defender* headlines synonymous with the play and its main character: "Bigger Invades Hollywood" announced a *Defender* headline when Lee earned a breakthrough role in Alfred Hitchcock's *Lifeboat* in September of that year.[49]

Native Son's and Wright's seeming inexhaustibility as avatars of the black "cultural front" perhaps reached its defining moment in September 1941 when Oscar Micheaux, the popular black filmmaker, broke generic form by releasing his first novel titled *The Wind from Nowhere.* Based on the story of Martin Eden, the novel was advertised in the *Defender* under the intentionally shocking copy: "HAS THE NEGRO A CONTEMPORARY LIFE? 'NATIVE SON' gave you a sordid, vicious and distorted picture of him. Now try reading the romantic and amazingly different side."[50]

Micheaux explained his decision to write the novel as a desire to find a black book that would make a film "to be shown after the fashion of 'GONE WITH THE WIND.'" He had already rejected *Native Son* as the basis of a photoplay. *Native Son,* he wrote, was

> easily the most sensational, greatest and biggest in point of sale, of any novel ever written by a Negro. If you read "NATIVE SON" and try to picture all its vile horror, its sordid and distorted preamble of hatred, expressed in the words and actions of Bigger Thomas, moving across the screen then picture what the Chicago Board of Censors, and all the other many Boards of Censors; the Will Hays office, and the National Board of Reviews report would be after a screening of "NATIVE SON" as it reads in book form, made into a picture. That report would read: "Rejected in toto!"
>
> If, on the other hand, that which made it interesting and popular, was left out, and it would most surely have to be left out, there'd be nothing left to film.[51]

Micheaux's argument shows the extent to which his contemporaries would and did use Wright's novel to measure the parameters of the cultural front for black artists. Caught between the retrograde embarrassment of Margaret Mitchell and the commercially unsuitable Marxian politics of Wright's own novel, Micheaux's appraisal of the book dovetailed significantly with Hurston's review of *Uncle Tom's Children* and the Reverend Dr. Austin's sermon on *Native Son.* Its avowedly "centrist" politics, though built on commercial rather than feminist or Christian precepts, transformed the book into the vanguard text of a new black cultural commerce that could duplicate *Gone With the Wind*'s box office if not its racial message. Yet the conflation of the racist icon with the economic imperatives of a new black cultural capitalism demonstrated that the book itself had helped to inaugurate a kind of political bad faith. "Misreadings" of the Micheauxian variety were not only not uncommon but inevitable given the numerous readings available in the text of *Native Son,* as its critical reception had proven, and the dialectical debate within the black public sphere about the political utility of negative images of black life. Arguably, this conundrum was the subtext not only for Wright's 1941 complaint to Barnett, but the "next book" he promised to and did write.

In late 1941 Wright completed his draft of "The Man Who Lived Underground," excerpts of which were published in *Accent*. The story derived directly from Dostoyevksy's "Notes from the Underground" and was the most experimental and commercially inaccessible piece of writing he had done for publication since his early 1930s radical poetry. Gone were any hints of detective-story racial melodrama or "sordid" details of ghetto realism; in its place was an existential nightmare bankers' daughters (or black filmmakers) not only wouldn't weep over but likely wouldn't dare to film. The story's imagination of a black fugitive trapped in an allegorical underground successfully failed to excite Left critics who dismissed the story's abandonment of "social realist" principles.[52] Its philosophical pretensions and relatively "marginalized" publishing status also successfully kept it from the purview of readers of Wright's previous best-sellers. The story's calculated failure to subscribe to Wright's prior political themes and literary strategies was thus one interpretation of his black everyman's fugitive existence. Wright was figuratively in hibernation from his own success and its concomitant appropriations. Indeed the story was the *only* new piece of fiction Wright published between the reissue of *Uncle Tom's Children* in 1941 and publication of his autobiography in 1945. It was also the last major piece of fiction he was to write on American soil, excluding the expanded version of the same story published in Edwin Seaver's 1944 *Cross-Section* anthology. Given this, "The Man Who Lived Underground" illuminates Wright's 1941 complaint about readers "takin' everything he could give 'em" as a portentous lament about his own literal and figurative "consumption." In 1948, Wright wrote, "The Right and Left, in different ways, have decided that man is a kind of animal whose needs can be met by making more and more articles for him to consume."[53] By late 1941, Cross Damon, existential hero of Wright's 1953 novel *The Outsider*—the story "Underground" would become—already loomed over Wright's shoulder as the figure who could move him beyond the ideological and philosophical contradictions, conflations, and appropriations not just of American communism but of the political and commercial ironies of the black cultural front.

By 1942, according to Arnold Rampersad, Wright had "quietly" broken with the Communist Party over its refusal to press racial reform during wartime and its reputed attempts to "control" his work.[54] In 1943 Wright began work on *American Hunger*, the autobiography that would cast a plague on the houses of both the CP and the "lust for trash" of American consumer culture. Significantly, this period also coincided with Wright's attempts to retrofit his life and work to the Chicago school of sociology. Wright's connections to the Chicago school were initiated as early as 1936 in his research for the WPA. In 1940, Wright had begun a long friendship with Horace Cayton when the two toured the South Side for the first time so that Wright could compile notes and information for use for *Twelve Million Black Voices.* During his period with the New York Communist Party, Wright and Cayton routinely argued over the validity and significance of Marxism as a solution to black American social problems. After 1942, Wright increasingly identified himself as a *lifelong* adherent to the Chicago school, and to sociological orientation generally, in order both to shed his "Marxist" label and to reconstitute his racial identity in something deeper than its contemporary "notoriety." He dedicated himself to helping Cayton and Drake publish their masterwork *Black Metropolis,* and lent public support and praise to Gunnar Myrdal's liberal manifesto *An American Dilemma* when it was published in 1944. Both books—Myrdal's in particular—rejected Marxian analysis as a solution to the country's race problems. Attaching himself to Parksian or liberal sociological study of the black experience also allowed the upwardly mobile literary and commercial New York superstar to resurrect his lumpenprol roots and his identification with Chicago without revisiting his Marxist past there. By 1945 Wright was adamantly insisting on his life experiences as sociological case studies best interpretable almost *exclusively* through the lens of Chicago-style sociology. Not just *Twelve Million Black Voices* but *Native Son, Uncle Tom's Children,* and *Black Boy* were all books inspired in small or large measure, Wright wrote in the 1945 introduction to *Black Metropolis,* by the "scientific findings of men like the late Robert E. Park, Robert Redfield and Louis Wirth."[55] Writing of this adoptive strategy vis-à-vis *Black Boy,* published in 1945, Carla Cappetti has noted that Wright "was able to make that story representative both of the specific experiences of Black migrants and of the more general facts of 'social life' and 'human nature' in modern society. It is in this light, as both participating observation record and representative case history, that Wright's autobiography, written at such an early age and interrupted before his move to New York and concurrent fame, becomes clearer. By the time he was living in New York his life had become far from representative: it had become exceptional."[56]

Wright's retroactive and retrospective sociological masking of both his red roots and his black "exceptionalism" can be seen as final stages in his gradual disengagement with both American communism and the broadscale popular reformation of black cultural politics during the Popular Front/Negro People's Front. Indeed Wright's reformulation of his own political and cultural "personae" to shed them of the conflicts, appropriations, and cooptations endemic to his writing and reception between 1937 and 1943 necessitated the creation of a mythic moment prior to it, or as near as possible, that could define the beginnings of his new autobiographical self-image as a migrant hero wise to contradictions of both modern Marxism and the commercial tendencies of American life. That moment was his remembered 1936 break with the Communist Party in Chicago that began this chapter. The consequent confusions in Wright's writing about the time and place of events—New York or Chicago, before or after his break with communism—are reflections of strains in Wright's own attempted revision of his relationship to history. The subsequent articulation of a "Wright school" of influence in Chicago—one Wright interestingly never claimed credit for—bears these signs as well. Wright is thrown into "representative" relief, while Chicago's renaissance is cast as comprised primarily of remnants of Wright's earlier "leftism" prior to 1936 and his "sociology" after 1943. "Wright school" theories have also ignored evidence that during the years of an alleged renaissance in black writing in Chicago white liberal writers—rather than black or left ones of either race—most benefited from and were influenced by Wright's critical and commercial success. Between 1940 and 1943, with the exception of J. Saunders Redding's *No Day of Triumph,* Wright's *Twelve Million Black Voices,* and Margaret Walker's *For My People,* no significant work by a black writer—or black Left writer—was published. Wright's influence on Redding's autobiography was obviously negligible; Walker clearly idolized Wright from the moment of her 1936 meeting with him, but her first book of poems was written in an entirely original voice and different genre.

In 1947, *Defender* columnist and ex-Communist Earl Conrad proposed that *Native Son* had actually *discouraged* publishers from addressing the "Negro-white situation" by addressing social phenomena that neither white editors nor publishers were fully ready to touch.[57] Conrad's argument had in fact been raised before, in September 1943, by *Chicago Defender* book columnist, editor, and white radical Ben Burns. In an installment of his weekly book column entitled "Wanted: Negro Authors," Burns noted the commercial success of two recent books about blacks, a biography of George Washington Carver and Roi Ottley's *New World A-Coming,* a survey of Harlem's political culture. Burns cited forthcoming title lists to demonstrate that the success of the books was leading to a "flock of fiction and non-fiction" about the "Negro problem," *almost all of it by whites.* Sterling Brown's *A Negro Looks at the South* was the lone black-authored title on major publishing lists, which included *Brown Americans* by Edwin Embree, president of the white liberal philanthropic Rosenwald Fund; *Strange Fruit,* Lillian Smith's anti-lynching novel; *Race and Rumors of Race* by Howard W. Odum, head of the University of North Carolina School of Anthropology, and Earl Conrad's biography of Harriet Tubman. Of these white authors only Conrad had radical credentials.[58] Nearly two years later, in February 1945, Burns would repeat the lament, this time noting the absence of blacks (and prevalence of white liberals) on the spring 1945 publishers lists, which included books again by Lillian Smith, Howard Fast, Henrietta Buckmaster, Ralph Korngold, and Edwin Embree. Of this list only Fast could claim a politics as near-left as Burns's own. "Nothing in the way of books," wrote Burns, "came from Richard Wright, Langston Hughes, W. E. B. Du Bois, Zora Neale Hurston, Walter White, J. Saunders Redding or Roi Ottley."[59]

Burns's impatience with the publishing industry attested to a failed opportunity for the full-scale revolution in black writing Wright's first two books had seemed to anticipate. This frustration crested in his March 3, 1945, review of Wright's new major work, *Black Boy.* For some months prior to its publication Burns had noted both the delays in its publication and the titillating advance publicity for the autobiography. More than once he cited the advance "leaked" news that the book would explicate even further Wright's now public "break" with communism that had constituted the heart of his 1944 *Atlantic Monthly* essays "I Tried to Be a Communist." No disinterested party himself, Burns teased readers in his January 27, 1945, column that "Wright has promised to whack thoroughly all and sundry in his Book-Of-The-Month Club selection and early reports on his work indicate that there will be many critics who will be reciprocating. Wright has already stated that he expects 'the race' to be mad about his frankness."[60]

The publicity machine for African-American radical political culture that Wright had nearly single-handedly inaugurated was coming full-circle in eerily self-consuming fashion. Advance publicity for the book hinged on Wright's "break" with his two formative constituents of the 1930s—blacks and white radicals. Thus by 1945 Wright's life was taking on the self-conscious shape of the serial political potboiler conveyed in the Hollywood-garish title of his *Atlantic Monthly* pieces. Ben Burns's *Defender* review of *Black Boy* rose to the bait set by the advance notices on the book. His first sentence—"When Richard Wright writes, he commands perhaps the widest white audience of any Negro author today"—foretold the review's unhidden agenda of proving *Black Boy* as Wright's "sellout" and deliverance to a false literary consciousness. The book was a "study in sadism," a "startling, shocking and sometimes weird series of autobiographical episodes." Because of his racial exclusion in the

South, Wright had become "a self-centered anti-social rebel. He is that unto today, uncomfortable with people, living to himself, almost suffering from a persecution complex."[61] Despite his common suffering with others, wrote Burns, Wright "is without feeling of solidarity with the Negro people. He is a lone wolf, wily and wise to the ways of the white man, yet still so suspicious and wary of his own that he cannot bring himself into common struggle with them." This "inner, subconscious distrust" is the reason for Wright's failure to find identity with Communists and for his "sorry slander of Negroes" generally as evidenced in his complaint about the "strange absence of real kindness" among blacks. Burns, a Jew, also charged the book with anti-Semitism and self-pity. "'The essential bleakness of black life' of which he speaks is more an accurate chronicle of his own life rather than symbolic of Negroes generally." Burns closed the review by suggesting that *Black Boy* might be an epitaph not just for Wright's still-young career but for the radical political promise of that career itself: "In Black Boy he is again erring as he did in Native Son in his emphasis on the hopelessness of the Negro's lot, in his total failure to see that the clock of history is moving ahead, not backward. As he himself states it, he is 'running more away from something, than toward something.' In his dread of life, he has lost the zest of living."[62]

Burns's implicit charge of "bourgeois subjectivism" against Wright was reiterated across the Left press, as in Isidor Schneider's *New Masses* review, which also attacked the book's failure to delineate or promise black political progress. "No reader would learn from it that there were any Negro cultural institutions or influences; or that Negro culture, even at the folk level, had made major contributions to American culture. . . . or that Negro struggle and protest was a proud strand in the American chronicle."[63] Wright's failure to demonstrate or embrace black progressive culture in *Black Boy* was for leftists like Burns and Schneider an implied failure of everything the Popular Front and Negro People's Front had hoped to forge and forward. Wright had abandoned even his own faith in the "folk" in *Black Boy,* while his radicalism was left out entirely. The book was a narrative that would fit into no viable black-Left framework for 1945.

Yet as the rest of this book will show, Burns and Schneider's frustrations with Wright's anti-communism and disassociation from Popular Front/ Negro People's Front movements was not merely party-style carping (though it was also that). In cities like Chicago and New York, where Burns and Schneider lived respectively, African-American cultural politics as practiced in 1945 had virtually *nothing* in common with either Wright's public political anomie or its literary "representation." Yet by 1945 Wright's life and work constituted a potent and confused symbol. Review after review of *Black Boy* conflated Richard Wright the author of *Black Boy* with Richard Wright the child of the autobiography with Bigger Thomas, and all three with the relationship of the "race" to the "Left." Two interpretive images—one from his time, one from ours—help to illuminate how the 1945 model of "Richard Wright" had become a cultural narrative freighted with significance far larger than any individual life could reasonably bear. "Many migrants like us were driven and pursued, in the manner of characters in a Greek play, down the paths of defeat; but luck must have been with us, for we somehow survived" wrote Wright in the 1945 Introduction to *Black Metropolis;*[64] and Carla Cappetti has argued that Wright's writings on communism through *American Hunger* act out a powerful personal crisis as political myth: "Through a collective process of projection the Communist Party became a symbol for the individual's loss of identity and for the fear of losing oneself in a changing social reality. As in a modern version of the passion plays, the Communist Party was made to bear the cross for a society plunging headlong into postwar affluence and alienation. The party was the lamb sacrificed on the altar of modernity."[65]

Like monolithic critical accounts of Wright's career and work, these two images have an appealing telos suggesting that Richard Wright must embody the "end" of some cultural and political story, that he attain archetype, be it as Greek myth or passion play, Great Migration warrior or cold war martyr. They thus mimic the mythic drive and logic of Wright's own stories—fear, flight, fate—conflating critical taxonomies, fictional strategies, and political interpretations. In doing so they help reduce Wright himself to a set of Manichean dualisms: Chicago and after-Chicago Wright; "folk" and modern Wright; Communist and anti-Communist Wright; native and exiled Wright; the socially committed Wright and the existentialist Wright. African-American literary and cultural history since Wright has in turn been infected by the taxonomic tendencies of some Wright criticism. Craig Hansen Werner has aptly characterized this phenomenon:

> Whether phrased in terms of the "School of Wright" or of "protest literature," criticism of the intervening decades focused almost obsessively on Richard Wright. In turn, criticism of African-American literature of the fifties frequently posited a simple reaction against Wright. In such frameworks, Wright became a writer of sociology, a naturalist with leftist inflections; Baldwin and Ellison appear as champions of a nonracial "universalism"; black women writers are marginalized (Hurston) or distorted (Ann Petry as

naturalist, the early Brooks as universalist). . . . The "sociological" approach to Afro-American literature, like its deracinated "universalist" double, established an interpretive framework—reflected in both academic criticism and the mass media—that continues to undervalue the work of artists who cannot be reduced to familiar categories.[66]

The remainder of this study will seek to "defamiliarize" these familiar critical categories by recovering the work of artists—and other cultural workers—who cannot be reduced to them. Doing so will necessitate further recuperation of specific categories, like communism and radicalism, and the refinement of others, like black mass and popular culture—which thus far have been largely excluded from the discussion of South Side Chicago cultural politics after Wright's departure. It also will require undermining the logic of cultural histories formed around both "great authors" and "great men"—an undermining well underway but still unfolding in the recuperation of voices from the black and left margins of American cultural history. For perhaps the greatest political legacy of Wright's Chicago reputation is its literal and political *centralization* of these margins symbolized by the equation of the author with the city and its cultural life.

To begin reconstituting these margins we might begin—and end—with the way one of its most representative voices of the "Wright years" viewed the events with which we began this chapter. Frank Marshall Davis first met Wright in 1936 when he became one of the original members of the South Side Writers' Group. Davis had first come to Chicago in 1927 after a stint as a reporter and editor at the *Atlanta Daily World*. He began his career writing commercial fiction "for bread and beans" using pseudonyms to publish action and crime fiction in publications like *National Magazine* and *The Light*.[67] In 1935 he published his first volume of poetry, *A Black Man's Verse*, producing two more volumes by 1948. Davis remained behind in Chicago long after Wright's departure, working as a reporter and editor for Claude Barnett's Associated Negro Press, serving on the board of directors of the South Side Community Art Center, working with the Allied Arts Guild, a Sunday morning culture club, and heading the publicity section for the 1940 National Negro Exposition in Chicago. By his own account, Davis also moved from liberal to radical between 1940 and 1945, allying himself with Chicago Communists because, in his own words, "The genuine Communists I knew as well as others so labeled had one principle in common: to use any and every means to abolish racism."[68]

In *Livin' the Blues,* his memoir, Davis recalls his reactions to Wright's notorious 1944 public "breaks" with the Left: "I thought his resultant series of articles in widely read publications was an act of treason in the fight for our rights and aided only the racists who were constantly seeking any means to destroy cooperation between Reds and blacks. What Dick had done was throw the full weight of his worldwide prestige into a position which, while it gave him emotional release, damaged our battle."[69]

Davis contrasts the decision of Wright to Angelo Herndon, who he recalls refused to sell his own "break" with communism story to the Hearst papers. In his own reviews of *Black Boy* for the Associated Negro Press in 1945, Davis raised these charges of opportunism and betrayal against his old friend, "and I never saw or heard from Wright again. And the irony of it all is that despite his continued Redbaiting during his final years, his writing showed that basically he was still a Marxist. When you get down to the nitty gritty, he had merely quit the organization and dumped his former comrades, not the ideology."[70]

Davis's interpretation of Wright's career provides an angle of vision—from the streets of Popular Front/Negro People's Front Chicago—much Wright criticism and black cultural history has consciously and unconsciously erased. Davis's editor John Edgar Tidwell has written that Davis himself "virtually disappeared from American literary history after 1948" despite ranking from 1935 until that year as one of the most celebrated black poets of his generation, and one of its foremost journalists.[71] The story of Frank Marshall Davis and other "former comrades" is merely one in the long black shadow of Richard Wright, a shadow that the remainder of this book will attempt to lift. Doing so will provide a revised shape for Chicago's "renaissance" as well as bring into focus the fuller dimensions of Chicago's Negro People's Front.

# 2 Turning White Space into Black Space: The *Chicago Defender* and the Creation of the Cultural Front

If the February 29, 1940, death of *Chicago Defender* founder and publisher Robert S. Abbott overshadowed the publication of *Native Son* in Chicago, it was in part because Abbott's death signified a crisis in black capitalism instantaneously perceived by the homeboys and newsboys of Chicago. The crisis had in fact been a long time coming, foretold in Abbott's legendary life and management of the paper.

The son of slaves born on St. Simon Island just after the Emancipation Proclamation, Abbott left his missionary upbringing in Georgia for the Hampton Institute, where he came under the influence of its most famous alumnus Booker T. Washington. During Abbott's tenure at Hampton, according to Abbott's biographer Roi Ottley, Washington frequently returned to lecture to undergraduates on the importance of Negro industrial education. Abbott, who was studying the printing trade, came to worship Washington; Ottley says the latter "became his hero."[1] Around 1900, Abbott left St. Simon permanently for Chicago with "25 cents" in his pocket according to island lore, and in 1905 founded the *Chicago Defender*. From 1905 until the outbreak of World War I, Abbott more than any other African American embodied the entrepreneurial ethos for black upward mobility set down by Washington. Abbott's first employee and managing editor, J. Hockley Smiley, had at the paper's inception created an ad hoc circulation system meant to capitalize on the nascent Great African-American Migration from south to north. Noting that railroad workers were the only blacks who traveled from place to place on regular schedules, Smiley offered them a chance to increase their incomes by selling the *Defender* along their train routes.[2] Dining car waiters later joined Pullman porters as "delivery boys," throwing bundled *Defenders* off moving trains to waiting agents for distribution in small or secluded locales, especially in the rural south.[3]

Rudimentary production techniques at the *Defender* mirrored its impro-visatory consumption in the early years. Pullman porters also served as itin-erant reporters, kept on salary by Abbott to deliver news-bits to the paper upon arrival in Chicago. Some were given press cards "which they carried in their wallets and proudly flashed to those they wanted to impress."[4] In this way beauty parlor and barber shop gossip along the migration route found its way back "up north" into the *Defender*'s pages, where Abbott lifted a marketing strategy from Washington's entrepreneurial contemporary, Wil-liam Randolph Hearst. Losses and gains of the migration were often trum-peted in screaming red headlines derivative of the tabloid style of Hearst papers like the *San Francisco Herald-Examiner,* from which Abbott had pi-rated his editorial style and packaging. So similar were the profit-motive strat-egies of the papers and their publishers that in 1918 Abbott's *Defender* was accused of being a "front" for Hearst's organization,[5] which sued the *Defender* for emulating the masthead on Hearst's own Chicago papers, the *Herald-Examiner* and *Evening-American.*[6]

For Abbott, the Great Migration was black journalism's economic water-shed. The migration had created an ever-growing black readership for the paper's city and national editions who could be lured by advertisements and articles for the "better life" up north. Black rural migrants, their children, single mothers, unemployed itinerant laborers, and the elderly constituted a burgeoning demographic pool for the consumption of articles and advertise-ments for housing, jobs, and equal opportunity in Chicago. Chicago, in turn, was to "civilize" the southern migrant, and Abbott's *Defender* was to be the migrant's book of dreams and etiquette. Ads for the former and products for the latter—including hair straighteners, skin whiteners, and modern appli-ances like the Frigidaire—dominated the newspaper's growing advertising sections in the 1920s and 1930s. Describing himself as an "interracialist" who rejected black separatism and Garveyism, Abbott also routinely published a set of "Things That Should Be Considered" in the newspaper, rules of con-duct for incoming black migrants to Chicago. These included "Don't use vile language in public places"; "Don't act discourteously to other people in public places"; "Don't allow yourself to be drawn into street brawls"; and "Don't use liberty as a license to do as you please."[7] These rules symbolized Abbott's anxiety about the potential gap between his own bootstrap ascent and the rest of black America, between his emblematic status as the definitive Chicago "race man" and the "race" itself.[8] As he put it to his biographer Roi Ottley, "When I consider the whole range of our social behavior, I am almost tempted to say that we are just a little more than educated apes."[9] Enoch P. Waters, who worked under Abbott through much of the period of his ascent, notes that by the time of his death in 1940, Abbott's brownstone mansion on Chicago's Grand Boulevard and his fleet of limousines had made his only rival empire in America that of the late Madame C. J. Walker, the titan of the black cosmetics industry.

Abbott's passing suddenly foregrounded what a younger, post-Washingtonian generation of black and white Chicago intellectuals, journalists, entrepreneurs, activists, and cultural workers perceived as the *Defender*'s legacy and onus: the need to make-over its militant face. Despite the enormous and crucial strides made for blacks through the paper's attacks on racism, economic inequality, and Jim Crow in the early years of the century, its tendencies toward white emulation, monopoly fiefdom, gaudy self-promotion, journalistic sensationalism, and at times embarrassing racial patronization were by the late 1930s untenable means for the production of black political culture. By Abbott's 1940 death South Side Chicago had moved from migration to settlement; from street cars to automobiles; from dime novels to *Native Son;* from field hand to trade union; from unemployment to WPA; from Third Period to Popular Front radicalism. In addition, the 1936 election of Roosevelt that had begun the black voting swing from Republican to Democrat had begun to solidify black participation in modern electoral process and at least the promise of Democratic commitment to black causes, as signified by the appointment of increasing numbers of blacks to positions in the Roosevelt administration. Locally, South Side electoral politics had by 1940 produced black congressmen (William Dawson), black aldermen (Earl Dickerson), and black appointed officials in prominent places in city government. Each of these changes had come in part through the progressive alliance of black politicians, cultural workers, and artists with black and white radicals working under the aegis of organizations like the NAACP, Urban League, National Negro Congress, the Communist Party, and the CIO.

Abbott's death in 1940 unleashed the full force and implications of these events at the *Defender.* The progressive and radical-led reforms of the post-1935 era had made Abbott-style journalism and capitalism especially vulnerable to attacks from two Chicago flanks merging at the time of his death: a restless class of new black entrepreneurs—including journalists—eager to expand and capitalize on the newspaper's growing influence and profits, and an increasingly militant black Left seeking to seize the most popular and accessible vehicle of black public opinion for support of radical causes. These arms crossed in the negotiation of what the paper itself called a "cultural front" after 1940, one that synthesized the leading edges of the Negro People's

Front campaign in Chicago: against "white chauvinism" and racism at home, and for the redistribution of wealth into black working hands. Under the new leadership of Abbott's nephew, John H. Sengstacke, the newspaper undertook a revolution in personnel, editorial strategy, and marketing that foregrounded these goals. While it retained its generally conservative "core" of young local black talent, it also sought to hire national figures in black and white politics and culture who could recast the newspaper as allied with the most progressive forces in the country in other major cities the second city now sought to emulate—like New York and San Francisco. These moves coincided with the paper's attempts to link itself commercially with a cooperative black-only network of black papers and media outlets across the country by forming all-black national press organizations like the Negro Newspaper Publishers Association.

From 1940 to 1945, these principles—and marketing strategies—constituted a new modern black protest voice in the mass media, one that echoed and resonated with Chicago's most radical Negro People's Front interracial alliances and organizations. Inspired in part by small and left-wing magazines and newspapers of both the Third Party and Popular Front eras and by black innovations in political organizing at the local level, the *Defender* assaulted commercial and journalistic convention in order to undermine representations of white hegemony. It blurred generic separations between "journalism" and other genres like poetry and fiction. Borrowing from Popular Front-style propaganda wars, it erased distinctions between advertising and "news" as a means of fostering a proactive cultural front between black capitalism and black journalism. Similarly, mainstream standards of journalistic "objectivity" were exposed as fronts for white power and oppression undermined by the shrill conflation of "opinion" and fact in the newspaper's pages. In this the *Defender* became something of a black pastiche of journalistic practices and strategies at fraternal white-dominated papers like *New Masses* and *PM*, gleefully exploiting every possible opening for black militancy while fueling black capitalist experiments that it viewed as corollary aims of a new cultural vanguardism.

Viewing the *Defender* in this light challenges and expands scholarly consensus on the black press during World War II. Lee Finkle iterates that consensus in the only full-length book on the subject by concentrating on the famous "Double V" campaign initiated by the *Pittsburgh Courier* in 1942 and followed up by papers like the *Defender*.[10] The "Double V," calling for black victories against fascism abroad and racism at home, was indeed part of the *Defender*'s wartime editorial program and the equation of domestic and international "fascism" a crucial thematic line in the newspaper's coverage. Yet Finkle's emphasis on the black press's push for "assimilation" and "democracy" and narrow focus on its coverage of World War II obscures the more intricate influences of Left black and white activists during the war struggling for the soul of black journalism. This narrow critical framework for viewing the black press, like reductive sociological or canonical paradigms for studying Chicago literature and culture, reflects a persistent cold war anxiety among historians of the black press to engage in and recognize the struggles and contradictions interracial Left influence brought to a boiling point within black American culture during the war years. Indeed by the end of World War II the *Defender* was both "redder" *and* more profitable than any other newspaper in the country outside of the Communist press, and had easily overtaken the *Pittsburgh Courier* as the most militant voice for black racial reform. This achievement culminated in its becoming both a target for FBI inquiry and the safe haven—at least temporarily—for new red blacks like W. E. B. Du Bois and old white reds like Earl Conrad. Thus rather than "substitut[ing] militant rhetoric for its lack of innovative direction,"[11] the *Defender* frequently made specific recommendations and programs, often in overt or covert sympathy with the CP or radical Left, for innovative political direction that South Side Chicago routinely adhered to and followed throughout the war years. The newspaper's increasing circulation during these years is only the most obvious evidence of this. The city's own multifaceted reform of interracial race relations, Left-black alliance, and radical cultural practices given heavy coverage and editorial support by the newspaper (subjects of this and future chapters), is the remainder of the story.

Consequently more than any other area of black capital and cultural venture during the Chicago Negro People's Front period, the *Defender* emblematized the transformation of black cultural politics from a local to a national front, from monopoly to cooperative production, from retrograde stereotype to "modern" Negro, from "white space" to "black space." In so doing it helped wartime and postwar African-American media facilitate both a new "image" of black American life and new markets and means for its distribution that were seldom without ideological tension and contradiction. It was, in short, a black cultural revolution not televised, but one black Chicago could and did read all about.

John H. Sengstacke, the son of a minister and nephew to Robert S. Abbott, began the work for the transformation of the *Chicago Defender* on the eve of his uncle's death. After earning his degree in business administration and working summers at the *Defender* while in college at Hampton Institute, Sengstacke had moved to Chicago, taking courses at the Mergenthaler Linotype School and the Chicago School of Printing. The training and family connections earned Sengstacke appointment in 1934 as vice-president and general manager of Abbott Publishing Company. He had been in that position six years when on January 6, 1940, he wrote to Claude Barnett, founder and president of Chicago's own Associated Negro Press, the country's first black news service. Sengstacke sought a meeting of Negro publishers to discuss what he perceived as a brewing crisis and opportunity for the black press:

> The Negro newspaper has weathered the storm of the depression, as well as, if not better than, any commercial enterprise manned and controlled by our race. This has been accomplished despite the fact that we as publishers have not been organized in any fraternity for the common good and welfare of all. I believe you will agree that this is not the case with other business organizations of either local or national scope; for instance, insurance men have a common fraternity, religious groups have their yearly conferences. Even the masses whom we lead and serve have their clubs and fraternities that meet regularly.
>
> The Negro newspaper is recognized as the mouthpiece through which the entire race speaks, yet we seem to be the most disorganized body in the entire set-up of Negro business.[12]

Sengstacke had carefully chosen Barnett as the target for his letter. Barnett had developed the idea for the ANP in 1919 while traveling the South working for the *Defender,* just two years after Abbott had launched his own Defender News Service in the spring of 1917.[13] As his strategic emulations suggested, Barnett was an even more direct disciple of Washington than Abbott, having studied at Tuskegee Institute and spent the years between 1920 and 1940 building up two commercial empires, one in publishing, the other in the cosmetics industry. By 1940, Barnett was Abbott's mirror and rival in more ways than one. Not only had Barnett created the second most important journalistic enterprise in Chicago, but he had revolutionized the relationship between the black press and black capital. As Linda Evans notes, Barnett's "key innovation" as director of the Associated Negro Press was to link the service to an advertising exchange. Because most newspapers did not have ready cash, they exchanged "white space"—unused advertising space in their publications—in return for ANP service. Barnett also aggressively looked to black companies for advertising business, and had arranged an advertising exchange with his own firm, the Kashmir Chemical Company, manufacturer of Nile Queen, a hair and skin product. When Kashmir failed after a dispute with the manufacturer of Cashmere Bouquet toiletries over their similar brand names, Poro College beauty products, one of the first million-dollar black cosmetics companies, replaced it as Barnett's first major advertising client. "Through this exchange system," writes Evans, "advertisers reached local markets wherever the black population was large enough to support its own newspaper. The newspapers enjoyed the benefits of ANP service in return for publishing the advertisements."[14] By the late 1930s Barnett was one of Abbott's few financial rivals and was the only Chicagoan capable of the dream and ambition to purchase the *Chicago Defender.*[15]

Sengstacke's letter was thus in part an invitation to join forces before a potential *Defender*-ANP editorial and economic war deepened. It was also a clever subversion of the principles—and ideology—both Abbott and Barnett had used to make their fortunes. Sengstacke's call for a "common fraternity" of publishers national in scope challenged Barnett to reconsider his ANP fiefdom as part of a larger cooperative struggle for black capital, both cultural and economic. His invocation of "the masses whom we lead and serve" also had a distinctly different cast than his uncle's missionary racial rhetoric. Though no radical, Sengstacke was reframing "reformist" language and an organizational zeitgeist up from the South Side streets into a cosmetic parlance Barnett would be sure to understand. The appeal was simple: it was high time that the black press not simply lead but *follow* the example of its mobilizing constituency of readers.

On January 13, Barnett responded favorably to Sengstacke's letter. The two agreed that a three-day conference should be held to discuss and delineate the issues facing the black press. On February 7, Sengstacke wrote to Barnett to say that more than seventy-five publishers had agreed to meet and had chosen Chicago by "consensus" as the logical meeting site. On February 29, March 1, and March 2, the week of Robert S. Abbott's death and the week preceding publication of *Native Son,* the first National Conference of Negro Publishers convened at the Chicago Wabash Avenue YMCA at 3763 South Wabash. Among the seventy-five publishers were editors and publishers of virtually all of the major African-American newspapers in the country, including leading *Defender* rivals like the *Baltimore Afro-American,* the *Cleveland Call,* and the *Pittsburgh Courier.* Like the *Defender,* whose circulation stood in 1940 at forty thousand, these other papers had seen steady growth in circulation during the Depression. National circulation for black papers in 1940 stood at an all-time high of 1,265,000.[16] Yet circulation gains were

story with a "frame up" for bringing criminal contempt charges against Patterson for his role in the strike.[22] Higher in the same issue, the *Defender* ran a story applauding a Chicago appearance by New York Congressman Vito Marcantonio, representative of the radical American Labor Party and president of the International Labor Defense, the organization black readers still fondly recalled for its Scottsboro defense. Still another prominent item featured a photograph of the Communist-led National Negro Congress moving into its new headquarters at 309 E. 47th Street. Pictured were Chicago Council President Lillian Summers and Ishmael Flory, chairman of the third congressional drive and a celebrated figure in the paper's pages during and after 1940 for his leading role against rent-gouging and for new public housing on the South Side.

The conflation of these editorial and economic "moments" in the 1940 *Defender* begins to give scope and dimension to the "common fraternity" that would help sustain the drive for the black press's cultural front. Indeed Patterson, Marcantonio, and Flory, on one hand, and the Communist Party, American Labor Party, and National Negro Congress, were not simply objects of *Defender* reports but active agents in influencing the paper's editorial politics from 1940 until the end of the war. Their impress on the newspaper was already manifest in July of that year, when the paper presented its editorial "program" for social and economic reform. It called for keeping America out of the war; passage of an anti-lynching bill and anti-poll tax bill; broadening and improving social security; passage of Marcantonio's American Standards Act providing three million jobs through public works programs; democratization of the American armed forces; a federal housing program; cash grants and loans to small farmers; maintenance of the Labor Relations Act and a Wages and Hours act; and passage of the American youth act.[23] With the exception of its failure to articulate equality for black women, the *Defender*'s program represented an updated and reformulated version of the platform inaugurated by the National Negro Congress 1936 session and which James Ford reiterated to black and interracial Communist Party audiences between 1936 and 1940.[24] Ford's speech at the Tenth National Convention of the CPUSA on May 29, 1938, had listed these as the "democratic issues of the Negro people come to the fore in the Democratic Front": the fight against discrimination in employment; full civil rights and citizenship; the right to vote; the right to sit on juries and hold public office; the enforcement of the Thirteenth, Fourteenth, and Fifteenth Amendments; the passing of the Anti-Lynching Bill, and the "defeat of all reactionary forces." Like the *Defender*, Ford also routinely singled out for praise labor's Non-Partisan

League, the CIO, and "other labor, liberal and progressive forces" like the NNC for its fight for passage of anti-lynching legislation.[25]

The incontrovertible conjunction between the *Defender* editorial "platform" in mid-1940 and the formulation by one as removed from its day-to-day practice as James Ford gives further substantive dimension to a singular claim of this book: that well after and beyond its formal 1939 "dissolution," Negro People's Front and Popular Front politics were central to the African-American agenda for social change in cities like Chicago. How exactly did it happen? In the case of the *Defender* the record is both clear and compromised. Ben Burns, who came to the newspaper in 1942, contends in his memoir *Nitty-Gritty* and in correspondence with the author that aside from himself and *Defender* editor Metz Lochard no *Defender* staffers were directly linked to the party. Enoch Waters, the only other editor beside Burns to leave a memoir, notes that "*The Defender* applauded many of the activities and declarations of the Communist Party but withheld endorsement of the party and its candidates."[26] Burns and Waters's combined accounts suggest something of the nature of a front-like defense consciously enacted during and after the *Defender*'s 1940s days against the acknowledgment of Communist influence on the paper—a denial understandable given the federal government's monitoring of red influence in the black community dating to World War I and, in Burns's case especially, his own bitter break later with the CP. Yet its marks are everywhere in the public record.

Burns's own life and tenure at the paper is the best case in point. Until the publication of his memoir in 1996, Burns was perhaps the best kept and strangest secret in the history of interracial American radicalism. The first and only journalist in the United States to work on three different Communist daily papers in the 1930s, Burns began his career at the copy desk for the *Daily Worker* in New York after graduating from Northwestern's journalism school. He was subsequently hired in 1938 to work for the first and only Communist daily in Chicago, the *Midwest Daily Record,* moving on to the *San Francisco People's World* after the *Daily Record*'s financial collapse. It was at the *Daily Record* that Burns met and worked under coeditor William L. Patterson. They were reunited in Chicago in 1941, when Patterson recommended Burns as a publicity assistant to South Side alderman Earl B. Dickerson. Dickerson, who was according to Burns "anything but a CPer," "met periodically on strategy" with Patterson,[27] while Burns cooked up publicity memos and statements for Dickerson's 2d Ward office. Some time in 1942, Patterson convinced his friend Metz Lochard to interview Burns for a job at the *Defender.* According to Burns, Patterson thought Burns's journalistic experience and training could be useful in the *Defender*'s plans to compile a "Victory Edition" of the newspaper in support of the war effort. Though he claims in his memoir to have been "off the Communist payroll" by 1941, Burns says Patterson's other motive for recommending him for a job was to place a "party member" in a position of influence in the South Side community.[28]

In "Nitty-Gritty," Burns suggests the parameters of political reformism the non-Communist Sengstacke brought to the *Defender* in 1940. Sengstacke, he says, favored his presence at the paper because of his desire to sweep out its "old guard." Despite constant harassment by the federal government, including direct threats by Frances Biddle, Burns also notes that Sengstacke "never . . . in any way sought to curb or tone down either our news reports" about racial clashes in the military or editorial attacks on discrimination.[29] As for Lochard, who had been at the paper for years, Burns writes that he "carefully played the middle,"[30] cultivating "a broad spectrum of contacts in the South Side community that included friendship with Communist leaders, no less than Catholic priests."[31] Indeed, Lochard was an open supporter and member of the board of directors of Patterson's Chicago Popular Front/ Negro People's Front project, the Abraham Lincoln School. The school was a fraternal companion to the South Side Community Art Center; both will be discussed in more detail in my next chapter.

Burns's memoir and correspondence is at best equivocal on whether he, Lochard, or the *Defender,* consciously chose to use the paper as a vehicle of party-influenced thinking or ideas. Party influence came, when it did, "mostly in suggestions and critiques of editorial positions and ideas for news coverage" passed along to Lochard and Burns by Patterson and Flory, the latter described as "an obnoxious, unwanted presence but difficult to keep out of the office."[32] "In any case," writes Burns, "the threats had no effect on any possible support of radical politics, like the CP, since never at any time was such supportive thinking either editorial or otherwise even contemplated. Only insofar as the CP might have represented a movement fighting against racism was there any common ground."[33] Yet in a summation of the newspaper's relations to the CP Burns opens up perhaps the largest possible space for understanding. Referring to the war years, anti-fascism, and the popularity of Russian War Relief in the United States, Burns concludes that for Dickerson, Lochard, and other black progressives to be friendly to known Communists was "in keeping with the wartime trend and spirit of the country, which was marked by open U.S.-Soviet cooperation in many areas even if individual communists in the U.S. were still very much subject to antagonism in many quarters."[34]

Burns's version of the *Defender*'s "position" on communism and Communist influence recalls the response of the parade crowd to the YCL float recounted at the start of chapter 1. The notion that for black Chicago the Communist Party stood as an emblem of interracial reform, particularly in the area of race relations—a notion so understandable to U.S. historians of the CP and the black community prior to 1939—was still a working and workable one well into the 1940s. Indeed, the cautious assimilation of both radicals and radical thought at the *Defender* described in these accounts suggests how during and after the Popular Front black institutions and leaders like the *Defender* began to *absorb* American communism into a new black framework for describing the conditions of black America. If James Ford was correct that blacks and the Communist Party during the Popular Front were "natural allies," then not just symbiosis but osmosis from red to black cultural politics was possible. Indeed, Abbott's passing of leadership of the *Defender* to Sengstacke may be an apt example of what Cayton and Drake described in 1945 as the passing of so-called safe leaders in Bronzeville. "Challenged on one hand by the Communists and on the other by the racial radicals," they wrote, "the 'accepted leaders' were forced to accommodate themselves to 'new techniques' of political and institutional organizing or to 'give way to men who could do so.'"[35]

From 1940 to 1945 at least Sengstacke and the *Defender* demonstrated a responsiveness to "new techniques" of both Communists and racial radicals. In these years these Communists, ex-Communists, or fellow travelers were either hired to the staff or contributed to the paper on a regular basis: Ben Burns, W. E. B. Du Bois, Earl Conrad, Jack Conroy, Langston Hughes, Grace Tompkins, and Margaret Burroughs. These writers, with the help of clearly sympathetic progressive non-party members like Lucius Harper and Metz Lochard, began a conscious campaign within the newspaper to extend favorable coverage of the radical Left, including the Communist Party, mainly out of respect for the party's long-time leading role in the fight against racism. Indeed, *at no time* during the war years does *Defender* coverage comply with popular accounts of black accusations of "betrayal" against the CP for its vacillating policy, structure, and positions on issues of race or the war. For example, the newspaper stood behind the party during its notorious "flip-flopping" on the war, supporting the Left's call for a move from pacifism to engagement after Pearl Harbor and the German attack on the Soviet Union in June 1942. During the years of Browderism and later the party's reorganization into the Communist Political Association, the paper remained a steadfast defender of the CP's reputation as a fighter against racial discrimination. In

March 1942 city editor Lucius Harper's name appeared along with those of Paul Robeson, Max Yergan, Richard Wright, Earl Dickerson, and Ishmael Flory in a full-page *Defender* ad published by the Chicago Citizen's Committee to Free Earl Browder calling for Browder's release from federal prison in Atlanta.[36] The ad was pitched to issues of "racial radicalism" the newspaper itself made recurring subjects of editorial assault in its 1941 and 1942 coverage: the Klan, the Bund, the Black Legion, and "Fifth Columnists" resistant to racial reform.

Placing Harper's name in a pro-Communist ad was in part a subtle evasion of editorial surveillance of the newspaper that the Office of War Information had already put the paper on notice for.[37] It was also a diversionary strategy common to 1930s Left journalism more commonly documented in the *New Masses* or *Daily Worker,* where published "petitions" calling for the release of political prisoners, like Angelo Herndon, reconstituted "advertising" as propaganda. In its May 23, 1942, editorial celebrating Browder's release from prison, the paper reiterated this Popular Front logic, mediating support for the "democratic gesture" of Browder's release through the lens of international racial radicalism. "We are not Communists," the editorial declared, "but we believe that Browder's release—though coming rather late—will remove any suspicion that Soviet Russia might have as to the sincerity of our country in the struggle for human freedom."[38] In releasing Browder, Roosevelt, the editorial continued, "is indirectly rebuking the Peglers, the lynchers, the industrialists who would rather destroy democracy than accord equality to the Negro."[39]

The editorial's own calculated "indirection" was clearly pointed toward the creation of an imaginary black political space where FDR, Stalin, Browder, and the Scottsboro Boys could inhabit something like a communal collective consciousness of the centrality of race and racial reform to 1940s America. This fantastic recombining of ideological possibilities so characteristic of the Popular Front translated into an intriguing conundrum for the production of black political culture in the black press during the 1940s, as witness the *Defender's* April 11, 1942, editorial call for "A Unified Press":

> The struggle of the Negro masses to attain democratic parity with the whites on those basic principles that give meaning to American citizenship, would be advanced to fruitful ends were the Negro press, which controls a considerable body of public opinion, willing to consolidate its energy, unify its aims and concentrate on a practical strategy for a sustained frontal attack on issues, institutions and personalities which are blocking the progress of the race.

> ... Too many, far too many of our newspapers are working at cross pur-
> poses. There are so many editorial contradictions that it is difficult for a
> reader who is not a member of the Negro race to ascertain through the pages
> of the Negro press what the masses of our people really want. ...
>
> We need a program of action on which all of us can act with unanimity
> and force. This should not be difficult of accomplishment [*sic*] if we can put
> aside petty intrigues and unprofitable competition.[40]

As the editorial makes clear, the attempt to balance a radical or progressive agenda for racial unity with the "unprofitable" constraints of liberal
capitalism was the *African-American dilemma* during the late 1930s and early
1940s. The paper's complaints about economic and political "competition"
demonstrated both the opportunities and the limits of Popular Front reformism for the black press. Resolving this dilemma inevitably demanded disman-
tling the structural relations of culture *to* capital by creating and facilitating
alternate means of "value" and exchange for black cultural work. One example of this was the formation of a "cooperative" black newspaper economy
through organizations like the Associated Negro Press that could freely exchange "white space" for black space outside of the rigors of white capitalism. For writers, artists, and journalists, the left cultural arm to the business
side of "cooperative" enterprise required rethinking the limitations of cultural forms (like a newspaper) that fostered "unprofitable competition" and
ideological division. From 1940 onward, Chicago's black literary and journalistic culture responded to this challenge more vigorously than any other
American city.

As early as its September 28, 1940, issue, for example, the *Defender* began
to revise and invert mass media convention as a means of revaluing its cultural work. The paper included a mock "Extra" section titled "Blitz Over
Georgia." Under the headline "Blitz Hits U.S.: Race in Revolt," the lead story
began thusly: "Heavily guarded, Adolph Hitler was moving northward from
here Sunday after a small expeditionary force which made a surprise land-
ing here Saturday night by air and sea had completely wiped out approxi-
mately 2,500 Negro troops in a tragic one-sided massacre which is perhaps
without parallel in the history of the world."[41] Forward dated "September
25, 1943," the story reported that "The easy victory of the Germans was attributable to the fact that the Negro troops when they arrived here were
armed only with picks and shovels." "There is little doubt," the story continued, "but that the effort would have been successful had the soldiers had
proper arms and support, the only items, besides possibly training, that they

lacked." As a result of the invasion, the story said, Congress had taken refuge in "Wayunder, Alasippi," an erewhon left (barely) to the imagination of black readers. In addition to reconfiguring the war as a dystopic racial nightmare for its Jim Crowed readers, the *Defender* "fantasy" also extended toward race war. The Hitler assault is a "story of treason in high places that will shock America, and cause widespread revolts among the Negroes," the story reported. "It's the same old story of aristocratic fifth columns that was seen unfolded in Norway, England, and France. White landlords, businessmen and politicians sold out the South and opened the gates to Hitler. In other words, they were traitors to America."[42]

"Blitz Over Georgia" had more than passing similarity to another dystopic Popular Front-style media hoax, Orson Welles's 1939 "War of the Worlds" broadcast.[43] Hitler's army was described as descending like a "huge amphibian, the like of which had never been seen here before," and the story included illustrations in a style best describable as WPA Gothic portraying Nazi forces running rampant over Goyaesque southern blacks.[44] Like "War of the Worlds," "Blitz Over Georgia" was an assault on American cultural and political hegemony. Like Welles's broadcast, it also configured mass media as both a site of this hegemony and its potential disruption. A sidebar to the "Blitz" story, "Release of 500 Martyrs is Demanded," wrote that "A committee of 500 prominent Negro newspaper editors wired President Willrose in Alasippi this week in a new demand for the release of 500 Negro conscientious objectors who have been in a concentration camp since the spring of 1942."[45] Once allegory, the story here returned readers to the *realpolitics* of Chicago, whose own wartime martyrs included the black sociologist St. Clair Drake and the racial radical Ralph Bunche, both of whom had publicly declared themselves conscientious objectors in opposition to an imperialist and racist war. "Blitz Over Georgia" was thus a kind of (black) magic realism. The paper's transgression of conventional journalistic boundaries was a metaphoric crossing of the geographical and ideological boundaries of Jim Crow Chicago and Jim Crow America. Bound on four sides by a hostile white publishing world, and still divided north and south within the city's racial demographics, black space in the black press could explode the small square of white real estate into which Bigger Thomas is symbolically driven in *Native Son.* Following the logic of South Side "Dream Books," which offered numeric systems named after faraway locales—Paris, Las Vegas, Haiti—generic experiment held out the promise of subversion and escape from white reality and its oppressive conventions.

## NEGRO TROOPS SLAUGHTERED AT SAVANNAH

Scene during Savannah massacre showing Negro troops from Fort Benning battling invading Nazis with picks and shovels. Over 2,000 soldiers who attempted to resist the Germans were slaughtered in a battle which is having historic repercussions in Congress which has taken refuge in Wayunder, Alasippi.

*Figure 1.* "Negro Troops Slaughtered at Savannah." This illustration appeared on the front page of a mock section of the September 28, 1940, edition of the *Chicago Defender.* The section described an imaginary assault by Nazis on Savannah, Georgia, in which black soldiers combatted the fascist army with hand tools. The incident was said to have stirred a "race revolt" across the South and sent Congress into hiding in the imaginary town of Wayunder, Alasippi. Reprinted courtesy of the *Chicago Daily Defender.*

This transgressive logic informed other *Defender* practices during the early 1940s of abandoning lines of demarcation between traditional journalistic categories: news versus opinion, poetry versus prose, fact versus fiction. After 1940, the paper consciously revised its sensationalism formula of the Abbott years in favor of what Cary Nelson has called after Bakhtin a "dialogic" journalistic discourse characteristic of 1930s style radical writing in the Left press.[46] A defining example of this appeared in the February 14, 1942, edition of the *Defender*. Beneath its lead story of A. Philip Randolph's reception of the 1942 Spingarn Award, the paper ran a boxed poem by Benjamin Franklin Bardner entitled "This is Dixie," in tribute to the victims of a lynching in the town of Sikeston, Missouri, weeks earlier. The lynchings had earned serial coverage in the *Defender* and national black press prior to the February 14 edition, and the paper routinely added the words "Remember Sikeston!" to its "Double V" campaign boxes that appeared periodically during the war years. Bardner's published poem now carried the superhead "Remembering Sikeston, Mo.," an editorial flourish meant to weld the paper, the reader, the poem, and the event in common cause:

Eenie! Meenie! Minie Mo!
White man? Black man? We don't know,
Any nigger, though will do,
This is Dixie—carry thru!

Hang the black brute to a tree
Openly so all may see;
When he's dead, then cut him down,
Drag his form through nigger-town.

Stop at his old Mammy's place,
Let her see his damn dead face.
If she sheds a tear or two—
This is Dixie—carry thru!

When the darky church we reach—
Where the niggers shout and preach,
Leave him there for them to view,
This is Dixie—carry thru!

When the sheriff comes 'round your way
Don't have one damn word to say,
If they try to make you tell—
This is Dixie—what th' hell![47]

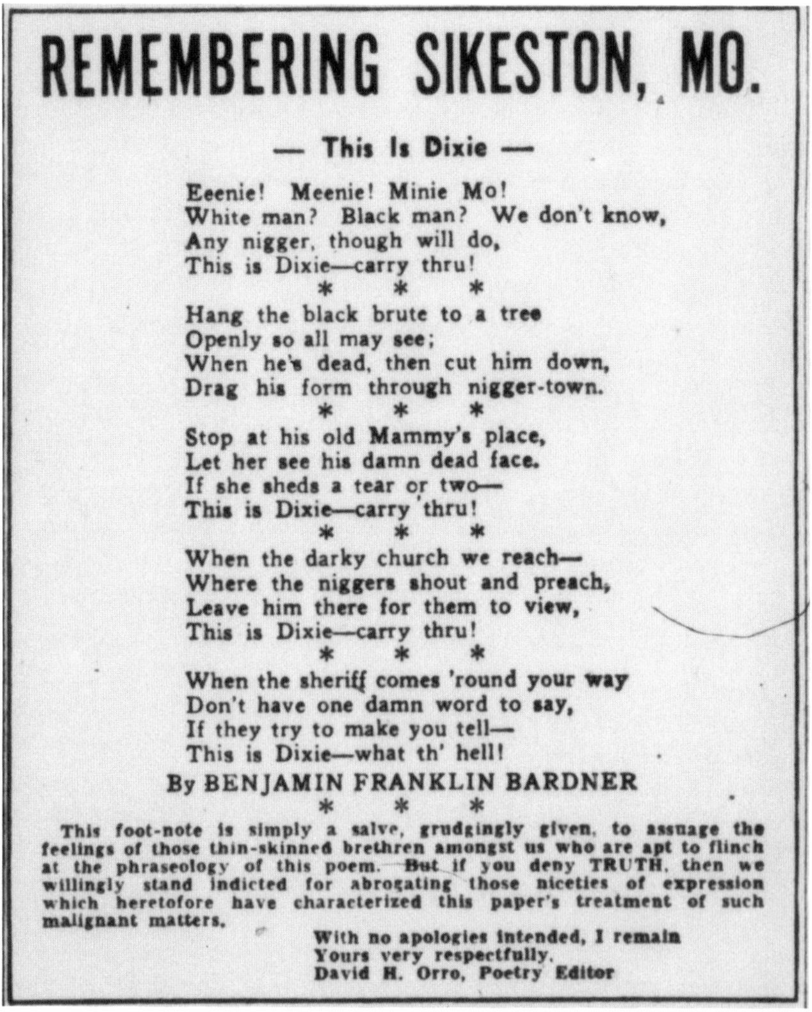

# REMEMBERING SIKESTON, MO.

## — This Is Dixie —

Eenie! Meenie! Minie Mo!
White man? Black man? We don't know,
Any nigger, though will do,
This is Dixie—carry thru!

   *    *    *

Hang the black brute to a tree
Openly so all may see;
When he's dead, then cut him down,
Drag his form through nigger-town.

   *    *    *

Stop at his old Mammy's place,
Let her see his damn dead face.
If she sheds a tear or two—
This is Dixie—carry thru!

   *    *    *

When the darky church we reach—
Where the niggers shout and preach,
Leave him there for them to view,
This is Dixie—carry thru!

   *    *    *

When the sheriff comes 'round your way
Don't have one damn word to say,
If they try to make you tell—
This is Dixie—what th' hell!

### By BENJAMIN FRANKLIN BARDNER

   *    *    *

This foot-note is simply a salve, grudgingly given, to assuage the feelings of those thin-skinned brethren amongst us who are apt to flinch at the phraseology of this poem. But if you deny TRUTH, then we willingly stand indicted for abrogating those niceties of expression which heretofore have characterized this paper's treatment of such malignant matters.

With no apologies intended, I remain
Yours very respectfully,
David H. Orro, Poetry Editor

*Figure 2.* "Remembering Sikeston, Mo." by Benjamin Franklin Bardner. Bardner's poem, inspired by a lynching in Sikeston, Missouri, appeared on the front page of the February 14, 1942, *Defender.* Reminiscent of Langston Hughes's 1930s and 1940s occasional poems on racial incidents across the United States, Bardner's poem also signified on the famous racist southern rhyme "Eenie meenie minie Mo." Reprinted courtesy of the *Chicago Daily Defender.*

For black readers with long-term memories, Bardner's poem could and did conjure up moments in black cultural politics as old as the 1931 Scottsboro case, or Richard Wright's breakthrough lynching verse "Between the World and Me," or perhaps the corpus of Langston Hughes's more radical 1930s verse like "Christ in Alabama." Yet the faithful sing-song recreation of the South's most notorious racist rhyme also marked the poem's intervention as an angry parody of the serial—or mass cultural—celebration of lynching that made it one of Dixie's most exportable products to blacks. The *Defender's counter* serial coverage of the lynching, capped off by its mock-poetic representation, signified like "Blitz Over Georgia" a war of mass cultural worlds, one black, one white. The unusual transgression of publishing poetry on page one of a newspaper could be seen as the cultural fault line of this divide. Indeed, the *Defender* included a "disclaimer" to the act for its readers acknowledging the possible abrogation of both good taste and good journalism. Poetry editor David H. Orro added a footnote to the poem, which, he explained, "is simply a salve, grudgingly given, to assuage the feelings of those thin-skinned brethren amongst us who are apt to flinch at the phraseology of this poem. But if you deny TRUTH, then we willingly stand indicted for abrogating those niceties of expression which heretofore have characterized this paper's treatment of such malignant matters."[48] The *Defender's* creation of a new journalistic "vocabulary" to describe racial horror was concomitant with a reaffirmation of the paper's racial radicalism, a literal and figurative revealing of old wounds. The poem established a synchronous, dialectical relationship between "news" and poetry as well as the relationship between newspaper readers and political activism. Journalistic "truth" and "poetic" truth were merely functions of the same cultural work.

Such was arguably the specific inheritance to the *Defender* of Langston Hughes. Before coming to work for the *Defender* as columnist in 1942, Hughes had already established himself as the "documentary" poet of the black Left. Hughes's occasional poems on racist atrocities against blacks during his most overtly red and radical years of the 1930s made them the obvious prototype for "This is Dixie." Prior to his being hired as a full-time columnist at the *Defender,* Hughes was in fact already publishing poems in the paper written expressly for syndication by the Associated Negro Press operated by Claude Barnett, a friend of Hughes's. Some of Hughes's early poems ran in a *Defender* op-ed page space appropriately titled "Lights and Shadows" and subtitled "A Little Bit of Everything." The column title signified the expansiveness of the black press as the obverse of the more traditionally generic and conventional white media. This transgressiveness included an outreach to white radicals. Lucia Trent, for example, poet and editor with husband Ralph Cheney of *Unrest! The Rebel Poets' Anthology* in 1931, more than ten years later contributed "Coleman Goes Out Free" to the February 14, 1942, "Lights and Shadows" space, a poetic tribute to a falsely accused black convict imprisoned at San Quentin, exhorting miners and red caps to rise up in his defense.[49]

By 1942, when his work began to appear regularly in the paper, Hughes was already scrambling to fight off blacklisting and attacks for his earlier radical verse and denying party affiliation. Yet characteristic of the plight of both black and white radicals in the post-1939 era, Hughes's radicalism—racial and otherwise—found safe expressive haven under the cover of avowedly "non-Communist" papers like the *Defender*. Indeed, many of Hughes's ANP poems were *about* the black press as a source of radical inspiration and protection. Poems written for the ANP like "The Mitchell Case," commemorating the Supreme Court ruling against segregation of interstate train cars, used headline-style titles as if the poems were literary transcriptions of black newspaper accounts. This strategy was reinforced by the recurring opening line of many of Hughes's ANP poems: "I see by the papers." So began "Governor Fires Dean," an attack on the much-despised governor of Georgia who was a recurring villain in the *Defender*'s pages. The poem takes the governor to task for firing a university administrator who supported integration. It concludes:

> Ain't it funny how some white folks
> Have the strangest way
> Of acting just like Hitler
> In the U.S.A.?[50]

Like the "Sikeston" poem, Hughes's Talmadge piece was the product of a cycle of cultural production beginning and ending with the black press. Like Barnett's attempts to trade "white space" with his own cosmetics company, or the *Defender*'s call for a national network of black newspapers, the poem demonstrated black cultural politics finding safe haven in the *self*-production of new forms and varieties of American radicalism. It was a process inverse to the commercial fate of *Native Son* and Richard Wright, but one far more characteristic of the pattern of black cultural politics in Chicago in the war years. After 1942, unlike Wright, Hughes refused to trade in his radical credentials for a set of new political clothes. Despite claims by critics that his poetry and prose lost its "radical edge" during the 1940s, works like "Governor Talmadge" and Hughes's *Defender* columns up through the 1940s and 1950s demonstrate that his renunciation of communism did not result in a break with all organizations of the Left and that he continued to support groups that fell victim to McCarthyism well into the 1950s.[51] Indeed, Hughes's *Defender* columns up to and throughout the war years hinged on two central tenets of his 1930s radicalism: support for the Soviet Union and its avowed racial equality, and sympathetic representation of the black working class. Hughes's ANP poems and *Defender* columns have until recently been ignored or typecast as examples of the failings after the 1930s of black radicals to maintain their Left allegiances. Hughes's racial radicalism in the *Defender,* and the *Defender*'s own in publishing him, have in turn been overshadowed by conventional accounts and periodizations about black radicalism's "end" after *Native Son,* a book whose influence and reputation among Chicagoans was limited in relation to Hughes's prodigious output in the widely read *Defender.*

In addition to refining and challenging narrow accounts of political quietism and accommodation in the black press during the war, reclaiming Left-influence and practice at the *Defender* provides a way of blackening the story of American mass media and its relationship to the pre–McCarthyite Left. Communist influence during the Popular Front and early 1940s in the American Newspaper Guild, Radio Writers Guild, Dramatists Guild, WPA, American Artists' Congress, and the American Writers' Union helped to provide an opening for a black cultural front in a variety of mass media during the war years. This influence reflected the institutionalization of the incursion of American radicals into mass culture—even the Popular Front *Daily Worker* expanded and regularized its "cultural page" to include focus on movies, theater, and book reviews.[52] During the late 1930s, as we have already seen, Wright, Hughes, and Robeson in particular entered this widening space for black progressive mass culture. In early 1940, for example, Hughes, still much identified with leftist causes and politics, was commissioned by the CBS "Pursuit of Happiness" program to write a drama based on the life of Booker T. Washington to star Rex Ingram. In August of that year, Hughes, Ted Ward, and Owen Dodson were featured speakers on a program celebrating the work of six black playwrights from the Negro Playwrights Company at the Golden Gate Ballroom in Harlem. The pageant included Wright speaking on *Native Son;* Robeson singing; speeches by Alain Locke and Edna Thomas, acting executive director of the Negro Actor's Guild; Gwendolyn Bennett, director of the Harlem Art Center; George B. Murphy Jr., publicity and promotion director for the NAACP; and Dr. Max Yergan, president of the National Negro Congress. Though small-scale gatherings of black radicals like these were barely reported outside of the scope of black media like the *Pittsburgh Courier* and *Chicago Defender,* they were far more characteristic of black cultural insurgency than singular blockbuster moments like the publication of *Native Son.* They also anticipated the accelerating trend during the 1940s for black entree into mainstream cultural forms and the gradual "radicalization" of those forms. In their lamentably narrow history of the Communist Party, for example, Irving Howe and Lewis Coser argue that "only during the war years, when it could fuse American and Russian patriotism and penetrate a great many wartime institutions, did it [the CP] seriously begin to approach the centers of American political power."[53] Coser and Howe offer the "fellow traveling" *PM* magazine in New York, or the 1943 issue of *LIFE* magazine devoted to "Soviet-American cooperations" as emblematic moments of the unspecified target of this institutional insurgency—American mass media.

Yet after 1940 black mass media were already in the vanguard of black-Left alliance, revision, cooperation. From 1940 until early 1943, *Defender* editorials persistently lobbied for—and sometimes received—stronger FEPC investigation of discriminatory unions; pushed for—and helped to achieve—hiring of black women workers denied wartime jobs in plants like Armour and Company; and reported tirelessly on restrictive covenants and tenant violations on South Side apartments, information in turn used in key Supreme Court cases during the war years. The paper also supported NNC and CIO union gains and tirelessly covered both groups' rallies and meetings, contributing to an upsurge in union membership in Chicago; waged investigative series into rent and other price-gouging on the South Side that led to some real estate reform; and relentlessly criticized both the NAACP and Roosevelt administration for perceived slow downs in New Deal reforms that might benefit blacks. This proactivity belies claims that the paper's editorial "rhetoric" was in lieu of specific recommendations for social change, or that the *Defender* hued to anything like a go-slow editorial stance.

Yet especially as the war deepened the paper also increasingly reflected the Popular Front habit of couching its largest political "front" offensives in expansive inclusionary programs that likely diluted the particularity—and radical potential—of its own agenda. The July 11, 1942, issue of the paper devoted significant space to promotion of the "American Negro Music Festival" at Soldier Field at which black tenor Napoleon Reed sang excerpts from

"Aida," and both Duke Ellington and Canada Lee—by 1942 a committed progressive—would speak.[54] The program was in conjunction with a South Side "Win the War Program" that included a "Peoples Victory Forum" at Washington Park, long the South Side's public flashpoint for speeches and demonstrations by black Garveyites, Communists, unionists, and other radicals. These ratios of entertainment and politics mimicked recurring *Defender* front-page layout and design strategies in which a photograph of, for example, Lena Horne enticed the reader's eye into the page only to discover a blast against racism in industry. Three weeks later, in its August 1 issue, the paper gave page-one promotion to Paul Robeson headlining a "Win the War" rally at the Grant Park Band Shell with backing from Philip Murray, Steel Workers Organizing Committee president, and R. J. Thomas, president of the United Auto Workers.[55] The same issue presented a Chicago CIO Industrial Union Council ad for a "Second Front Now!" calling for direct strikes against Germany. Speakers ran the political spectrum of Chicago, from Mayor William Kelley to Ishmael Flory. Again front-style medium and message merged: the ad included a reminder to readers to "Listen to CIO Radio Broadcasts Every Night" for breaking information on the labor situation.[56]

The *Defender*'s attempts at balancing radical reformist coverage and a "higher" appeal to national unity through cooperative political and cultural consumption was most severely tested by the events of the summer of 1943. The rioting that struck black ghettoes in Detroit, Los Angeles, Beaumont, and New York that year emerged from conditions that virtually mirrored Chicago's: massive discrimination in access to private and public housing; routine harassment and violence by city police against citizens; union discrimination in industry; disproportionate crime, poverty, and unemployment. Leading up to the riots the paper had aggressively reported on these incidents, fanning a range of political responses and initiatives. When the Detroit riots broke out in June 1943, the paper gave them sensational but thorough coverage, including full-page photospreads of bloodied black victims of police brutality. Yet throughout the tense weeks of June 1943, the paper stood steadfastly for calm. Its July 3, 1943, editorial "A Hopeful Sign," praised the coming together of the CIO, NNC, and Chicago Council of Negro Organizations with the mayor's newly formed Council of Race Relations seeking to study the causes of the Detroit riot and prevent their recurrence in Chicago. The editorial also cited a telegram from John Sengstacke to Roosevelt appealing for increased attention to black inner-city conditions.[57]

In retrospect, the *Defender*'s response to the riots delineates a crucial moment in the evolution of black cultural politics after 1935. To paraphrase

Malcolm X, the Popular Front had come home to roost. The appeal to Chicago's new coalitions of radicals, black organized labor, white political establishment, black capitalists, both progressive and conservative, to "stave off" rioting symbolized the simultaneous autonomy of a new black progressivism and its ambivalence toward its most radical flank and roots. The tension between the paper's flamboyant news coverage of the riots and its editorial call for peace marked again the paradoxes and parameters of the black cultural front. This paradox was the unintended subtext of the *Defender's* September 4, 1943, editorial "Why Hoodlums?" The editorial opened with the question: "Are Negro newspapers and leaders bending over backwards in their current 'good conduct' campaign?" Noting black papers' support for measures to curb "unbridled elements" among the black population, like zoot suiters and pool players, the paper argued that "to blame bad Negro behavior for any race riot is sorry logic of the cart-before-the-horse variety." Instead, the paper focused blame on "white America," which "insists on segregation and jim crow which gave the Negro refugee status in his native land." The product of this segregation, the paper tried to suggest, should not be the object of black bourgeois scorn: "In the Harlem riots, we have the picture of thousands of Bigger Thomases running berserk instead of the one so aptly described in Richard Wright's novel. . . . Our battle is not against the results, but the cause—not against the Bigger Thomases, but the Bilbos and Rankins."[58]

The *Defender's* confused and confusing appropriation of Wright's most famous character as both race rebel and race pariah, "native" outcast and native son, reconstituted the ambivalence in Wright's novel between the "appeal to liberal capitalism" and the urgency of its overthrow as a crisis embedded in the black press's representations of black space in white America. As the *Defender* "Hoodlums" editorial made clear, the riots constituted a looking-glass for black Chicago—and black America—conjuring up images of real and imagined, historical and stereotypical black "militancy" dating from the 1919 Red Summer to *Native Son*. It was in part the available representations of the riot themselves through black mass media (including literature) that created the self-surveillance reflected in the *Defender's* call for peace. The rioting vicariously constituted a visceral "display" of Chicago and the black media's own Janus-faced contradictions—part Sengstackian entrepreneurship, part Hughesian militancy—contradictions more deeply rooted and fully developed by 1943 in Chicago than in any other black American city. Following the internal logic of these Negro People's Front occupational hazards, the paper and the city agreed to lay down the sword and shield. Both rallied around institutional democratic politics, supporting the mayor's call for a committee to investigate racial reform. Though the committee was oft-accused of a "go-slow" politics in the newspaper's pages in the months after its formation, the *Defender* dutifully supported its aims throughout. The South Side stewed but never duplicated the violence of New York, Los Angeles, and Detroit.

The Chicago strategy for peace mirrored aspects of the shifting national black consciousness toward increasing black "Americanism" as A. Phillip Randolph called it, and a future-oriented postwar consensus.[59] Six months later, the paper had turned its attention almost entirely to two issues: black participation in electoral reform in the 1944 election, and postwar jobs. These concerns undergirded the paper's formation of its last wartime "front," the Non-Partisan League. The name and organizing model evoked the agrarian, labor-based, and previously mostly white Non-Partisan League that had successfully fought racism and lynching from World War I until well into the 1930s. The "new" league gave its address as 3435 South Indiana Avenue, home of the *Defender*. In-house ads for a "Non-Partisan Roosevelt Unity Rally" in the fall 1944 *Defender* were undersigned by numerous Communist-controlled or influenced and heavily black Chicago unions like the United Auto Workers; Joint Council of Dining Car Employees; United Packing House Workers CIO; International Longshore and Warehouse Union CIO; and United Radio and Electrical Workers CIO.[60] Yet the ads reached well beyond a labor or CP base, quoting Wendell Wilkie, by 1944 the only Republican placing race reform near the top of the party agenda, and the progressive Henry A. Wallace, whose attacks on the poll tax and job discrimination had endeared him to black progressives. Local endorsements ranged the Chicago political spectrum, from Robert Taylor, chair of the Chicago Housing Authority; to Willard S. Townsend, by 1944 a firmly anti-Communist CIO organizer; to radical CIO and NNC organizer Ishmael Flory; to the ANP's Frank Marshall Davis, who in *Livin' the Blues* attributed his own turn to radicalism to the fallout from the 1943 Detroit riots.

This distinctly "un-American" coalition, its apparent rapprochement with the state, as well as the political debate in which it was engaged was distinctly recast in the paper's 1944 election editorials and endorsements. "Where Negroes Belong: Liberalism or Reaction?," the paper's October 7, 1944, editorial, put the matter bluntly: "Negro America has but one road ahead—the path of liberalism, of unity with Wallaces and Wilkies, with recognized spokesmen for the people's progress, with the foremost liberal of America, President Roosevelt."[61] In its most decisive presidential endorsement ever, the *Defender* showed the precarious ground upon which it was made. Liberalism had become the default mode of black cultural politics at a time when the African-American, and American, definition of liberalism itself had reached a horizon point of indeterminacy. The editorial's conflation of Wilkie, Roosevelt, Wallace, and the "people's progress" was as semantically and ideologically mercurial as Browder's infamous Popular Front rallying cry "Communism is Twentieth-Century Americanism." The same craving for legitimation that had pushed the party into supporting Mother's Day during the Popular Front had pushed black cultural politics into a nativist political corner from which, beyond bipolar party politics, there now seemed to be no exit.

Yet as with Richard Wright's symbolic value for the black cultural front, stories about Negro People's Front Chicago that offer "closure" are quickly pried open by contradictions they cannot easily contain. Despite its 1944 editorial sleight of hand in endorsing "liberalism," the *Defender* found itself *returning* Left immediately after the 1944 elections. Governmental failure to support the permanent establishment of the Fair Employment Practices Commission, the beginnings of black layoffs in wartime industries during re-conversion, and the continued wafflings of labor on union discrimination cast the war's end as a cloud over racial progress. "Is V-E Day the Negro's D-Day?" the paper asked in May 1945.[62] The paper also found itself defending black radicalism, now under open attack as domestic fears of the Soviet Union's postwar role escalated. It gave extensive coverage and editorial support to Communist Ben Davis's 1945 attempted reelection to the New York City Council, where Davis fell under opposition and attack by Republicans, Democrats, and anti-Communists. On the local front, deteriorating housing conditions and continued application of restrictive covenants earned numerous editorial blasts from the paper and Chicago activists like Horace Cayton, who singled out the mayor's Committee on Race Relations for foot-dragging and retrenchment of Supreme Court mandates.

Events like these fired enduring black cynicism and old-Left suspicions of liberalism, providing the outlines of a new internationalist racial radicalism. Dispirited and wary that the war on racism at the home front could be lost, *Defender* coverage, particularly its editorials and columns, began to resurrect the specter of international racial solidarity, one not seen in its pages since the days of Mussolini, Ethiopia, and the war in Spain. Copious attention to the fate of European colonies, African partition, and the plight of nonwhites, including black soldiers, in England and France in the news pages were complemented by columns by W. E. B. Du Bois, Earl Conrad, and Langston Hughes attuned to the Soviet Union as a model of racial equality for the United States in the postwar world. Even the *Defender's* book pages took on a distinctly internationalist cast. Jack Conroy and Ben Burns devoted many of their 1944 and 1945 reviews to new books on revolution in China and the colonial question in Europe, while Burns in particular was venomous in attacking books by American liberals, like Hodding Carter's *The Winds of Fear*—for their cautious antidotes for American racism. For black and white progressives and radicals on the *Defender* staff, the postwar world soon took on the outlines of a racist hegemony even more daunting than the prewar world, with American conservatives at home, and imperialists and colonialists abroad, arming themselves with atomic bombs and a UN Charter to permanently divide the world into white and nonwhite, master and slave, colonizer and colonized.[63]

The urgency of this alarm, along with the serial drama of the war, the election, and the success of the Double V campaign, made 1944 and 1945 the apex years of circulation for the *Defender* and the black press generally. By the end of the war circulation for the *Defender* and other black weekly papers had risen 43 percent from 1940, from 1,276,600 to 1,808,060.[64] By 1945 the black press had also successfully lobbied the Office of War Information into granting the first-ever press credentials providing White House access, as well as the first-ever overseas war correspondents. Sengstacke and twelve other editors and publishers from ten black papers had successfully presented a twenty-one-point statement on black war aims and postwar aspirations to the president in a thirty-five-minute meeting in February 1944.[65] By 1945 the *Defender* was proclaiming credit for the coming to fruition of a two-year campaign to integrate the major leagues in the person of Montreal prospect Jackie Robinson. Black papers had also earned the respect and, more importantly, advertising dollars of white businesses after 1942, when a new federal excess profits tax had convinced major American companies like Philip Morris, Pepsi-Cola, Pabst Blue Ribbon, and Old Gold to begin advertising in the black press.[66] Finally, black media cooperation and access was at an all-time high. In February 1944 the NNPA had begun a series of "Newspaper Week Broadcasts" on NBC, CBS, and the Blue Network to celebrate Negro Newspaper Week initiated by the NNPA. Show topics included "The Negro in the Defense Industry," "The Negro Press and the War Effort," hosted by C. B. Powell of the *Amsterdam Star-News,* and "Statement on the Negro Press" by John Sengstacke, still president of the NNPA. The broadcasts included entertainment in the form of music by Duke Ellington's orchestra, radio plays on exploits of Negro naval heroes, and music by a glee club training station and orchestra.[67]

It was these images of African Americans as conspicuous producers and consumers on the new "cultural front" that had in large part mobilized the state into renewed oppression of black radicalism as early as 1940. Throughout the war, as both Patrick Washburn and Lee Finkle have noted, the FBI built its elaborate machinery for surveillance and observation of black America largely through its monitoring of the black press. Passage of the Smith Act and Espionage Act during the war years were targeted directly at black newspapers. FBI surveillance of the black press's alleged ties to Communism and Japanese and German intelligence constituted the brunt of Office of War Information investigations by director Francis Biddle from 1939 to the end of the war. According to Washburn, the *Defender* was one of seventeen papers listed by Military Intelligence as carrying inflammatory articles by Communists in 1942.[68] In that year, OWI came close to a blanket suppression of the black press until Biddle "decided quietly" that no black publishers would be indicted for sedition during the war.[69] The government's culmination of its wartime surveillance of black America was its 1943 "FBI's Racon," a 714-page survey of black "subversive" activity in the United States, including thirty on the black press.[70] Ben Burns, in his memoir, recounts the discovery of his own FBI file in 1941. Langston Hughes, meanwhile, spent much of his 1940s career fending off allegations of party ties from conservatives, universities, right-wing groups, and eventually the House Un-American Activities Committee. W. E. B. Du Bois declared his Marxism while still writing a column for the *Defender* and was subsequently ousted from his post at Atlanta University. In 1951 he was denounced by the *Defender* itself as a turncoat to Americanism.

As Robert Hill has noted, the wartime period thus sowed the seeds of the FBI's Counter-Intelligence Program and the permanent establishment of formal surveillance of black America in the postwar period. As this chapter has demonstrated, the *Defender*'s role in the birth of this trend was as tragic as it was earned. Despite its recurrent pledges of unanimous support for Roosevelt as early as 1942,[71] and even its offers of cooperation in assisting the federal government with wartime press censorship programs,[72] the *Defender* emerged from World War II as one of the best pieces of evidence the FBI had for what Naison calls the "deep-rooted appeal" of Popular Front-style radicalism to black America. Ironically, this appeal has frequently been characterized by historians of the black press as a fundamental "conservatism." As with critical taxonomies of Richard Wright, such implicitly binary descriptions of the newspaper reproduce the anxieties about black radicalism that the *Defender* itself succumbed to in its 1943 riot editorials, its 1944 presidential endorsement, and its 1951 attack on Du Bois. Clearly, the categories of culture and politics were opened far beyond such binary opposition in the pages of the *Defender* between 1935 and 1943 especially, creating a moment of creative friction perhaps unrivaled in the history of the black press.

Yet like *Native Son,* the *Defender* might also be said to mark the beginnings of black critical anxiety about its companion phenomenon, the creation of African-American mass consumer culture. Its construction of a black capitalism built out of the shattered pieces of the Depression, an emerging black entrepreneurship, and liberal economic and political reform undergirded the production of cultural images of a new black protest idiom dependent on cultural icons—from Joe Louis to Lena Horne to Paul Robeson to Richard Wright to Bigger Thomas—whose oppositional "meanings" were ultimately subsumed under a larger drive to satiate the new black marketplace for ideas about itself. Perhaps the most ironic and descriptive image of that trend lies in its figurative progenitor, Robert Abbott. In 1942, two years after his death, the *Defender* led a fund-raising drive in Chicago to create a Liberty ship in Abbott's memory. Serially, for weeks on end, the paper urged readers to donate money for construction of the USS *Abbott.* Funding came from all quarters, including the Communist-led Abraham Lincoln School. At the 1943 christening of the ship in California, Sengstacke, Metz Lochard, and Abbott's widow—who had lost a royal battle for control of the paper to the "reformist" Sengstacke in 1940—were on hand.[73]

In 1945, near war's end, the ship was turned over to the Soviet Union as part of a lend-lease agreement. In an editorial marking the transfer, the *Defender* noted the symmetrical justice of the "race man's" battleship steaming towards the place the paper was still celebrating as the utopian end point of racial equality. "It is altogether fitting," the paper wrote, "that a ship named after him should fly the flag of the one country in the world where racial discrimination is prohibited by law; where self-determination of peoples is written into the constitution; where color of the skin has no more significance than color of the eyes as far as citizenship rights are concerned. Robert S. Abbott would have been proud that the Liberty ship that honors his name is sailing the seven seas for the country that honors the principles for which he fought."[74]

Abbott's symbolic "transformation" during the course of the war from black bootstrap entrepreneur to defender of Soviet-style racial equality was a culminating moment in the Negro People's Front/Popular Front's "Black and White Unite and Fight" aspirations. That this moment took symbolic form bespeaks less the tendencies toward compromise and assimilation of the black press than the recurring, and perhaps inevitable, displacement and reinvention of black political aspiration into the production of culture during this period. The "seven seas" of an imagined Soviet racial harmony was in 1945 still an alluring metonym of the unfinished drive toward a free, public, and expressive black space where the "unprofitable" contradictions of democratic capitalism and institutional racism could perhaps be left behind.

# 3  Artists in Uniform: The South Side Community Art Center and the Defense of Culture

On July 4, 1940, four months after the death of Robert S. Abbott and the publication of Richard Wright's *Native Son,* the American Negro Exposition opened at the Chicago Coliseum on the city's near South Side. Planned to commemorate the seventy-fifth Anniversary of the Emancipation Proclamation, the eight-week exposition, funded in part by a $75,000 grant from the Illinois State Legislature, showcased the achievements of black writers, journalists, musicians, and visual artists. Though national in scope, its location reflected Chicago's centrality to the exposition's aim of demonstrating the changing scope and direction of African-American culture. The Illinois Federal Writers' Project, for example, had by 1940 produced the outlines of the largest single WPA study of black life, the "Negro in Illinois" project, featuring the talents of some of Chicago's best black writers: Arna Bontemps, Richard Wright, and Willard Motley. Similarly, no fewer than twenty-one black Chicago visual artists had by 1940 participated in the Illinois Federal Art Project, the greatest black participation in an FAP in any American city. The Art Exhibition of the Negro Exposition included work by Charles White, Eldzier Cortor, William Carter, Joseph Kersey, George E. Neal, Henry Avery, Charles Davis, William Farrow, Bernard Goss, Walter Ellison, Archibald Motley, Charles Sebree, Margaret Taylor Goss Burroughs, Marion Perkins, and David Ross, all of whom had studied, trained, and worked in Chicago before and during the Depression. Though their style and subject matter varied broadly, almost all had concentrated—like their Federal Writers' Project comtemporaries—on documenting the quotidian conditions of Chicago's Depression-sieged South Side.

Alain Locke, chairman of the exposition art committee, used his introduction to the Exhibition of the Art of the American Negro to revise and

update prevailing African-American cultural imperatives he had done much
to establish in his 1925 *New Negro* collection, the ur-text of the Harlem Renaissance. Locke's introduction formally announced a new black visual aesthetic emerging from the social and political traumas of the Depression
whose onset had coincided with the end of Harlem's artistic boom:

> Not too many yet know how this present generation of younger artists are
> maturing and catching the stride of the national awakening in art by which
> a characteristic native American art is being developed. An art that adequately
> reflects America, must, of course, include the American Negro, and artists,
> with their more liberal tradition and spirit, have not been slow in realizing
> this. In contemporary American art of this generation, both the Negro and
> the White artist stand on common ground in their aim to document every
> phase of American life and experience. More and more you will notice in their
> canvasses the sober realism which goes beneath the jazzy, superficial show
> of things or the mere picturesqueness of the Negro to the deeper truths of
> life, even the social problems of religion, labor, housing, lynching, unemploy-
> ment and the like. For today's beauty must not be pretty with sentiment but
> solid and dignified with truth.
>
> Nor is the Negro artist of today so very different from his brother artists.
> Product of the same social and cultural soil, he is typically American after
> all. And yet, he must somehow reflect what he sees most and knows best, his
> own folk, and his own feeling of life. In so doing, he can teach us to see our-
> selves, not necessarily as others see us, but as we should be seen. Finding
> beauty in ourselves, we can and must be spiritually stronger, and in conse-
> quence, socially and culturally more worth while.[1]

Locke's Introduction recast what he had called at the 1937 Philadelphia
National Negro Congress the "cultural racialism of the art philosophy of the
1920s" into a new paradigm for a black folk-cultural revival. His invocation
of the exhibition's "sober realism," of the drive among black artists for interracial cultural production, of the "documentary" calling of the Negro artist
and the stress on social protest against racial and economic injustice was a
more cautious summoning of what his NNC address had deemed "the class
proletarian art creed of today's younger generation."[2] Locke's use of distinctively Popular Front rhetoric—the Negro artist is "typically American after
all"—also echoed both the Left's post-1936 cultural front policy and James
Ford's recurring references to black cutural workers as the vanguard of the
"democratic front." Locke's 1940 application of these tenets reflected not just
the persistence of Depression-like circumstances in South Side Chicago well

into the late 1930s, but a lag time in official recognition of black artists and their role in "proletarian" aesthetics the American Negro Exposition was meant to overcome.

No single artist in the 1940 American Negro Exposition better represented these circumstances than Charles White. His epic "A History of the Negro Press" (pp. ii–iii) executed for Barnett's Associated Negro Press Exhibit, had won first prize in the exposition's mural competition. White had also won a first prize in the black and white category and an honorable mention in water color painting. The winning works reflected White's absorption of numerous political and aesthetic strands available to Depression-era South Side artists. In 1936, the year he graduated from Chicago's South Side Englewood High School, White had taken part in his first exhibition, sponsored by the Art Crafts Guild of the South Side. According to Margaret Burroughs, another member, the guild was an art club of primarily young, poor, black artists who met every Sunday afternoon in each other's homes.[3] Its president was a sign painter, William McGill. In 1936, members of the guild had begun private tutelage under George E. Neal, a black painter immersed in both the "social realist" tendencies of better-known white artists like Ben Shahn and other currents of Western painting: landscape, still life, abstraction. Because informal Jim Crowing of galleries gave black painters no places to show, guild members worked and exhibited at "whatever space [was] available" according to Burroughs, including YMCAs and church basements.[4] The precocious talent displayed by White in the 1936 guild exhibition earned him a scholarship to the School of the Art Institute of Chicago, making him one of the first South Side artists to penetrate its nearly exclusively white walls.

In 1938 White was hired to the Mural Division of the Illinois Federal Art Project, one of the first blacks hired to the project. The hiring coincided with the easing of restricted access for blacks to Illinois FAP jobs under its notoriously conservative director Increase Robinson, who after a three-year reign was replaced in 1938 by the more progressive George Thorpe. In the mural unit White and fellow black Chicago artist Archibald Motley worked with the white artists Edward Millman, Edgar Britton, and Mitchell Siporin—the latter a former member of the Chicago John Reed Club. The dominant muralists of the Illinois FAP, all three had by 1938 traveled to Mexico to work with Diego Rivera, Jose Clemente Orozco, and David Alfara Siquieros, Mexico's vanguard revolutionary artists. In 1923, Siquieros had written the manifesto of the Mexican muralist movement. Published by the Syndicate of Technical Workers, Painters, and Sculptors, it read in part:

Exhibition
of
# THE ART
# OF THE
# AMERICAN
# NEGRO
(1851 to 1940)

ASSEMBLED BY THE

American Negro
Exposition

ON VIEW
JULY 4 TO
SEPTEMBER 2
1940

TANNER
ART GALLERIES

AMERICAN
NEGRO
EXPOSITION
CHICAGO, ILLINOIS

PRICE TWENTY-FIVE CENTS

First Award in Black-and White
"There Were No Crops This Year"
by Charles White, Illinois.

*Figure 3.* Program cover, "Exhibition of the Art of the American Negro" for the 1940 American Negro Exposition in Chicago. Charles White's first prize black-and-white "There Were No Crops This Year," pictured on the program cover, indicated White's prominence as the most representative artist at the Exposition. Reprinted courtesy of the Estate of Charles White.

The art of the Mexican people—is the highest and creates spiritual expression of the world-tradition which constitutes our most valued heritage. It is great because it surges from the people; it is collective, and our own aesthetic aim is to socialize artistic expression, to destroy bourgeois individualism. . . .

We repudiate the so-called easel art and all such art which springs from ultraintellectual circles, for it is essentially aristocratic. . . .

We proclaim that this being the moment of social transition from a decrepit to a new order, the makers of beauty must invest their greatest efforts in the aim of materializing an art valuable to the people, and our supreme objective in art . . . is to create beauty for all, beauty that enlightens and stirs to struggle.[5]

According to George Mavigliano and Richard Lawson, Millman, Britton, and Siporin sought an "Americanization" of the Mexican muralistic aesthetic, linking Orozco's anti-capitalist roots in the 1910 Mexican revolution to the radical democratic socialism of Walt Whitman.[6] White's own murals and late 1930s paintings constituted a distinctly African-American revision of this aesthetic. In place of Whitman and other white American "democratic" heroes, White, as had Rivera, wove black historical struggle and its icons into a representational strategy that Locke would call in 1940, in a virtual paraphrase of Siquieros, a beauty "not . . . pretty with sentiment but solid and dignified with truth" ("beauty that enlightens and stirs to struggle"). In addition to his award-winning journalistic mural on the heroes and history of the black press, a virtual paean to the Mexican muralists, White's other 1940 exhibition works included the watercolor "Fellow Worker, Won't You March With Us" and the prize-winning black and white "There Were No Crops This Year." The latter, used as the cover art for the exhibition catalog, depicts a wearied black farm couple against an archetypally stark Depression-era sky. The woman, foregrounded, lists leftward with an empty grain bag extended; her partner, in the background, holds his left hand to a furrowed brow, his right hand reaching down empty towards the ground. Typical of both Mexican mural painting and what Michael Denning calls the "proletarian grotesque" it helped to produce in American art,[7] the laborers' hands are enlarged to symbolize both the enormity of their work and the scope of their want.

White's empathic rendering of the black proletarian "folk" for a northern urban expo and its selection by the exhibitors as both the most outstanding and representative work of the exhibit bespoke a new black visual aesthetic of 1940 grounded simultaneously in the indigenous catastrophe of black slavery and a new interracial and international solidarity for black artists looking to frame that experience seventy-five years later. White's work, its roots its Mexican vanguardism, and his struggles against segregation and discrimination in Chicago's own Depression-era art scene was thus the exposition's best evidence of the need for late 1930s black visual artists to take up what Earl Browder, James Ford, Alain Locke, and David Siquieros were in different places and times demanding of vanguard artists around the world: a defense of culture. Indeed White's work and the American Negro Exposition were retrospective markers of a host of 1930s demands and gains by black Chicago visual artists for access to political and cultural capital fueled by black experience of the Depression: not just positions on the Federal Art Project, for example, but access to the Jim Crowed gallery and museum world of Chicago. These demands had since the mid-1930s been fed locally by grassroots organizations like the interracial Chicago Artists Union and its black-only Arts and Crafts Guild, and nationally by the emergence of Popular Front organizations like the American Artists' Congress.[8] Within the South Side artistic community, reception for these demands had been supported by radical or progressive white artists and gallery owners like Morris Topchevksy, Si Gordon, John Walley, and Peter Pollack, who up to and after 1938 and well into the 1940s provided example for Locke's 1940 claim that the "Negro and White artists stand on common ground" in their efforts to document American life.

These local collaborations of progressive black and white artists and cultural workers in Chicago were also emblematic of larger Popular Front-style cultural politics symbolized by the broad-ranging coalitionism that had produced the 1940 Negro Art Exhibition: the state and local funding support for the exhibit, which included both WPA and National Youth Administration money; its broad publicity in the black and white Chicago press, most especially the ANP and *Defender;* the success of gimmick exhibition attractions like the Miss Bronze America national beauty contest; and the exposition appearance of black mass entertainers from Duke Ellington's band to Paul Robeson. This swirl of giddy entrepreneurialism and vanguard cultural production had made the exhibit by its September 2, 1940, closing Chicago's *own* Negro People's Front avatar: a progressive cultural and political party drawing enormous mixed-class crowds from black Chicago eager to realize the city's potential to supplant New York as the capital of Negro progressive culture.[9] Heady with this vast menu of possibility, black and white visual artists led a charge to the future after 1940 beholden both to the promise of revolutionary vision forged as far away as Moscow and Mexico City, and to the purse strings of a new Negro (and white) patronage without whom that vision would be economically if not politically bankrupt. Yet as this preliminary account also suggests, the battleground for that charge had already been established prior to the 1940 Exposition in the dilemmas and opportunities for black artists during the Depression. Those dilemmas and opportunities were rooted in and played out in the more extenuated, dramatic, and permanent struggle for political control and artistic direction of Chicago's Negro People's Front artistic crown jewel: the South Side Community Art Center.

The obscurity of the story of the South Side Community Art Center reflects the extent to which Chicago's black "renaissance" has been narrowly construed in previous cultural histories. Outside of George Mavigliano and Richard Lawson's passing and incomplete account in their book on the Federal Art Project in Illinois, the history of the Art Center exists mostly in internal commemorative records produced by the center, its surviving members, and the city of Chicago itself.[10] Yet arguably no black cultural institution better documents both the mid-century absorption and revision of 1930s American cultural and political radicalism into black public space. And as my concluding chapter in particular will show, no Chicago institution also reflects more overtly the enduring scars of internal black struggle for provenance and sovereignty over the direction of postwar black political culture.

Officially, the Art Center was a product of the WPA's Community Arts Center Program, which during its tenure opened more than eighty community art centers around the country. The conflicting communal lore illuminating its origins begins to delineate especially the tensions in black cultural politics that it came to symbolize in Chicago's Negro People's Front. In a commemorative fiftieth anniversary program published in 1991, for example, James Graff offers the history of the Art Center as a "rich commentary on civic dedication in the changing world of the black middle-class."[11] Graff writes that the decision of the WPA to establish a Community Arts Center in Chicago was initiated by Peter Pollack, a North Side gallery owner, who in 1938 was a staff member on the Illinois Federal Art Project. Margaret Burroughs remembers Pollack as a progressive Jew whose North Michigan Avenue gallery had been the first to exhibit South Side black artists on the North Side, including herself, Bernard Goss, Charles Sebree, and Joseph Kersey.[12] Graff and Burroughs's published accounts of the center's founding agree that Pollack and Illinois Art Project director George Thorpe mutually decided in 1938 to try and find new venues for the exhibition of black art. According to Graff, Pollack contacted Dr. Metz Lochard, *Defender* editor, asking to be put in touch with some prominent South Side blacks who could help conceive, and pay for, the creation of a new exhibition space. Graff says Lochard took Pollack "unannounced" to meet Pauline Kigh Reed, a black social worker, who suggested to Pollack the idea of developing an art center.[13] Burroughs's account varies slightly but significantly: she contends that Thorpe and Pollack came directly to a small group of "leading" black citizens, including poor, young artists like herself, to discuss forming the art center. Burroughs recounts preliminary discussions at the South Side Settlement House, another itinerant exhibition space for members of the Arts and Crafts Guild. Graff's account has Reed inviting "four friends" to meet Pollack the next week: Frankie Raye Singleton, Susan Morris, Marie Moore, and Grace Carter Cole, none artists and all members of Reed's polite society. Here accounts more or less converge: Graff and Burroughs write that Golden B. Darby, a prominent South Side insurance salesman, accepted an invitation to become chairman of the Art Center Sponsoring Committee. Shortly thereafter, a South Side Community Art Center Association was organized to draw together the broadest range of the South Side's money and talent: Mrs. Katherine Marie Moore, federal judge of the Virgin Islands, was elected president; other invited members included William Yerby, U.S. consul to France; J. Livert Kelly, flamboyant leader of the local 444 AFL Waiters, Bartenders and Cooks union; Patrick Prescott, according to Graff the "biggest Republican in town"; Earl Dickerson, the biggest Democrat. All together more than sixty South Side citizens and organizations signed on to the sponsoring committee.[14]

In 1938 and 1939, according to Burroughs, more than forty planning meetings were held at various South Side locations including the Urban League and a funeral parlor at 55th Street between Michigan and Wabash Avenues.[15] In the fall of 1938, the center's first fund-raiser was held at the Savoy Ballroom beside the Regal Theater at 47th and South Parkway. In style, esprit, and turnout, the first annual "Artists and Models Ball" was both derivative and reminiscent of other socials and fund-raisers for the Spanish Civil War and defense of Ethiopia sponsored by the Communist Party and other progressive South Side organizations. The ball featured a combination of food and politics, music and art, highbrow social posturing and grassroots cultural work. The 1938 ball, for example, coordinated by black society woman Frances Moseley Matlock, featured costumes, decorations, and artwork by artists like Burroughs, Joseph Kersey, and William Carter, and drew financial support from South Side CIO chapters. Using this formula, the balls became annual events after 1938, drawing huge crowds largely from the black bourgeoisie.

On October 25, 1939, the Art Center Committee met again at the South Side Settlement House. George Thorpe reported that if the South Side community could find a facility for an art center, the Federal Art Project would fund renovations. It would also pay the salaries of the staff, teachers, and maintenance crews. The center would need to raise funds for utilities. Edgar E. Mitchem, an insurance man, was according to Burroughs named chairman of the finance committee. Henry Avery, an artist, was named chairman of the site committee. Burroughs herself recalls standing on the corner of 39th and South Parkway (now Martin Luther King Drive) collecting dimes in a can as part of "A Mile for Dimes" campaign to raise center funding.[16] A membership campaign initiated thereafter enlisted, among others, the sculptor Simon Gordon, Thelma Kirkpatrick Wheaton, a social worker, and a number of mostly female black schoolteachers and social workers who comprised the progressive spectrum of Chicago's "race women." On May 4, 1940, the nationally recognized sculptress and Harlem activist Augusta Savage lectured in Chicago on "Crises, Past and Present" as part of a fund-raising tour for the art center. Less than a month later, a brownstone mansion at 3831 South Michigan Avenue in Chicago's old Gold Coast district was purchased for about $8,000. The three-story coach house featured a huge first-floor living area to be converted into a gallery and two other floors for workshops, studios, and classes.

Between June and December 1940, WPA funds and the sweat equity of South Side artists transformed the South Michigan mansion, the painters and sculptors literally scrubbing floors and walls in preparation for the scheduled May 7, 1941, dedication by Eleanor Roosevelt. In December 1940, these same artists received the first fruit of their labor at the informal opening of the Art Center Gallery. White, Avery, Davis, Motley, Cortor, Carter, Kersey, Gabriel, and Bernard Goss were featured in a show of seventeen artists and forty-two oils and watercolors. According to the *Chicago Defender,* four hundred attended the opening.[17] The show marked not only the successful remodeling of the Art Center but another step in the ongoing renovation of the national image of the black artist initiated by the 1940 Chicago Exposition. In February 1941, Alonzo Aden of the Art Gallery at Howard University, who had curated the 1940 Exposition Art Exhibition, reprised part of it in an "Exhibition of Negro Artists of Chicago" at the Howard University Gallery of Art. The exhibition featured all of the prominent Chicago artists and many of the works from the Chicago exposition, including Henry Avery, William Carter, John Collier, Edward T. Cortor, Eldzier Cortor, Charles Davis, Katherine Dorsey, Raymond Gabriel, Bernard Goss, Margaret T. Goss, Charles T. Haig, Fred Hollingsworth, Joseph Kersey, Clarence Lawson, Frank Neal, George Neal, Marion Perkins, Charles Sebree, Earl Walker, and Charles White.[18] Sebree and Carter were also fresh off of an exhibition of watercolors marking the nineteenth season of the Art Institute of Chicago.

In September 1940, Alain Locke met with other members of the Art Center's sponsors' committee to continue planning for its opening. In November, "The Associates in Negro Folk Education" published Locke's *The Negro in Art: A Pictorial Record of the Negro Artist and of the Negro Theme in Art.* Chicago artists were again central to the book's conception: Avery, John Carlis Jr., Carter, Cortor, Davis, William McKnight Farrow, Bernard Goss, Joseph Kersey, Clarence Lawson, Archibald Motley, William Edouard Scott, Earl Walker, and Charles White were all featured. As he had in his 1940 introduction to the American Negro Exposition Art Exhibition, Locke revised both the locus and the mission of black cultural production. He equated the black artists' task of "self-delineation as part of a maturing program of racial self-expression" with the development of Negro art "as an important chapter in the development of a fully representative and native American art."[19] Reflecting an even more dramatic inversion of Harlem Renaissance aestheticism, "The Ancestral Arts," demonstrating African influence, was the last section of the book; the first, "The Negro As Artist," was dominated by 1930s images by black artists reflective of what Locke called "a vigorous, intimate and original documentation of Negro life."[20] Locke also reprised, verbatim, his Art Exposition copy on the "deepening significance" and "sober realism" of the new Negro art, while adding kudos for the move toward the creation of public black space for the arts with which he was now intimately connected in Chicago. "Never having had generous support from private patronage," he wrote, "it is particularly vital to the Negro artist to have some considerable measure of public and popular support. Important as it is to heighten the productivity of the Negro artist, it is even more important to broaden the base of popular art appreciation and use."[21] Locke cited WPA-funded Community Art Centers in Harlem, Chicago, and "even more strategic places in the South,—Greensboro, N.C., Memphis, New Orleans," which would carry this task. "They will also further," Locke wrote, "the equally important job of carrying the Negro artist, too long isolated from the folk, back to one of the most vital sources of his materials."[22]

Locke's wistful, and wishful, celebration of northern black urban artists and Art Centers as the new homes of the black "folk" encapsulated ideological and historical revisions in the black aesthetic Chicago's South Side arts scene embodied. Between the Harlem Renaissance and the early years of black northern migration and the 1936 reformulations of Popular Front policies into Negro People's Front activism, black artists had discovered a new vernacular for old black troubles. The merging of modernism, primitive technique, historical black sources, and a radical documentary impulse evident,

for example, in Jacob Lawrence's stirring series on the life of Toussaint-
Louverture completed in 1938 and prominently featured in Locke's book, or
even more obviously in Lawrence's more famous "Migration Series," were
meant to literally and figuratively indicate the distance the "folk" as subject
and technique had traveled by 1940. Locke's introduction, like Lawrence's
series, White's mural on the historical evolution of the black press, and the
convergence of artists in the manual labor of preparing the Art Center were
thus complementary articulations of a collective black claim on a new communal space meant to mark the end of one historical journey and the beginning of another. As had been the case with the influential Mexican muralists, the "social transition from a decrepit to a new order" in the minds of
Chicago painters and national figures of prominence like Locke had come
to be symbolized in the need to historicize, house, protect, and reproduce
racial experience, from field to factory, cotton to canvas. Logically, the Taller
de Grafica Popular printmaking center in Mexico City was one model for this
attempt. Created in 1936 to institutionalize the revolutionary teaching and
practices of the Mexican vanguard muralists, it was by 1940 already an aesthetic influence and safe haven for artists like Siporin, and soon for black
artists like Charles White and Elizabeth Catlett. Still another was the Harlem
Art Center, then headed by the leftist painter and writer Gwendolyn Bennett,
later ousted from her position for those same politics. These sites, well prepared by the ground-breaking work of the 1923 Syndicate manifesto and the
vanguard organizing of the Harlem Renaissance, were models Chicago could
by 1940 feel well prepared to emulate, or transcend.

Yet the Art Center's 1941 dedication also served to crystallize not just ideological but organizational tensions in Chicago's black cultural front. The dozens of poor painters and cultural workers who saw the Art Center as a chance,
in Burroughs's words, "to stop shining shoes all week and just paint on Sundays"[23] found themselves pushed to the margins by the numerous black socialites who had come to attach themselves to this sudden institutionalization
of black culture. Just prior to Roosevelt's arrival, the artists were told that they
wouldn't be able to speak formally as part of the dedication ceremony.
Burroughs, whose artistic brio, organizing ability, and radical political instincts
perhaps embody the creative energy of Chicago's Negro People's Front better than any other figure, hurriedly wrote out a "Statement" on behalf of the
artists present and asked David Ross, a fellow painter, to read it to Mrs.
Roosevelt and the crowd. Insisting on the economic and political differences
between Chicago's black Left bohemia and its aspiring patrons, it invoked the
Depression struggles of black painters as a microcosm of the seventy-five years

since Emancipation and a warning not to forget or allow the struggles of either to be appropriated by deep pockets or "false consciousness":

> Now, in this period of wartime, we have our own plans for a defense—a defense of culture. . . .
>
> We were not then and are not now complimented by the people who had the romantic idea that we liked to live in garrets, wear off clothes and go around with emaciated faces, painting for fun; living until the day we died and hoping that our paintings would be discovered in some dusty attic fifty years later and then we would be famous. . . .
>
> . . . We believed that the purpose of art was to record the times. As young black artists, we looked around and recorded in our various media what we saw. It was not from our imagination that we painted slums and ghettos, or sad, hollow-eyed black men, women and children. They were the people around us.
>
> We were part of them. They were us. Thus, the coming of this Community Art Center has opened up new hope and vistas to all of us.[24]

Burroughs's call for a "defense of culture" was not simply an injured artist's response to a social slight, but a rallying cry to Chicago's black visual artists to march with other vanguard cultural workers locally and internationally. Indeed, "defense of culture" was also the rallying cry for the International Association of Writers for the Defense of Culture, a Paris-based Popular Front organization formed in June 1935. While the Soviet Writers Union constituted the largest single affiliate to the IAWDC, American writers had responded in large numbers to its 1937 call for international support of Republican forces in Spain and the larger war against fascism. Members of the American affiliate League of American Writers included virtually all of the preeminent black authors of the era, including the core of Chicago's emerging army of literary talent. Along with Richard Wright and Langston Hughes, who would serve temporarily as league vice-presidents, Chicago-affiliated black league members included Arna Bontemps, Illinois Writers Project colleague to Jack Conroy; Frank Marshall Davis, editor of the Associated Negro Press and from the outset a founding supporter of the Art Center; Alain Locke, who in addition to his role at the dedication ceremony penned the catalog copy for the first-ever art exhibit at the Art Center in 1941; Margaret Walker, veteran of the late 1930s South Side Writers' Group; and Gwendolyn Brooks, who by 1941 had already written her first poems and contributed to a short-lived South Side magazine called *Youth*, edited by a young John H. Johnson, future founder and publisher of *Ebony*.[25]

Burroughs's Art Center manifesto also synthesized nearly a decade's worth of ideas and events in the gradual radicalization of herself and many of her artistic contemporaries. In 1933 she had marched in an anti-lynching parade instigated by the Communist Party's famous Scottsboro Boys defense. In the late 1930s, along with the painters Charles White and Bernard Goss, she regularly attended public forums at the South Side's Washington Park. There, in her own words, black artists joined in "rap sessions" with white artists like Si Gordon and Morris Topchevsky—another Reed Club veteran—about the writings of Marx, Lenin, and Trotsky, and studied the lives of black freedom fighters like Harriet Tubman and Frederick Douglass.[26] In the late 1930s, Burroughs became a contributing writer to the *Chicago Defender*. Her August 31, 1940, column, "A Negro Mother Looks at War," demonstrates in microcosm ways in which black Chicago artists and intellectuals hewed to and reformed 1930s radical politics in defining the Negro People's Front. Echoing the Communist Party's recurring 1940 attacks on the "imperialist" World War, Burroughs delivered to readers a "red" message tinged both black and feminist:

Who is the god of War? The god of war is greed. Money-hungry mad men make the wars. Always the poor people are forced to fight in the wars.

This is not a people's war.

The British and French imperialists are fighting the German imperialists. The people pay the price. Innocent men die while the profit-hungry war makers grow richer. Many people here just as in the World War are anxious to get us into this war. They see a chance to reap a fine harvest, to build up fortunes for the future.

The black mothers may continue to be poverty stricken but it will be such a consolation to have their sons with them, to see their sons grow up under the watchful eyes of their fathers.

If all of the black men and women would mass themselves in a solid flank, to abolish the poll tax in the south; to end lynching and peonage; to do away with jimcrowism and segregation; to enforce the Constitution as it is written—if all black men and women would mass themselves in solid opposition to war we would see America really being America to BLACK AMERICANS. . . . Fighting for this ideal black women would be laying a firm foundation for the future of this country lifting ourselves up and off the lowest rung of the economic ladder and insuring that one-third of the nation which is ill-housed, ill-clothed and ill-fed [gets] a new birth.[27]

Burroughs's 1941 Art Center proclamation cited earlier might be read as a reapplication of the international wartime class struggle to the homefront

*Figure 4.* William Smith, "Poverty and Fatigue." Smith, Dox Thrash's Pennsylvania Federal Art Project colleague, featured this 1940 linoleum cut at the May 1941 Art Center opening. As Leslie King-Hammond has noted, Smith's 1930s and 1940s prints, including the 1938 linoleum cut "Native Son," reflected the tendency of African-American printmakers to depict the black Depression downtrodden as isolated individuals rather than crowds. From the Collection of Dave and Reba Williams.

cultural front in Chicago. Indeed, the manifesto's verbal commitment of artists to shared struggle with the working and unemployed proletariat of the South Side was in many ways visually realized by the "National Negro Art Exhibition" the center featured at its dedication. Among the works selected for exhibition were Charles Davis's "Back Streets," Burroughs's "Street Scene" and "Neighborhood," Ramon Gabriel's "Restaurant," George Neal's "Across the Street," and William Stewart's "Side Street." This insistence on Chicago's South Side *public space* as the site and source for the "defense of culture" was itself a metonymy for the seizure and transformation of the former Gold Coast white mansion into a site of black struggle and creative work. Following this same logic, the paintings themselves frequently rendered Chicago's South Siders alternately captured in moments of black labor and its discontents: Frank Neal's "Hat Makers," Charles White's "Fellow Workers," Vernon Winslow's "Barber Shop" on one hand; White's "Fatigue," a portrait of exhaustion, and Eldzier Cortor's "One Alone" on the other. Like the poems of Gwendolyn Brooks's *A Street in Bronzeville* these paintings visually foretold, these works deployed tensions between the communal and commercial potential of Chicago black public life with the isolation and encroaching despair of race-based poverty endemic to it.

Complementing these portraits were the contributions of other artists like William E. Smith and Philadelphia WPA artists like Raymond Steth and Dox Thrash, whose style and subject inversely evoked the spirit of Horace Cayton's claim, "Understand Chicago's black belt and I would understand the black belts of a dozen other large American cities."[28] Smith's linoleum cuts "Poverty and Fatigue," "War Fatigue," and "Native Son," a portrait of black adolescence predating Wright's book by two years, captured the stark despair of black urban poverty—their generic locations are both everywhere and nowhere.

Similarly Steth's 1943 lithograph "Despair" might have also been alternately titled "Bigger's Blues" for its rendering of emotional collapse on a city street—here most likely Philadelphia's South Side rather than Chicago's. Steth's starkly dark graphics demonstrated the collaborative influence of Philadelphia WPA colleague Dox Thrash, a graduate of the School of the Art Institute of Chicago. During his WPA/FAP tenure of 1939 and 1940, Thrash had invented the "Carborundum" process of printmaking. The technique drew its name from the trade name for a coarse, granular industrial product made of carbon and silicone used for grinding and polishing. According to Leslie King-Hammond, Thrash experimented "by manipulating various grades of Carborundum crystals until he achieved a wide range of tints and tonal variations."[29] Visually, Thrash's work was the chiaroscuric endpoint of

*Figure 5.* Dox Thrash, "Boats at Night." Thrash's carborundum technique and its capacity for stark graphic rendering is captured in this 1940 print on display at the May 1941 exhibit marking the dedication of the South Side Community Art Center. Thrash executed the piece while employed on the Pennsylvania Federal Art Project.

WPA graphic experiment with shading, shadowing, and black and white contrast. Images like "Boats at Night," "Coal Yard," and "Surface Mining" on display at the 1941 exhibition literally and figuratively blackened the comparatively bright "American scene" paintings of contemporaries like Thomas Hart Benton with the tools and residue of black manual labor: carborundum. Thrash's labor-intensive process reconstituted the aesthetic of manual/artistic labor in ways inseparable from the larger black revisions of "proletarian" work, culture, and technique Chicago artists had themselves demonstrated. The same talented hands that had cleared space for the Art Center in turn dexterously represented the black economic struggle and unemployment literally and figuratively surrounding it.

The tensions between the Art Center's vanguard working artists and its black patronage class manifested at the May 7 dedication were also echoes of 1930s battles within the WPA and the South Side Chicago arts scene. Chicago's own Artists' Union during the late 1930s, for example, was itself divided into "conservative and activist" factions according to Mavigliano and Lawson.[30] John Walley, head of the Art and Craft Project in twelve Illinois districts on the Illinois Federal Art Project, was a veteran of the Artists' Union when he joined the South Side Art Center teaching staff in 1941. In an un-published draft of an article on the history of the Artists' Union of Chicago between 1935 and 1943, Walley noted that Increase Robinson, first project director, "unwittingly was the chief organizer of the artists union by her iso-lated concepts and restricted social ideas," including her refusal to give WPA jobs to black artists.[31] In protest, Wally recounted the union forming a picket line around the Art Project gallery at 433 E. Erie Street for its refusal to ex-hibit minority artists. Eventually, because of the protests, several black art-ists served on the union's executive board.[32]

Fresh from these insurgent actions, Wally and other progressive whites like sculptor Si Gordon and Sophie Wessel came directly to the Art Center as teachers and advisors at its 1941 opening, as did Morris Topchevsky, one-time friend to Richard Wright and by 1942 United American Artists Union's national president. Their experience fighting racial discrimination and their commitment to a proletarian political aesthetic within WPA made their immediate natural allies among the black artists Burroughs, Charles White, and Bernard Goss. This group formed the openly progressive core of a larger group of black painters assigned to teaching posts at the center in 1941: Henry Avery, Eldzier Cortor, Walter Ellison, Ramon Gabriel, Charles Davis, and William Carter. The fluid nature of radicalism among these artists was a pronounced feature of their collaboration. As both Goss and Burroughs re-call it, while few of these Art Center artists were Communist Party mem-bers—both claim fear of retribution as early as 1941—all were supporters of the CP's fight against racial discrimination. "People, like myself, who were sympathetic were considered 'Progressive or Liberal,'" notes Burroughs.[33] In opposition to this "progressive" group was the slate of black bourgeoisie socialites headed by Pauline Kigh Reed administering the board and officers. Gordon Parks, who came to Chicago from Minneapolis in 1941 and was hired by Exhibition Manager David Ross to be the center's first in-house photog-rapher, remembers constant uprisings and turmoil between these parties, reflective of the South Side's larger class and culture wars.

Indeed, Parks recalls first visiting the Art Center in 1941 to absorb the "graphic protests" of the work of Charles White, Ben Shahn, and Isaac Soyer, the "grim paintings of the jobless and oppressed," which "had forsaken the pink ladies of Manet and Renoir, the bluish-green landscapes of Monet, hang-ing at the Art Institute several miles to the north on Michigan Avenue."[34] In November 1941, Parks was featured in a one-man show at the Art Center meant to "bag sponsors" for his application for a Rosenwald Fund Fellowship. Jack Delano, a Farm Security Administration photographer who also inspired his work, was in attendance. As Parks recalls, "It seemed that half of Chicago was there. The elite, dressed in their furs and finery, rubbed elbows with some of the people I had photographed in the poor quarter; I had invited as many of them as I could find."[35]

The Art Center's status as a contested site for both class struggle and its representations in Chicago's black cultural front is also manifest in its programming for 1941. In addition to serving as an exhibition space, the center regularly hosted club meetings and special activities throughout the year. In April 1941, the center hosted the Negro Press Club, National Negro Youth Club, and an Urban League Tea. In June, meetings of the Alpha Kappa Alpha sorority, of which Pauline Kigh Reed was a longstanding member, and the "Copacetic Club," a black sorority that included several center trustees, were sandwiched around a "Cultural Fiesta" sponsored by the cultural committee of the National Negro Congress. Through Ishmael Flory, the congress and organized labor had provided financial and advisory support for the center prior to its May 1941 opening. Flory was himself a neighbor and friend to Goss and Burroughs. The still Communist-dominated congress's choice of an international motif for its 1941 program was, as with the influence of Mexican muralists on Charles White, no cultural accident. The program's theme, according to the *Chicago Defender,* was "social significance." It featured William Franklin, star of the WPA "Mikado" and "Chimes of Normandy," singing songs from those shows; Winifred Ingram, a "research worker," performing an original interpretive dance about Phyllis Wheatley; Alpheus Merchant, Hyde Park high school student and member of the American Youth Congress, playing boogie woogie music and singing "Negro songs of protest." Highlighting the evening was the group singing of the United Cannery, Agricultural, Packing and Allied Workers union commemorating the organization of dispossessed Negro and white sharecroppers in Missouri, and the debut performance of the new People's Group theater. Modeled on 1930s-style grassroots dramatic guilds like the Workers' Theater and Negro People's Theater, the group put on two original skits written by local talent: "Draft Board No. 5" and "Picket Line Prance."[36]

The congress "fiesta" demonstrated the lingering support of center progressives not only for American labor, as evidenced by its hosting of a Union Workers Party, Artists Union Party, and reception for the International Workers Order in July and August 1941, respectively, but for an internationalist political and cultural aesthetic. In October, Lorraine Williams lectured on "An Artist in Mexico"; in December, Kathleen Blackshear lectured on

"African Sculpture." In November 1941, the annual Artists and Models Ball was dedicated to the theme "Pan-American." The program featured latinized black rhythms in the form of "Boogie La Conga" dance numbers dedicated to the famous Chicago danseuse Katherine Dunham, and art work by Lorraine Williams, Margaret Taylor Goss Burroughs, John Carlis Jr., and Charles White to accompany Elizabeth Hunt's singing of "Frenesi." The highlight of the program was the choosing of the Queen of the Ball. Five contestants, all out-of-towners, competed in costumes representing foreign countries. Miss Maxine Tanner, representing Mexico, from Maywood, Illinois, won third place and a house-coat; Miss Roxie Jones, representing Argentina from New York, took second prize, a dress. First prize went to a young Miss Elizabeth Catlett, a teacher of art at Dillard University in New Orleans and holder of a master's degree in art from the University of Iowa. Catlett had come to study at the Art Center that summer, where she met and shortly thereafter married Charles White. She had also won first prize in sculpture at the American Negro Exposition under the name Alice Elizabeth Catlett for her "Negro Mother and Child," a black pieta reflective of her precocious talent and formal art school background. According to the *Chicago Defender*'s report of the 1941 ball, her award-winning costume "was 'Mexico' itself, even to detail of accessories." *Defender* reporter Diana Briggs also revealed in an "interesting sidelight" that "at 3 o'clock on the afternoon of the ball Miss Catlett had not the faintest idea of what her costume would be." "The skirt," wrote Briggs, "which was one of the most Mexican features of her costume was in reality made from draperies in a friend's apartment. Most of the accessories were corralled from among friends who had visited Mexico this past summer."[37]

Beyond its prize-winning appeal, Catlett's spontaneous, collaborative improvisation on a Mexican theme foreshadowed the influence of Mexican vanguard aesthetics taking hold in the life and work of herself and her artistic colleagues on the South Side. In part through the influence of the already radicalized White, Mexican lithographic and muralist technique was beginning to inform a revision of her classical art school training.[38] Between 1941 and 1945, Catlett began to move away from traditional Western art school formalism and toward experimentation in social realist graphic design. In 1945 she earned a Rosenwald Foundation Fellowship to travel to Mexico, where she became affiliated with the Taller de Grafica Popular. In 1946, she executed "Mother and Child," a lithographic revision of her 1940 pieta. Here, Madonna and child are rendered in stark black and white geometry, the mother's body functioning as a protective cocoon for a hollow-eyed male child. In the background, a blighted tree stands beside a road heading to a

*Figure 6.* Elizabeth Catlett, "Negro Mother and Child." Catlett's 1940 limestone, created under the name Alice Elizabeth Catlett, won First Award in Sculpture at the 1940
Exhibition of the Art of the American Negro. The black pieta reflects Catlett's early
training in classical Western motifs. © Elizabeth Catlett/Licensed by VAGA, New York,
N.Y.

*Figure 7.* Elizabeth Catlett, "Mother and Child." This 1946 print was made after Catlett's first visit to Mexico. The revision of her 1940 pieta reflects the early influence of the vanguard political aesthetic of the Taller de Grafica Popular created by the Mexican muralists Rivera, Orozco, and Siquieros. The work is representative of Catlett's body of work done after her permanent move to Mexico after World War II. © Elizabeth Catlett/Licensed by VAGA, New York, N.Y. From the Collection of Dave and Reba Williams.

vanishing point on a flat plane. It is probably a lynching tree, as used in Charles White's 1947 "Hope for the Future," an even more overtly pessimistic pieta revision—the tree includes a noose.

Catlett's appearance and award at the 1941 Artists and Models Ball "Pan-American" in many ways suggests the fortuitous cast of radical black cultural politics described in this book. Catlett's 1946 appropriation of international leftist aesthetics dating to Siquiero's 1923 vanguard manifesto completed a cycle of influence from Mexico City, through Chicago, and back to Mexico, the country to which she would declare her permanent exile and later citizenship. After 1946, Catlett formalized her allegiances to radical politics in theory and practice: her portraits of black women workers like "I Have Always Worked Hard in America" were nationalized renderings of her growing internationalist consciousness as reflected in her 1947 linoleum cut "My Role Has Been Important in the Struggle to Organize the Unorganized."[39] Like many other black artists and cultural workers described here, Catlett was in comparison to her white contemporaries a late bloomer to the causes of American and international radicalism as measured against standard histories of the 1930s U.S. Left and African-American culture.[40] Yet contact with black artists like White, Burroughs, and others connected to the South Side Community Art Center directly pushed her to the frontlines in the African-American "defense of culture." Catlett's improvised Mexican skirt might, viewed in the spirit of its making and wearing, thus be seen as a significant "uniform" for the black artist of 1941. Part political education, part artistic brio, the skirt, like the oppositional cultural politics and practices of the Art Center's vanguard, was once worn not easily cast off.

In *Report from Part One,* her autobiography of her early years in Chicago, Gwendolyn Brooks sustains the metaphor of the South Side and its Art Center as a political party to which virtually all of Chicago's progressive blacks were welcome. Brooks, stereotypically known as the purveyor of a modest formalism and of parochial Chicago attachment, cuts loose figuratively and literally from those images in recounting the years 1941 to 1949. "Poetry was not the whole of life," she writes of the decade of her breakthrough collection *A Street in Bronzeville.* "Nineteen forty-one through 1949 was a party era. . . . My husband and I knew writers, knew painters, knew pianists and dancers and actresses, knew photographers galore."[41] According to Brooks, the "most fascinating parties" took place above the Michigan Avenue barn where her friend and comrade in social arms Margaret Taylor Goss Burroughs lived:

> You might meet any *Per-sonality* there, white or black. You might meet Paul Robeson. You might meet Peter Pollack. On any night you might meet Frank Marshall Davis, the poet, Robert A. Davis, the actor, artists Eldzier Cortor, Hughie Lee-Smith, Charles White, Elizabeth Catlett; sculptor Marion Perkins. . . . once every couple years you might get lucky enough to run into Margaret Walker. . . . In Margaret's barn apartment sculpture, rich fabrics, books, paintings and paint addressed you everywhere. Margaret, then a rebel, lived *up from the root.*[42]

Gwendolyn Brooks's cautious memory of the seductions of Margaret Burroughs's "rebel" life bespeaks a way of seeing and reading Brooks's own poems of the 1940s that few critics have explored. In chapter 6 I will take up this endeavor in full. Here, Brooks's portrait of Bronzeville's bohemian Left gives fuller dimension to both the cultural and political reach of the Art Center, the central exchange of Burroughs's party cast. Brooks had herself come through its doors in 1941 an aspiring poet already published in John Johnson's *Youth.* The impetus was the announcement of a new poetry class at the Art Center to be offered by Inez Cunningham Starks. Starks, a resident of Chicago's wealthy white Gold Coast, from 1933 to 1938 was also a first reader for the important modernist magazine *Poetry.* From 1936 to 1940 she was president of the Renaissance Society of the University of Chicago, where she helped to bring the work of Le Courbusier, Leger, and Prokoviev to the United States. Like Nancy Cunard, to whom she bears striking historical parallels,[43] Starks's modernist aesthetic was buttressed by political imperatives of the 1930s Left—she had also helped refugees fleeing the Nazis find haven in the United States. In 1941, Starks began offering on Wednesday evenings from 6 to 9 P.M. a class in the writing of poetry. Brooks, her future husband Henry Blakely; the same Robert Davis from Burroughs's party; William Couch; the painter John Carlis, Burroughs herself, and Margaret Danner Cunningham were the initial members. As Brooks remembers it, Starks read to the class from Robert Hillyer's *First Principles of Verse* and gave a subscription to *Poetry* to every one of its members.

Starks's workshop inspired and helped to launch the most celebrated book produced by a Chicago writer of the 1940s, *A Street in Bronzeville.* Yet the lesser-known accomplishments of its other members bear out the more representative contours of Chicago's South Side cultural upsurge of the early

1940s. William Couch's poems appeared not primarily in literary journals but in the "Lights and Shadows" column of the *Chicago Defender* alongside and beneath those of Langston Hughes and Lucia Trent; Margaret Cunningham, using the pen name Jessica Danner, published in both *Crisis* and *Opportunity* and won second prize in a 1945 poetry contest sponsored by the Midwestern Writers Conference before herself becoming an editor for *Poetry.* Because she found through the workshop she could not write sonnets, Burroughs began writing free verse and juveniles. In 1947 she published *Jasper, the Drummin' Boy,* one of the first children's books by an African-American writer to be published by a commercial press (Viking). In 1942 Starks relinquished control of the poetry class to Miss Katrina Looser of the staff of *Poetry* magazine. The newly named "Poetry Research Clinic" met every Thursday evening at 8 P.M. at the Art Center. From the class a young South Side socialite, teacher, and aspiring short story writer and publisher, Miss Alice Browning, began soliciting for a new magazine titled *N.Y.P.S. (Negro Youth Photo-Script).* A glossy magazine billed as a "creative outlet for Negro youth," *N.Y.P.S.* was short-lived, but published other poems by Burroughs produced in the Art Center workshops and inspired a more lasting periodical, *Negro Story* magazine. Robert Davis, meanwhile, went on to become a Hollywood film actor under the name of Davis Roberts, while John Carlis, who had already shown at the American Negro Exposition, moved to New Jersey, where he became a notable among African-American painters and book designers.

The entrepreneurial reach of the Art Center into virtually every corner and medium of the South Side's—and black America's—political and cultural life was reflected in its 1941 Director's Report for WPA Illinois District 3. Peter Pollack reported that more than fifty thousand visitors had passed through the Art Center's exhibitions, classes, and lectures between December 1940 and December 1941. The *American Magazine of Art, Art Digest,* and *Art News,* the country's leaders in arts coverage, had devoted space to the center's art exhibits. During the year the center had also cooperated with the Library of Congress, New York galleries, the Oklahoma Fine Art Center, the American Federation of Arts, and Howard University to make possible national Negro art exhibitions that received attention from *Time, Newsweek,* and *The New Yorker.* The twenty-four teachers furnished the center by the Illinois Art and Craft Project of the WPA had taught more than two thousand students under sixteen, and 647 adults. An advisory committee composed of schoolteachers in the community had linked the Board of Education and the center, while public schoolteachers had enrolled hundreds of students in center art classes. Even the Chicago Art Institute School of Fine Arts had tentatively agreed to send senior students to the Art Center for their practice teaching credits.[44]

Written just after the declaration of war by the United States, Pollack's director's report also attempted to reformulate the "defense of culture" theme for black artists and cultural workers. In a section titled "What the Art Center Can Do in '42," Pollack wrote, "That art plays a vital part during war has been proved by England's experience with its artists." He cited a *London Studio Magazine* report that murals were being painted on public buildings and air shelters to counteract the "grimness of war," and other reports of art clubs with traveling exhibitions and art classes available to "evacuated" women and children. Following suit, Pollack recommended that the Art Center "offer our institutions to be used for the stabilization of civilian and morale defense." He recommended exhibitions in the following areas for the defense programs: (1) Consumers education; (2) Exhibitions of specific community defense programs; (3) Interpretation of the life of the armed forces to the community; (4) Exhibition of defense on the war front, the morale front, and the civilian front with emphasis on how the community fits into this program.[45]

Yet just as the *Defender*'s wartime support for national unity was interpellated by the "unprofitable" side effects of capitalist competition, the Art Center's recognition of the obsolescent value of progressive black culture came with the early 1942 announcement of June 1 WPA funding withdrawals from the Community Art Center program. Rumors of WPA cuts and job losses had circulated in the news and editorial pages of the *Defender* as early as 1939 and had escalated during 1940 and 1941 as Congress and Roosevelt debated funding levels and support for WPA programs. On April 18, 1942, the newspaper attacked the possible withdrawal of Art Center funding as a betrayal of black electoral support and undermining of good faith reciprocity between the black community and the federal government. Echoing Pollack's director's report, the newspaper argued that "High morale in the civilian population is essential during war time. . . . We therefore must exert every effort to assure the continuation of this vastly important cultural institution. The Center must be saved."[46] In May 1942, the center announced the opening of a national campaign for membership to forestall possible closure after the June 1 WPA cutoff. Yet the effects of WPA funding withdrawal were immediately pronounced. Between June 1, 1942, and April 1943, the center's programming was severely restricted and turned decidedly conservative in an attempt to maximize economic returns. A one-man exhibit of the internationally known sculptor Richmond Barthe, whose work and reputation preceded the younger generation of Chicago artists who had established the center's cultural vanguardism, opened November 23, 1942. Barthe had died in 1937, making his the first posthumous (and canonical) exhibit of a major black artist. Nearly six months elapsed before the center's next major exhibition, the works of Henry Ossawa Tanner. Tanner, the son of an A.M.E. bishop, had earned his fame in the late nineteenth and early twentieth century for his treatment of religious subjects: "Christ with Mary and Martha," "The Holy Family," and "The Three Marys" were some of the Tanners on loan for the exhibit. The Tanner exhibit, guaranteed to attract a broad interracial and more traditional art audience, was thus an expedient show with which to attempt to jump-start the center's fund-raising.

In this same period of cultural and financial retrenchment at the Art Center, its most progressive vanguard, reminded by WPA funding withdrawal of the absent middle ground in the defense of culture, began to reinstitute ties with other South Side institutions similarly situated. As early as December 1941, the end of its first year of operations, the center's most progressive artists had held an exhibition and sale at the Communist-influenced Abraham Lincoln Center at 700 East Oakwood Boulevard. White WPA muralists Edward Millman and Mitchell Siporin, Morris Topchevksy, Charles White, Eldzier Cortor, Charles Davis, Charles Sebree, and Bernard Goss were all featured in the exhibit, whose openly radical setting constituted aside from the Art Center the only free space for interracial cultural expression in that year. The exhibition had also marked symbolically the parallel missions of the Lincoln Center and the Art Center. Both were grassroots South Side institutions dedicated to interracial programming, the fusion of progressive politics and culture, and public educational outreach to the community. In 1942 the Lincoln Center's affiliated Abraham Lincoln School had inaugurated its "Workers School," which featured lectures by William Patterson on the war's potential for increasing or retracting civil rights and its effects on equality for blacks in America, the West Indies, and Africa. In his autobiography Patterson remembers the school as "broad, nonpartisan . . . for workers, writers and their sympathizers," offering classes intended to educate southern migrant blacks and white European workers on class struggle and racism.[47] Throughout 1942 and 1943, the school and the Art Center shared and exchanged teachers and artists and helped to promote each others' activities.

These informal and fraternal exchanges were formalized in early 1944. The Abraham Lincoln School announced the opening of classes on the topic "The Negro People." The classes addressed the increasingly urgent questions of discrimination, unemployment, housing, and civil rights in the postwar period. Instructed by school assistant director Patterson, still advertised by the school in 1944 as "formerly head of the Defense of the Scottsboro Boys," the course featured guest lectures by Metz Lochard from the *Defender* and Frank Marshall Davis.[48] Other Lincoln School courses for 1944 included "Trade Unionism" taught by Ishmael Flory, 1944 international representative of the Mine, Mill, and Smelter Workers of America CIO, and a course on the works of Leadbelly by Arthur Stern, former director of art for the United Auto Workers of America in Detroit. Flory and Stern were in 1944 established supporters of the Art Center's progressive cadre of artists; Davis, an amateur photographer in addition to being a poet and journalist, had been associated with the center since its 1941 inception, taking part in and coordinating its photography contests and exhibitions. In July 1944, Lochard, a devout supporter of the center, was named to its board of directors. One month later, on May 24, Patterson began offering a new companion course to "The Negro People" at the Art Center titled "Negro People in the World Today." Patterson's own promotional copy for the course stressed the persistent need for application of prewar racial radicalism to black intervention in wartime politics and their aftermath:

> The character of this war has released new forces which are changing the thinking and actions of people all over the world. White supremacy is cracking in its very stronghold—the reactionary South. The defeat of Rep. Joe Starnes in the Alabama primaries, the victory of Claude Pepper in the Florida primaries, Martin Dies' "resignation" from political life are all victories for the forces of progress and were made possible by the steadily increasing unity of Negro and white America especially within the labor movement.[49]

The symbiotic relationship of the Lincoln School and the Art Center was in 1944 definitive, if belated, evidence of the fluid rapprochement of radical political thought and black cultural production the 1936 opening of Chicago's Negro People's Front had aspired to. Arguably, this symbiosis reached its peak in Chicago six months later when the *Chicago Defender* reported an upcoming event at the Educational Building of Sinai Temple at 4622 South Parkway, a one-day "Interracial South Side Cultural Conference" portentously titled: "The Present Day Problems of South Side Poets, Writers, Painters, Sculptors, Dancers, Singers, Musicians, Actors, Entertainers and Playwrights."[50] The conference organizing committee, chaired by Frank Marshall Davis, was a representative roster of the South Side's cultural and political lights: Gwendolyn Brooks; her husband Henry Blakely; Arthur Stern; the social worker and South Side Writers' Group veteran Fern Gayden; the playwright Theodore

Ward; Margaret Taylor Goss Burroughs; the sculptor Marion Perkins; the radical white Hyde Park artist Sophie Wessell; the writer Joseph Johnson; the white artist Elizabeth McCord; and the poet Margaret Cunningham, veteran of Inez Starks's Art Center poetry class.

In a ten-page unpublished recollection of the November 26 conference, the only written record of the event, Margaret Taylor Goss Burroughs writes that all of its participants, "both black and white" could best be described as "'progressive.' That meant being from Left wing to Communist."[51] She recalls that the topic, "The Role of the Artist," was meant to raise the consciousness of South Side artists about "social problems" as reflected in the participation of many Abraham Lincoln School veterans. The program was keynoted by A. C. Spettersky, literary editor of the *Chicago Sun*. Following the opening session, the conference was divided into four panels, each with an honorary chairman and speaker. Chair of the music panel was Grace Tompkins, *Chicago Defender* music critic and public school music teacher. CIO veteran Arthur Stern issued the panel's report. Other speakers included Ruth Allen Fouche, a music teacher and musicologist and one of the founders of the South Side Community Art Center; James A. Mundy, a choral director who had directed a one hundred-voice choir at the 1933 World's Fair; Marl Young, a musician; Charles Collins, a labor and trade union leader; and John Greene, a concert baritone, who according to Burroughs, lived at the Abraham Lincoln Center.[52]

The conference theater panel was chaired by Bertha Mosely Lewis, a Chicago public schoolteacher. Ted Ward, from whose new play in progress "Whole Hog or Nothing" two scenes had been read in August at the Art Center, provided the report. Other panel members included Brunetta Mauson, a Chicago schoolteacher and actress associated with a Chicago children's theater;[53] Frank Greenwood, member of Chicago's "Little Theater"; Marjorie Witt Johnson, a dancer and dance group leader; and Lester Goodman, another dancer and dance troupe leader. The writing panel was chaired by Metz Lochard; Frank Marshall Davis delivered the general report. Other speakers were Jack Conroy, author of the proletarian classic *The Disinherited*; Marjorie Peters, a white writer who succeeded Starks as a writing teacher at the Art Center; Ben Burns from the *Defender*; Henry Blakeley; Charlamae Rollins, a librarian at Hall Branch Library described by Burroughs as "very helpful" to aspiring black writers; Oneita Ferrell, a Chicago schoolteacher; Mavis Nixon, a writer, poet, and Chicago schoolteacher; and Gayden, editor of the recently inaugurated *Negro Story* magazine. The panel on visual art featured Morris Topchevsky, Art Center mentor and resident of the Abraham

Lincoln School. Margaret Taylor Goss Burroughs delivered the report to Marion Perkins, the painter Rex Gorleigh, recently named new Art Center director, and Tom Bracey, a commercial artist. "Resource speakers" for the panel included Eldzier Cortor; Clovis Fouche, a commercial art teacher at Dunbar Vocational Trade School; Edna Wolff Henner, a white artist and intimate friend of Burroughs and other black artists; and Sophie Wessell. Closing remarks were made by William Patterson.[54]

The legacy and accomplishments of many of the participants of the 1944 Interracial South Side Cultural Conference have been well documented elsewhere—Gwendolyn Brooks, Jack Conroy, Margaret Taylor Goss Burroughs, Marion Perkins, Ted Ward, Eldzier Cortor, Rex Gorleigh, all were in the midst of or went on to distinguished careers in literature, painting, sculpture, and theater. Others, like Frank Marshall Davis and Ben Burns, have been subjects of recent books that reclaim their cultural work in Chicago during this period as well as their radical roots there. Still others listed here—Gayden, Tompkins, Lochard—are subjects of this book and thus additions to the horizon of Chicago's radical black "renaissance." Yet the persistent obscurity of many members of Chicago's most active and activist cultural workers of the war years group also marks them as what Frank Marshall Davis calls the "former comrades" Richard Wright has overshadowed in his famous abandonment of Chicago and public disavowal of American radicalism. Indeed, Wright's "I Tried to be a Communist" and his spectacular story of his fatal break with Chicago's Left had appeared in the August–September 1944 *Atlantic Monthly,* two months before what was one of South Side Chicago's culminating events of the Negro People's Front period. Perhaps wistfully, Burroughs wonders whether "McCarthyism" didn't prevent the conference from reoccurring, noting that even unpublished radical writers like Joseph Johnson succumbed to dismissal from a post office job not long after the end of the war.[55]

Yet clearly, the 1944 Interracial Conference program and the success of its participants in building and shaping their own culture and cultural work denotes the persistence and influence of radical and progressive political thought on black Chicago well after the end of the Depression and the official exhaustion of Popular Front policy on the American Left. The conference was a striking reincarnation and revision of the National Negro Congress, Negro People's Front, and Popular Front "defense of culture" theme transposed and translated into "The Present Day Problem" of virtually all of Chicago's most active and accomplished black artists. Indeed, black and white cultural workers and artists themselves had now seized the mantle of cultural reform and revolution from both party leaders and the congress, by 1944 embroiled in internal factionalism and loss of national prestige that would seriously dilute their effectiveness in the postwar period. The presence of schoolteachers, artists, social workers, and community organizers at the conference, few formally affiliated with the party but all committed to progressive cultural work, indicated the degree to which the boundaries of American radicalism had been expanded, erased, and remade in the course of the war years in Chicago. In true Popular Front/Negro People's Front spirit, South Side Chicago was now a political and cultural party without walls.

This spirit infused creative strikes by Chicago's vanguard black artists and institutions up to and through the conclusion of the war. In October 1944, the Du Sable Lodge 751 staged "Marching Down Freedom Road" at the Art Center, a dramatic adaptation of Howard Fast's *Freedom Road*. Also appearing on the program were Frank Marshall Davis, now firmly committed to Left and labor causes, and the white radical poet Meridel Le Sueur.[56] In May 1945, as the end of the war became imminent, Paul Robeson headlined a program entitled "San Francisco and Planning the Negro's Future" at Corpus Christi auditorium, blocks from the sight of the 1944 Interracial Conference. Robeson, appearing simultaneously in *Othello* at Chicago's Erlanger Theater, was the 1945 chairman of the Council on African Affairs, whose official representatives, concurrent with his performance, were attending the United Nations Conference in San Francisco. The newly formed council sought to obtain full democracy for African and colonial peoples in the postwar world. At Corpus Christi, Robeson spoke on the San Francisco conference along with O. O. Morris, executive secretary of the YMCA and chairman of the South Side Citizens' Committee on African and Colonial Affairs, a local branch of the New York-based organization.[57] Ishmael Flory served as its assistant secretary; Margaret Taylor Goss Burroughs as its executive secretary. At his May 20 performance, Robeson sang "Ballad for Americans," the Allied Opera Guild song whose "democratic" theme, as Michael Denning has shown, had become a keystone anthem of the Popular Front "cultural front" by 1945.[58]

Robeson's appearance and embrace by founding members and defenders of Chicago's South Side Community Art Center signified the common cause on which their work of the 1930s and early 1940s was grounded. Sterling Stuckey has summarized Robeson's aspiration toward a vanguard black cultural politics during this period in ways that help to illuminate this rapprochement:

With the lineaments and substance of Robeson's thought now accessible to us, it is evident that he made possible such intense reciprocity between cultural and political nationalisms that the two were rendered virtually indistinguishable. In fact, he perceived art as such a direct instrument of revolutionary change that any dichotomy between the cultural and political would be meaningless and false before his system of thought. Not dissimilarly, Robeson's vaulting conception of Negritude, his suffusing of the cultural with the political and the political with the cultural elminated any future need to label his form of Negritude merely, or even primarily, cultural. Thus, the whole of his ideology was political and cultural.[59]

Stuckey's illuminating conception of Robeson's "nationalism" is conspicuously devoid of the profound influence of Marxist thought on Robeson's ideology, life, and career. It also fails to document African-American cultural and political practices in the years of his study of Robeson—1914–45—that fall outside of his direct influence on black American culture. Yet the theory and praxis of black cultural politics on Chicago's South Side between the opening of the Popular Front/Negro People's Front and the end of the war bears uncannily the parochial mark and shape of Stuckey's formulation of Robeson's global ambitions. Margaret Burroughs's call for a "defense of culture" at the South Side Art Center was no less than a suffusion of the political and the cultural, as was the rapprochement between numerous black artists and the white-majority CP, between numerous black and white artists and cultural workers, between institutions like the South Side Community Art Center and the Abraham Lincoln School, between Charles White and Diego Rivera, between Elizabeth Catlett's improvised Mexican skirt and a life of radicalism in exile.

Robeson's well-documented influence on black nationalism and Marxism notwithstanding, Chicago's most militant South Side artists in uniform produced an equally distinguished mark on the history of radical black political and cultural struggle that even the great baritone could, and did, sing about.

# 4 Worker-Writers in Bronzeville: *Negro Story* and the African-American "Little" Magazine

Fern Gayden's role as organizer and participant in the November 1944 Interracial Conference on the Arts was emblematic of both the improvisatory spirit and deep roots of Chicago's Negro People's Front her life had by the time of that event come neatly to symbolize. Six months prior, the young social worker had bolted into prominence on the South Side's cultural scene with the publication of the first issue of *Negro Story* magazine. Coedited with her friend Alice C. Browning, *Negro Story*'s first issue was a plainly unadorned, sixty-four-page "Magazine for All Americans" available to readers at forty cents an issue. The first magazine dedicated to short fiction by and about black Americans, *Negro Story*'s debut was atypical of contemporary start-up publications in several other ways: it had no institutional financial backing, having been financed exclusively with a two hundred dollar loan from Browning's husband, Charles, vice-president of public relations for the *Chicago Defender;* its first issue had been assembled entirely by the editors in Browning's home at 4019 Vincennes Avenue; its distribution scheme, reminiscent of the early days of the *Defender,* was at best itinerant: readers were encouraged to recycle copies to black soldiers overseas, and Browning was nearly arrested for hocking the inaugural issue without a permit at Chicago baseball parks.

Yet *Negro Story*'s debut also included new work by three authors of note: Richard Wright's short story "Almos' A Man," originally intended as part of his unfinished proletarian-style novel *Tarbaby's Surprise;* "With Malice Toward None," a short story by Nick Aaron Ford, a teacher at Oklahoma's Langston University, essayist, journalist, and literary critic; and "Chicago Portraits" by Gwendolyn Brooks, a "Series of Sketches of Chicago Life" remarkable for being some of the first prose published by the poet. Ford and Langston Hughes also lent stature to the debut issue as advisers to the editors listed in the masthead. The remaining contributors were mostly unpublished Chicago novices chosen for inclusion by virtue of their friendship to Browning or Gayden, including Lieutenant William Couch, who had graduated from Inez Cunningham's poetry class to the military.

Richard Wright's seemingly incongruous appearance among such a largely undistinguished lot of writers was no accident. His granting of permission to Gayden and Browning to publish "Almos' a Man" was a payback for personal and literary debts long incurred. Wright had met Fern Gayden almost ten years earlier, when the latter was assigned as the case worker to Wright and his family. In 1935, she had helped Wright, his mother, his aunt, and his brother Leon move from their poorly suited South Side apartment to a new one at 3743 Indiana Avenue. Wright was then still a member of the Communist Party, and Gayden, who had come to Chicago from Kansas in 1927, had activist leanings already manifest in her attempt to organize the first social workers' union in Chicago. Gayden was also, like Wright, experimenting with writing short fiction. The two immediately struck up a friendship. In 1936 Wright invited Gayden to join his newly formed South Side Writers' Group, where she met among others Frank Marshall Davis, who described her in his memoir as "one of the most poised and gracious women I have even seen."[1] She was present at Wright's readings to the South Side Writers' Group of "Bright and Morning Star" and other stories in progress from what would become *Uncle Tom's Children*. Gayden was also a participant at Abraham Lincoln Center discussions attended by Wright and George McCrory, later labor reporter for the *Chicago Defender,* addressing questions like "Would Communism save you?"[2] After Wright's departure from Chicago in 1937 and the disbanding of the South Side Writers' Group, Gayden continued her work as a social worker and community activist, joining the board of the South Side Community Art Center shortly after its 1941 opening.

Sometime in the late 1930s or early 1940s, Gayden met Alice C. Browning. Browning, the daughter of a minister, was a graduate of Chicago's Englewood High School and Chicago Normal School. In 1931 she graduated from the University of Chicago. Some time in the 1930s she married Charles Browning, then director of the Division of Works Projects of the Illinois National Youth Administration. Browning's own emergence as a public cultural figure on Chicago's South Side bespoke both her black bourgeoisie roots and the entrepreneurial drive that would culminate in the appearance of *Negro Story.* On March 26 and April 2, 1938, Browning's by-line appeared under the new "Hmff! in Fashion" column in the *Chicago Defender.* An editor's note describing Browning as a "young socialite-teacher" reported that

"Following the example of Mrs. Marva Louis," wife of the heavyweight champion, Browning would be one of Chicago's "smart, well-dressed women" to
conduct a round-table column on fashion tips. Browning delivered hints on
spring fashion, tennis, beach wear, and horseback riding attire.[3] In 1941,
Browning left Chicago to take a master's degree at Columbia University.
There, under the tutelage of Vernon Loggins, she began study of the role of
black writers in American letters and her own career as a short story writer.
In 1941 she submitted a story called "Tomorrow" to *Esquire,* which rejected
it. Upon her return to Chicago, Browning aspired to settle the score by en-
terprising new periodicals for the publication of black writers. *N.Y.P.S (Negro Youth Photo Script)* was her first endeavor in 1942. Shortly thereafter, she
entered discussions with Gayden about starting a magazine that might cater
to their mutual desire to enter the short fiction market. The idea for *Negro
Story* was born.

Serendipitously, Wright had in 1940 purchased a house for his mother just
two doors down from the Browning's own Vincennes Avenue home. In early
1944, knowing Wright was visiting Chicago, Browning and Gayden visited
Wright at the apartment of Horace Cayton to ask permission to reprint a
story for their first issue, hoping to anchor its credibility in Wright's reputation. Wright's consent helped to inaugurate one of the most representative
moments of Chicago's Negro People's Front. The marriage of two minds so
differently contoured by the divergent strains and influences of 1930s and
early 1940s South Side Chicago produced a fortuitous if brief moment in
black literary history that has the shape of a crossroads. Gayden's ground-
ing in Left-influenced grassroots political and cultural work of the 1930s lent
a racial and class-based militancy to a new black magazine that attempted
to demonstrate the vital persistence of this ethos in black cultural entrepreneurship of the mid-1940s. Her connections to the 1930s interracial Left and
familiarity with incubatory black writing ventures like the South Side Writers' Group brought to *Negro Story* a pioneering radical literary sensibility
reminiscent and reflective of the Left "small presses," little magazines, and
vanguard cultural circles of an earlier era.[4] Browning's Columbia education
and "talented tenth" entitlement to rendering the economic and aesthetic
shape of contemporary black letters constituted both a complement and a
challenge to that ethos. From its inception and throughout its two-year publication run from May 1944 to May 1946, *Negro Story* provided a haven for
white and black radicals seeking to continue cross-racial alliances forged by
their experience and contacts with veteran Communists and socialists of the
1930s—Jack Conroy, James Light, and Earl Conrad, for example—while also

providing first-time commercial and cultural access to an army of black "worker-writers" drawn from the ranks of Chicago's teachers, social workers, soldiers, nurses, and domestics. Hewing to this formula, the magazine by 1946 had altered the direction of black achievement in the short story in particular, crystallized in 1930s-style "little magazine" form the radical and progressive agenda of Chicago's interracial wartime Left, and helped to create the outlines of a postwar "canon" of African-American writers.

In "A Letter to Our Readers" in the magazine's inaugural issue, Gayden and Browning reported that in their own attempts to write short fiction dating to the late 1930s, "the idea struck us that among thirteen million Negroes in America, there must be many who were eager to write creatively if they had a market."[5] The editors also voiced a desire to use the short story as a tool for social uplift for black readers, and as a way to involve black literature in the national and international crises of the war: "We believe good writing may be entertaining as well as socially enlightening. . . . we emphasize the belief that the future of the world is at stake during this World War II. But we also believe that Negroes have a great opportunity to achieve integration with the best elements of our society. We, the editors, as Negro women, not only welcome the opportunity to participate in the creation of a better world, we feel we have an obligation to work and to struggle for it."[6]

Gayden and Browning's "polite manifesto" wrapped the millenial rhetoric of the Mexican syndicalist drive for a "new order" and Margaret Burroughs's prescriptions for a "defense of culture" in the more cautionary sentiments of wartime patriotism and black social reformism. In so doing it reflected a compromise of their formal and informal attachments to Chicago's larger South Side cultural and political scene. Gayden, unmarried, was intimate friends to many of the South Side's most progressive artists like Burroughs and Jack Conroy. Browning's attachment to black bourgeois Chicago included her marriage to conservative *Defender* public relations man Charles. Press censorship, of which Gayden and especially Browning were keenly aware, also likely mediated their editorial tone. Attempted repression of the black press's most militant voices had begun as early as 1942, when Archibald MacLeish, director of the Office of Facts and Figures for the Roosevelt administration, had convened a conference of black newspaper editors to ask that they tone down calls for racial reform in respect for national wartime unity.[7] It was the first of a series of meetings on the topic between black editors and the Roosevelt administration, at one of which

Charles Browning accompanied *Defender* editor John Sengstacke.[8] These
threats were compounded by Justice Department visits to noncompliant
black publications like the *California Eagle,* edited by Communist sympa-
thizer Charlotta Bass,[9] as well as the vociferous *Pittsburgh Courier,* and by
government accusations that militant black papers were taking funds from
the Germans and Japanese.[10]

In addition to circumstantial evidence, direct evidence that Browning
and Gayden from the outset felt pressure to appear at least politically
diffident appeared in *Negro Story*'s pages. An early editorial noted that "questions have been asked" about the magazine's politics. The editors insisted
that the magazine was both "independent" and "non-political," and affirm-
ed their faith in both "Christian principles" and the democratic process.
Yet the contents of the magazine over the two-year course of its bimonthly
issuance bespeak at best a complication of this editorial line emblematic
of the fluid scope and entrepreneurial political strategies of Chicago's
Negro People's Front-style politics. Among the contributors, advisors, or
associates to *Negro Story* beginning with its May 1944 issue were these active Leftists, radicals, Communists, or fellow travelers: Earl Conrad, Langston Hughes, Jack Conroy, Chester Himes, Frank Marshall Davis, James
Light, Margaret Burroughs, Grace Tompkins, Ralph Ellison, Roger Mais,
Richard Wright, Joseph Johnson, Alden Bland, and Gayden herself. Organized labor was also a crucial financial contributor to the magazine from
the outset. The Federal Hotel Waiters Union, Local 356, donated to the first
issue. Subsequent issues were supported by donations from the regional
office of the Chicago District United Auto Workers CIO and the United
Electrical, Radio, and Machine Workers. In the second issue Ishmael P. Flory
donated $25 war bonds for the best short story and poem published in the
magazine. Not coincidentally, *Negro Story*'s *contents* revealed that, rather
than distancing themselves from earlier black and white political radicalism of the 1930s, as might have suited press censors, Browning and Gayden
consciously re-formed their critiques of capitalism, American race relations, and imperialism to suit the newly evolving political crises of the mid-
1940s, while adding to them a black feminist awareness they could have
hardly avoided.

From the outset, *Negro Story* included materials meant to hearken readers
and writers to an earlier era of African-American and American radical protest. In addition to Wright's uncompromisingly polemical "Almos' a Man"

in the inaugural issue, reminiscent of his more famous "Big Boy Leaves Home" from *Uncle Tom's Children,* the recurring appearance in *Negro Story* of Langston Hughes's poetry and prose, many with 1930s-style themes, evoked both the continuity of Depression-era circumstances for black American readers as well as Left-led strategies for black protest against them. Indeed, in and around 1944, Hughes faced an editorial dilemma comparable to that of the magazine he now advised: retaining a radical political literary voice while dodging allegations of Communist affiliation.[11] Typically, Hughes's *Negro Story* work featured a revised, muted, but poignant political energy updated to address the wartime circumstances for blacks as well as his emerging concern with the plight of black women. In the magazine's third issue, for example, October–November 1944, the editors reprinted four Hughes poems from *Common Ground*—Louis Adamic's Popular Front quarterly to which Hughes was advisor—titled "Madam, to You," later serialized in his 1949 collection *One Way Ticket.* The series featured the female protagonist "Madame Albert K. Johnson," a former beauty parlor owner who, put out by the Depression, is forced into domestic work. Feminist complement to Hughes's "Simple" series written concurrently for the male-dominated *Defender,* the poems featured ironic attacks on white wealth, male sloth, and the shortcomings of federal assistance to blacks. Here, "Madame Albert K. Johnson" asks her white employer, whose twelve-room house she cleans, "You trying to make a / Pack-horse out of me?" When told, ". . . Oh no! / . . . / I love you so!" Johnson can only reply: "That may be true— / But I'll be dogged / If I love you!"[12]

Hughes's poems gave voice to black female wartime domestics temporarily empowered by labor shortages brought on by industrialization to ask for increased wages and better work conditions.[13] The poems were in complement not only to other stories on working women in *Negro Story,* but to satiric editorial strikes in the *Chicago Defender* in the form, for example, of Jackie Ormes's "Candy," a serial comic strip about a pert black domestic's constant subversion of the racial and matriarchal order in her madame's home. The editors grounded this wartime setting for Hughes's more politically muted verse—the Communist Party and red imagery was at least no longer a part of Hughes's poetic diction—with poems by more openly militant and less assailable (because less well-known) Left writers whose work formally and thematically recalled the origins of Hughes's own militancy. In its second issue, for example, *Negro Story* reprinted Frank Marshall Davis's "For All Common People" from the February issue of *Free World.* Written concurrently with the author's leftward turn following the 1943 Detroit riots, the poem's anti-fascist internationalism was a powerful reconstitution of the Depression-era polemics in Davis's 1935 first book, *A Black Man's Verse.* In theme, spirit, and style, Davis's poem was also reminiscent of his work while associate editor for Jack Conroy's interracial proletarian *New Anvil,* another 1930s prototype for *Negro Story:*

> Let the common people smash all foes of the common people;
> Let the people fade fascism to a sour memory,
> Let the people snort goodbye to empire;
> Prepare soundproof cells for the hating rabble rousers,
> Plant the greedy in the earth they covet,
> Chase the munitions makers to the poor house,
> Spade soft soil over the warlords,
> Sterilize the minds of all Hitlers from Berlin to Birmingham;
> Then let us the people who never made this war mold a bombproof peace.
> Let us walk as kinsmen;
> Let us freeze a common dream;
> Let us extend life for plain John Smith!
> Are you ready, brothers?[14]

Davis's 1943 poem reconstituted the idiom of black "mass" and folk protest he and Gayden had helped Wright articulate for the 1937 "Blueprint for Negro Writing," one that would also inform fellow South Side Writers' Group member Margaret Walker's 1942 prize-winning *For My People,* a collection for which Davis's "For All Common People" was a virtual precis (Walker's own poem, "Dark Men Speak to the Earth," appeared in the same issue). In chorus to Davis's political raptures, *Negro Story* included other poems, like 1930s CPer, *Defender* columnist, and Harriet Tubman biographer Earl Conrad's "I Heard a Black Man Sing." Dedicated to Paul Robeson, Conrad's poem had originally been published by the National Educational Department of the International Workers Order. An editor's note to the poem's publication noting IWO permission to reprint indicated that of the four thousand copies printed, three thousand had already been sold, including one thousand to the National Negro Congress. Though less musical than Davis's work, Conrad's poem shared with his "Yesterday and Today" column in the *Defender* begun in 1945 an attempt to reanimate the themes and icons of an earlier era for application to black domestic and international interracial wartime struggle. As if in response to Robeson's vocal "call," Conrad's poem was a litany of the singer's performance:

John Brown was there and Tubman too,
    And Frederick Douglass great,
The Civil War and what is more
    The future of our State.

No Swanee opiate last night,
    No Old Virginny Home,
Down Among the Sugar Cane
    And no Magnolia poem!

"Nat Turner did not die," he sang,
    Nor Prosser, Old Man Brown,
Nor Vesey, Cato, L'Ouverture,
    Whose names they cannot drown.

. . . . . . . . . . . . . . . .

He voiced the repertoire of man,
    Of all, of Negro, white.
Amalgam of the people's song,
    Uniting day and night.

The Zulu chord, Brazilian song,
    The English, Jew, and Swede,
The Chinese and the Hindue song:
    All who would be freed!

The peat bog solider in the camp,
    The Joads out seeking food,
The black man breaking from his chains:
    He sang in fighting mood!

I heard a bell ring out last night,
    I heard an old chord clang,
And I shall hear no song again
    So long as "free" men hang.[15]

The political and rhetorical immediacy of Davis and Conrad's poems could not help but remind *Negro Story* readers of the "occasional" stories, poems, and reportage by writers of the 1930s interracial Left from which they had emerged, writings meant to commemorate strikes, lynchings, and political trials like the Scottsboro case. This immediacy was undoubtedly hastened by readers' familiarity with the journalistic writings of both writers in the black press. Indeed *Negro Story*'s ties to the *Defender* in particular were both ideologically and practically deep. In addition to Browning's marriage to Charles, other links to the newspaper included Julia Lochard, wife of Metz Lochard, and Myrtle Sengstacke, wife to John Sengstacke, both of whom were listed as "contributors" to the magazine though neither appeared with regularity. *Negro Story*'s attempt to fashion itself as the female and feminist cultural arm of the *Defender* was not, as in the case of "win the war" efforts, *pro patria* female muscle flexing. Rather, the magazine represented for female radicals an autonomous space for public voicing unavailable in male-dominated mass media or other Left circles. Grace Tompkins's contributions to the magazine are a good case in point. The regular music columnist for the *Defender* and participant in the 1944 Interracial Conference, Tompkins used the magazine as an annex in which to display responses to social conditions that her publisher and format couldn't allow. Indeed, Tompkins shed the conventional politesse of her *Defender* music column in favor of a polemical form of address often identified with male Left writers of her era. In the second issue, for example, she published the story "Justice Wore Dark Glasses," a terse tale of a black woman arrested for shoplifting and railroaded to a conviction.[16] The story was accompanied by a caricature of a judge wearing dark glasses emblazoned with swastikas. In the August–September 1945 issue Tompkins excerpted four poems from a book whose title, *The Birth Pangs of a New Order,* reflected a skepticism that was the dark obverse of Conrad's and Davis's bright revolutionary aspirations:

> The smell of death? I know it well.
> At Buchenwald, you say?
> I wasn't there. . . .
> But here at home . . . in Georgia
> I smelled it once
> Even before the hounds gave voice at his scent
> The hate-filled eyes . . . and curse upon the lip
> The coiled rope, the lash, the loaded gun
> And the stench of death clogged my nostrils.
> Just one man died
> Not thousands as at Buchenwald
> But each man dies but one death
> It is an individual matter
> And all the others
> Touch him not at al [*sic*]
> When his turn comes for dying
> Mass murder is appalling, yes,

But each death of the whole is one
The total makes the mass.[17]

Like Gwendolyn Brooks's wartime sonnet sequence in *A Street in Bronzeville*, to be discussed later, Tompkins adapted the roving "eye" of an ungendered narrator in order to allow the masculine territory of war (and lynching) into female poetic purview. Analogous to the *Defender*'s genre-bending use of front-page anti-lynching poetry, Tompkins's joint role as music critic and protest poet also linked black newspaper and literary work "arm in arm" on the cultural front. Indeed, on more than one occasion Gayden and Browning editorialized in *Negro Story* that their commitment to publishing short stories and poems based on breaking current events was both a conscious rejection of the political and literary hegemony of white-owned commercial magazines—what they called the "slicks"—and a desire to provide an arena for beginning writers to experiment with what they called "plotless realism." This "plotless realism"—deemed documentary or reportage fiction during the so-called proletarian moment of the 1930s—was the predominant literary mode for many of the novice black and white writers who regularly contributed to *Negro Story,* allowing them to transform racist and sexist acts around the country into fictional polemics meant to charge readers' political awareness. In Davis Grubb's "Rest Stop," published in the October–November 1944 issue, the story of a black solider killed by a white MP for approaching a white girl served to remind black readers of news accounts of several ongoing 1944 trials against black soldiers accused of rape and dubbed "Little Scottsboro" or "Army Scottsboro" cases by the black press.[18] In "Something for the War," published in the December 1944–January 1945 issue, a black domestic's blood donation is rejected by white nurses, reminding readers of the Red Cross's official wartime policy of rejecting or separating black from white blood donations. In Margaret Taylor Goss Burroughs's "Private Jeff Johnson," a young black soldier is tempted into a racial quarrel with harassing whites but draws the admiration of his black peers for restraint: he wants to save his fight for Hitler.

These three- or four-page "plotless" vignettes, by transforming the short story into anecdotal representations of everyday black suffering, prolonged the strategy of deploying literature in the quotidian guerilla war against class and race oppression initiated by small, independent journals of the prewar period like *Anvil, Challenge,* and *New Challenge,* launched in 1937 in collaboration between Dorothy West and members of the South Side Writers' Group. *Negro Story*'s stories and poems also sought to reconfigure poetry and short

story writing as literal and figurative black "work," reconstituting black au-
thorship and literary production as subversive interventions in both the
material and literary economy of wartime America. This attempt to move
the short story to the front line of black cultural defense was a product of
*Negro Story*'s unique application of Popular Front/Negro People's Front logic.
Caught between the Scylla of commercial white "slicks" that refused to publish them and the Charybdis of the militant left press that published black
short fiction to primarily white audiences, the editors devised a referendum
on the short story's role in the black cultural front. The magazine's fourth
issue, published in December 1944, published letters by three of the country's
veteran left cultural authorities in response to their query, "What Should the
Negro Story Be?" Earl Conrad began by praising the magazine's dedication
to the "Negro story" itself. His recommendations vacillated between integrationist pragmatism—"The universal of freedom is at the core of all human
experience"—and the more radical literary impulses and examples from his
CP past: "I would be experimental; I would look for the unusual and print it
when it came in; I would be anti-Fascist, and I would consider that this world
belongs to the Negro as well as to anyone else and keep the policy as broad
as that."[19] The second response was from the increasingly conservative Locke.
"Your best criterion, beyond a doubt, will be to base this material on a high
regard for originality and authenticity without the slightest regard for the
racial identity of the authors. We must not only have the single standard in
this field, but welcome, as I am glad to see you do, any contribution which
seriously attempts to penetrate Negro life and experience."[20] Locke's appeal
for color-blind "quality" was given a predictably more materialist inflection
by Jack Conroy. Conroy likened the dilemma of the magazine's editors in
choosing material about black life to the frequent readerly complaint "Why
can't you find something cheerful to publish?" when he first began editing
*Anvil* at the outset of the Depression. Responding to the harrowing conditions of their times, Conroy noted, "Writers were inclined to be bitter and
rebellious when recording these maladjustments, and hence were frequently
accused of undue pessimism or of inciting to revolution against the status
quo."[21] Conversely, writers who attempted a shift "from the negative to the
affirmative" frequently lapsed into revolutionary sentimentalism. "Negro
writers and white writers who explore Negro life for literary material,"
Conroy noted, "are confronted by a problem almost identical to this." While
the war had solved, "temporarily, at least," many questions agitating the
minds of primarily white industrial workers during the Depression, "the
Negro is still harassed by segregation and discrimination both in military and

civil life." Thus, concluded Conroy, like the "proletarian" writers of the 1930s, black writing responding to the "Negro's peculiar problem within a problem" attempting a true and full picture of the general black condition "is likely to be defeatist in tone."[22]

Conroy's articulation of a "proletarian" aesthetic and dilemma catching up with black writers of 1944 was commensurate with the belated appeal of Mexican vanguard radicalism to Elizabeth Catlett and Margaret Burroughs's 1941 reformulation of the Popular Front "defense of culture" theme. His evocation of the Negro's "peculiar problem within a problem" was also an echo of the "black nation within a nation" thesis of the early 1930s Left, reformulated now to the virtually colonized population of Chicago's segregated South Side. Typically, Conroy's contribution to these dilemmas and the short story's role in resolving them turned out to be more than rhetorical. Four of the students enrolled in his course "Problems of the Individual Writer" taught at Patterson's Abraham Lincoln School in Chicago in the fall of 1943 published in *Negro Story,* including Esta Diamond, Zena Dorinson, and most significantly James Light. Light, described by Douglass Wixson in his biography of Conroy as the latter's friend and drinking companion, was also throughout its two-year tenure one of the magazine's most important radical white voices. In addition to publishing several anti-racist stories, Light contributed a favorable review of Arna Bontemps and Conroy's migration study *They Seek a City.* A March–April 1945 Light review also savaged John Steinbeck's *Cannery Row,* accusing the author of producing a "joyous piece of whimsy" whose message, "don't bums have fun?" was seen as a sell-out and compromise of his tougher, if not revolutionary, 1940 bestseller *The Grapes of Wrath.*[23]

Conroy's prescient recognition of the historical and literary parallels of a "little magazine" emerging from 1944 black America also helps to provide a framework for understanding *Negro Story*'s revision of the "worker-writer" aesthetic it consciously kept alive. Browning and Gayden's commitment to publishing work by both black and white working-class and novice writers constituted one of the first commercial proletarianizations of African-American literature in the city's—and the country's—history. While many of the magazine's contributors had literary pedigrees through university training, many more were schoolteachers, social workers, or domestics. A characteristic example is Melissa Linn, the pseudonym of a Marietta, Ohio, college graduate who contributor's notes noted was forced to work as a domestic and waitress after receiving her degree from Ohio State. Linn's story, "All That Hair," appeared in the April 1946 issue of the magazine. A precursor to Toni

Morrison's *The Bluest Eye*, it describes a young black girl's attempt to straighten her hair as a way of measuring up to white beauty standards. The literal plight of worker-writers like Linn was figuratively represented by complementary stories about working women in the magazine by other amateurs. In the magazine's first issue Margaret Rodriguez's "I Had a Colored Maid" rendered the archetypal moment in black domestic life of a colored woman wrongly accused by a white master of stealing. Another popular story in the magazine's early issues was "Viney Taylor" by Lila Marshall, a Chicago schoolteacher. Marshall's protagonist was a "hardworking girl" in Nashville, Tennessee, who after years of working as a domestic for "white folks" had earned a job as a power machine operator. In short order, Viney's aspirations for a home with a flower garden, car, garage, and children are dashed when she discovers her husband Sam having an affair with a nineteen year old. The women literally fight it out in front of Taylor's home until two indifferent white police arrive to break it up. Frustrated by neither woman's willingness to turn the other in—"Shucks, these damn niggers ain't gonna tell on each other"—the police swagger off to a bar musing about women "Fightin' over some old no-good man."[24] The story was accompanied by an illustration by the black WPA painter and lithographer Elton Fax. The New Yorker Fax was a veteran of the Maryland Federal Art Project and former teacher at the Harlem Art Center. Famous by 1944 for his renderings of black industrial workers, his "Lunch Time," an oil, had been featured at the 1940 American Negro Exposition art exhibition.

Marshall and Fax's rendering of the common black female wartime "conversion" from domestic to industrial worker embodied the short story's reincarnation in *Negro Story*'s pages as a synecdoche of the African-American wartime work experience. Indeed, *Negro Story*'s most popular and frequent contributor during its two-year tenure was Chester Himes, whose career, as George Lipsitz has argued in *Rainbow at Midnight,* is representative of the plight of African-American working-class Leftists of the 1940s.[25] A former Ohio WPA worker, ex-prison inmate, bell boy, and manual laborer, Himes struggled throughout the war years to produce literary representations of his workaday experience written out of and between jobs. Six of Himes's wartime stories were first published in *Negro Story.* Characteristic of the stories is Himes's proletarianization of his solider/civilian protagonists, and implicitly of the author, whose Los Angeles experiences included close contact with Communist Party organizers. Himes's wartime stories demonstrate radical and satiric skepticism about racism and class oppression in wartime America. In his first *Negro Story* piece, for example, "He Seen It in the Stars,"

Himes's protagonist, Accidental Brown, like the author a wartime Los Angeles shipyard worker, falls asleep after a long day turn while watching a film called *Hitler's Children*. He wakes in Nazi Germany, where he attempts to save himself from execution by telling Hitler (punning on "slave's" colloquial meaning as "job") that he is the personal "slave" of the U.S. president. Hitler promptly hangs a sign on Brown's neck declaring him "President of the American Slaves." But because Hitler has told the Germans *all* Americans are slaves, the German masses believe Brown to be *the* American president. Punished for his own recognition, Brown is forced to march through the streets of Berlin wearing a sign saying "De Fuhrer Needs Babies for the New Order." Eventually, Brown tells Hitler he has had a vision of an American invasion against Germany led by Roosevelt, General MacArthur, Humphrey Bogart, and the mayor of Los Angeles. When the invasion occurs, Brown wakes up.[26]

Himes decrypted his brilliant allegory of native and foreign fascism in an essay published a year later in Bucklin Moon's *Primer for White Folks*. After attacking the racist polices of a U.S. Army "that sends unarmed Negro soldiers into a hostile South to be booted and lynched by white civilians," Himes asks, "Are we seeking the defeat of our 'Aryan' enemies or the winning of them?"[27] Himes's contention that the war represented a chance for African Americans to fight against domestic fascism was nothing less than a reformulation of the earlier Communist Party line on the "Negro Question" that viewed blacks as victims of interior colonization, a line variously debated throughout the 1930s and into the 1940s in the writings and speeches of Earl Browder and Doxey Wilkerson, who was the party's most visible black spokesperson.[28] It also acknowledged tacitly A. Philip Randolph's "Double V" wartime rhetoric, linking black civil rights at home to the rebellion of blacks in the Caribbean Islands and Chinese insurgency against Japanese imperialism.[29]

Indeed, as did the *Defender* and the Art Center, *Negro Story* routinely provided space for international racial radicals, linking the "defense of culture" at home to black, interracial, and anti-colonial struggles abroad. Twice in its two-year run, for example, it published work by the Jamaican socialist Roger Mais, who in July 1944, while a member of Norman Manley's People's National Party, published an anti-colonial tract in its political affairs journal *Public Opinion* that earned him a six-month jail sentence.[30] Two months earlier, Mais had published the story "World's End" in the first issue of *Negro Story;* in the second issue, published in the same month of his *Public Opinion* essay, Mais published an angry letter describing the apathetic response of Jamaican writers to his personal campaign to establish an "indigenous" anti-colonial literature on the island.[31] Mais's anti-colonial militancy was contextualized for American readers by domestic tales published in *Negro Story* like "Into the Wide Blue Yonder" by Bessie Scott. The story concerns a black war-bride who learns while playing a Hebrew slave in a local theater production that her husband has been shot down by fascists in the Ethiopia campaign.

Such archetypal connections between racial and gender oppression at home and racist colonialism abroad could not have been missed by *Negro Story* readers. The magazine's international circulation to black soldiers overseas reinforced this connection. Routinely, writers like Robert Davis, an army lieutenant and veteran of the South Side Community Center's poetry class, or William Couch, another, sent stories and poems back to the magazine reporting on the abusive treatment of black soldiers abroad. Reciprocally, the magazine kept careful watch on the wartime careers of emerging black writers overseas, citing William Attaway's military career or Ralph Ellison's stint in the merchant marines in its "Current Town Talk" as evidence of the deferral of an even more advanced black literary renaissance in the postwar period. Similarly, readers were regularly updated on the status of the formation of a black WAACs unit (Women Auxiliary Army Corps) and occasional overseas gains by black nurses and ground troops were reported as evidence of the success of what the magazine called, following liberals and Leftists from Roi Ottley to the Communist Party's black journal *Congress Vue,* a "People's War."[32] This international focus, circulation, and exchange of resources made the magazine still another important piece in the larger cultural front war for black media influence, growth, and cooperation in the assault on regressive images and treatment of African Americans inaugurated by the 1936 National Negro Congress. Indeed by 1945, as the *Defender,* Associated Negro Press, and *Negro Story* all demonstrated, World War II had become an occasion not simply for a black press "Double V" campaign on racism at home and fascism abroad, but for the creation of an international black publishing idiom in harmony with the voice of cultural and political emissaries to the world like Paul Robeson.

With the fourth issue of the magazine, January–February 1944–45, Fern Gayden left her editor's post at *Negro Story.* The magazine reported in its "Chat" section that Gayden's severe case load had necessitated the move. While there is no official record or memory by either Browning or Gayden to rely on, it is at least plausible that political differences hastened the split.

Browning's craving of celebrity and social standing was as unflagging as Gayden's commitment to radical causes. Upon leaving the magazine, Gayden, as had her vanguard artist friends separation at the Art Center, resumed affiliation with "former comrades." On April 29, 1945, she spoke on a panel at the Abraham Lincoln School dedicated to discussion of Wright's new best-selling *Black Boy*. Featured speaker for the discussion was Ben Burns, whose savage review of the autobiography was fresh in the minds of *Defender* readers.[33] Also on the panel was Arthur Stern in his role as literature instructor at the Abraham Lincoln School. Gayden's solidarity with white Leftists was sympathetic with her own fast support for other black Leftists during the 1940s like Robeson, William Patterson, and Du Bois.

Meanwhile, Browning devised new ways to capitalize on the magazine's increased circulation and influence. It was now distributed in New York and at a number of historically black colleges, its circulation perhaps as high as one thousand per issue.[34] In early 1945, Browning began sending press releases and photographs of herself to the *Defender* to promote forthcoming issues. A "Hollywood"-style headshot of Browning appeared on page one of the Features section of the February 24, 1945, edition of the paper, the same issue that debuted Earl Conrad's column.[35] In May 1945 she announced in the *Defender* the first anniversary issue of *Negro Story* and singled out for praise her own pseudonymous story "The Slave." In June 1945, Browning called a meeting of the new National Negro Magazine Publishers Association to which she had recently been appointed president. A sister organization to the National Negro Newspaper Association that had inspired it, the NNMPA met on July 30 and 31, 1945, at Harlem's Hotel Theresa. There Browning led the call for "adaptation in story and article form of case histories of Negro life to cover civil liberties, housing, individual health, socialized medicine, and fascism—native and foreign."[36] Attacking increasing wartime and potential postwar problems such as "riots, strikes and race relations," Browning was joined by the editors of *Opportunity, Color, Music Dial, Expression,* and *The African* in vowing that "magazines and newspapers should work together in a united front for the Negro."[37] Browning's rhetoric was a virtual echo of Sengstacke's 1940 appeal to Barnett to organize the black newspaper press, and the *Defender*'s 1943 call for black "unity" among its newspapers. Also in June 1945, Browning hosted a publicity committee meeting at her home to press the NAACP drive against restrictive covenants. In July 1945, Browning initiated a plan for "Negro Story Book" clubs and announced the publication of a new children's magazine, *Child Play*, published by the new Negro Story Press.[38] Derivative of the *Defender*'s "Bud Billiken" children's pages, the magazine was to include pictures, cartoons, and contests for children four to fourteen years of age. Margaret Taylor Goss Burroughs contributed material from her forthcoming children's book *Jasper, the Drummin' Boy* to its first issue. In August 1945, Browning announced another Negro Story Press book, *Lionel Hampton's Swing Book*.[39] The book was a *Variety*-style record of Hampton's life and career, splashed with photographs of the band leader named the *Defender*'s "Number One Band of the Year" in its 1945 polls. The Art Center painter and teacher William Carter provided artwork and promotion for the book. Meanwhile, the April 1945 anniversary issue of the magazine was its largest ever, featuring contributions by Conrad, Hughes, Vernon Loggins, Chester Himes, Ellison, Gwendolyn Brooks, Owen Dodson, and a variety of amateurs and friends.

Browning's frenetic entrepreneurial strategies were in part meant to attract a burgeoning middle-class black readership whose tastes were increasingly being shaped by John Johnson. In 1943, the first issue of Johnson's Publishing Company's *Negro Digest* had appeared on Chicago newsstands. Deliberately copying the look and content of *Reader's Digest*—reprinting articles on black Americans from the black and white press—the magazine's instantaneous success was followed shortly by Johnson's own watershed in black journalism, *Ebony,* a direct emulation of another white magazine, *Life.* Jacqueline Jones has argued persuasively that *Ebony*'s reporting on the displacement of southern farm workers and discrimination against blacks in unions distinguished it at least editorially from *Life,* calling its editorial politics "aggressively integrationist."[40] Indeed, Ben Burns's role as one of the first editors at both *Negro Digest* and *Ebony*—while still maintaining at least intellectual allegiances to the Communist Left—makes it another obvious product of the Popular Front/Negro People's Front. Yet Burns's recollections of both magazines' increasingly virulent anti-Communism and economic opportunism makes them more significant of a postwar cold war order in Chicago to be discussed in my final chapters. The calculated and unabashed "patriotism mixed with commercialism" of both *Negro Digest* and *Ebony* made Johnson's magazines the first to attract both black and white advertising.[41] *Ebony*'s early emphasis on what Burns cynically calls the magazine's "four basic subject areas: interracial marriage, Negroes passing as whites, sex, and anatomical freaks"[42] even helped to attract white corporate advertising accounts, something no other black periodical had yet to do. By 1944, circulation for *Negro Digest* was 150,000 monthly; *Ebony*'s October 1945 premier issue run of 25,000 sold out completely.[43] *Negro Story*'s reliance on hand-distribution, overseas subscribers, personal donations, and financial backing by organized labor were suddenly thrown into relief by Johnson as archaic strategies of an aggressive new black periodical market.

So too were its much more militant editorial politics that lingered long past Gayden's departure in part due to her replacement by Earl Conrad in the role of "associate editor." As funds from its limited resources grew short, so did editorial optimism and patience with a postwar political culture that could neither literally nor figuratively support *Negro Story*'s agenda. The radical biracial rhetoric that had motivated the magazine's editorial politics began to sound hollow by late 1945, which saw black workers displaced in rapid numbers by returning white war vets, failure by the Roosevelt administration to persist in application of Fair Employment Practice Commission policies preventing discrimination in industry, and an increasingly racist tenor in postwar discourse. In December, Browning wrote, "We have no rancor against sincere individuals, and we laud all of the fine liberals who are interested in working together to help solve America's problems, but we have no love for the general hypocrisy, deceit and false attitude of many Americans."[44] In April 1946, the final issue of the magazine appeared. Its contents were both portentous and retrospective of its radical roots: an installment of Conrad's anti-lynching novel in progress *Alabama Evening;* another lynching parable by Conrad's wife, Alyse; "Riot Gold" by Pearl Fisher, the sister of Harlem Renaissance notable Rudolph Fisher, about a reporter's coverage of the 1943 Harlem riots; "The Tact of Abyssinia" by Florence Lennon, who evoked the precolonial name of the heroic African nation as the moniker of a newborn child; and "One More Way to Die" by Chester Himes, a surreal, interior monologue from the point of view of a black urban worker watching himself repeatedly shot by police after hitting a white girl in a bar.

Yet like Himes's protagonist's, *Negro Story*'s death was offset by what might be called the foretelling birth of political and cultural capital its extinction at least symbolically marked. The magazine's last issue also included a review of Himes's recently released *If He Hollers Let Him Go,* whose 1945 publication made Himes the official angry and ironic national voice of the black working class; a review by Fern Gayden of *Negro Story* contributor Gwendolyn Brooks's first book, *A Street in Bronzeville,* a momentous occasion both for African-American women writers and for the city of Chicago; and a review of Ann Petry's *The Street,* whose progressive though bleak examination of black working-class female life was for black and white, male and female writers a welcome and necessary addition—one might even say correction—to the hostile misogyny and bitter renunciation of political hope forecast in Richard Wright's *Native Son,* a novel whose publication in 1940, with its fatalistic portrait of black-Communist alliance, had seemingly dealt a crushing blow to post-Depression attempts at formulating a radical black literature.[45]

*Negro Story*'s successful if short-lived incarnation of Negro People's Front-style cultural politics and its concomitant erasure from most accounts of African-American cultural history is also, by this point it is clear, no accident. Robert Bone's critical formulation of Chicago's black "renaissance" again provides the best example. Though one of the few critics perceptive enough to acknowledge the magazine's centrality to black literary culture of the 1940s—Bone calls it "for a brief moment . . . the focal point of black writing in America"[46]—he casts it as a minor by-product of the "Wright generation" and never acknowledges the ample evidence of its interpenetration by Marxist and other radicals of the late 1930s and early 1940s. In 1947, Earl Conrad provided a more prescient evaluation of the magazine's historical place both in his time and in ours. In *Jim Crow America*, Conrad pointed toward *Negro Story* as the nexus of a "Blues School of Literature" fusing proletarianism with the racial urgency of black wartime protest. "What is occurring is a flow of Negro writing comparable to the upsurge of socially enlightening literature that brightened but finally dominated the 'thirties," wrote Conrad:

> The proponents of blues writing have operated mainly on the basis of showing the negative in Negro life, with a view to reaching the positive conclusion of indicting a white supremacist society. "Compulsive violence" is the keynote of the writing. . . . "Oppress us," says this school of writing, "and we will strike back, sometimes at you, again at ourselves, sometimes at both of us."
>
> *Negro Story* . . . frankly presents all of the issues of segregation and protest, the complexities of Negro-white labor relationships, intermarriages, and all matters of color, "race," caste, class, and sex. The magazine, widely read in the publishing world, has been the means of launching a number of writers and books.[47]

Conrad's assessment of *Negro Story* helps to make clear its "crossroads" nature in twentieth-century black letters. As *Negro Story* comrade and supporter Jack Conroy had insisted, the magazine successfully reconstituted and sustained the themes, dilemmas, and obstacles of the 1930s interracial Left, of its proletarian and "worker-writers," its revolutionary aspirations, and cataclysmic frustrations. So, too, had the magazine's editors and writers absorbed, revised, rewritten, and recontextualized the political and cultural ethos of earlier black-Left alliances into a dazzling product—the black little magazine.

Presciently, too, Conrad's acknowledgment of *Negro Story*'s copious treatment of an expanded range of issues, adding sexual and gender concerns to the more dominant class discourse of the 1930s Left, signaled its foreshadowing of postwar black political culture and cultural politics. Though Gayden and Browning fell into obscurity after *Negro Story*'s demise, through the magazine passed not only the predominant African-American voices of the 1940s and 1950s—Brooks, Hughes, Ellison, Wright, Himes, Owen Dodson, and others—but increased national concentration on black women's work, voice, literary ambition, and participation in the traditional masculine preserve of black cultural capitalism. While *Negro Story*'s and the short story's preeminence at the crossroads of black prewar and postwar culture will be further illuminated in the following chapter, this preliminary account suggests that as a site of political and cultural rapprochement for black and white, male and female, national and international radicals of 1940s America, the magazine had few peers.

# 5  Genre Politics/Cultural Politics: The Short Story and the New Black Fiction Market

Chicago's enduring status as a synecdoche for a black "renaissance" in mid-century cultural expression begs the question of how geographic sites, their institutions, and their products become emblematic of larger discursive formations. In previous studies Carla Cappetti, Craig Hansen Werner, and Robert Bone have each posed possibilities and paradigms. For Cappetti, Chicago's 1930s and 1940s cultural rebirth signaled the deep impress of University of Chicago sociology on the literary imagination of Chicago novelists like Wright, Farrell, Willard Motley, and others.[1] Craig Hansen Werner, positing Chicago as the site of the development of an "Afro-modernism," reads its history as an ongoing reactive cultural formation by black artists incorporating and revising black cultural tropes like blues and jazz into a modern black urban landscape.[2] Robert Bone attributes the national significance of Chicago's renaissance, as to Harlem's, to its creation of a cultural repository for understanding the Great African-American Migration from the South.[3]

This study has used a rubric of "cultural politics" as a means of challenging critical narratives previously applied to Chicago in the period under study. Similarly, it has focused critical attention on means and modes of expression—journalism, magazine writing, manifestos, personal memorabilia—that destabilize conventional cultural hierarchies. Extending the logic of *this* line of interrogation begs a slightly revised version of the question that I began with, namely, to what extent may any *one* of these local products predict or help us to understand the nature of cultural politics in a given historical moment? Put another way, is it possible for a single or isolated mode of writing to reveal as much or more about the condition of cultural politics in a given era as the ideas commonly identified with that culture itself?

To date, perhaps the most illuminating treatments of this question are Cary Nelson's 1989 book *Repression and Recovery: Modern American Poetry and the Politics of Cultural Memory, 1910–1945,* and a companion essay "Poetry Chorus: Dialogic Politics in 1930s Poetry." Inspired in part by the canon debates of the 1970s and 1980s, Nelson's book and essay demonstrate the upsurge of radical American poetry in the early part of the twentieth century as a "localized" challenge to the aesthetic, literary, and political assumptions guiding western modernist articulations of poetic value. In *Repression and Recovery,* Nelson demonstrated how the proliferation of small, Left-wing magazines and newspapers during the 1910s and 1920s laid the foundation for a revolution in the production and consumption of poetry during the climactic "red" decade of the 1930s. Nelson offered the examples of mass circulation newspapers like the *New York Call, Appeal to Reason,* and *Daily Worker,* markets for Left-influenced poetry before and during World War I, as paradigmatic precursors of Depression-era Left magazines like *Left Front* and *Partisan Review.* Poetry written and poets writing for these magazines, Nelson argued, refashioned poetic value as political praxis. By writing poems inspired by political events like the execution of Sacco and Vanzetti, or the Scottsboro Boys case, poets like Joseph Kalar, Langston Hughes, Mike Gold, Genevieve Taggard, and others reconceptualized the "poem" as a living political artifact—the equivalent of the Workers' Theater "Living Newspaper" productions, for example—and poetry readers as mediating respondents between a poetic call for action and social change. Poetry became, according to Nelson, written to play an immediate role in public life.[4] Evidence of this process was manifest in the "thematic, rhetorical, and metaphoric" overlaps of different poems on the same radical causes, what Nelson called an "intertextual social conversation" in which "verbal echoes, reinforcements, extensions, and disputes actually permeate poems."[5] The recurring, repetitive use of newspaper headlines, anecdotes from the Left press, and other documentary "facts" in radical poems of this era was one example of an "intertextual" conversation across political and generic boundaries. Further evidence existed in the simultaneous publication of poems on similar themes in different journals and magazines, what Nelson calls after Bakhtin a "dialogic" exchange in which writers communally participated in a shared conversation about social and artistic change.[6] Ultimately, Nelson offered the example of radical poets in ongoing collaborative composition as evidence of a genre-centered challenge to poetry and poetic composition as individuated, elitist, and inconsumable icons detached from the everyday lives of American citizens. The genre itself, Nelson demonstrated, became the site for a much larger (both geographically and ideologically) struggle for control over the direction of American and western political culture.

Nelson's argument for the presence of an "other" modern American culture and cultural politics embedded in the revolutionary evolution of a single genre—its communal and collaborative production, its assault on literary convention, and its interweaving of oppositional publishing and political practice—might profitably begin a reconsideration of the larger significance of *Negro Story* magazine. The magazine's insistence on publishing amateur black and white short story writers whose primary "credential" was a commitment to progressive or radical race, gender, and class reform was clearly an effort by the editors to constitute what Nelson calls a "shift in the epistemology of composition"[7] in the short story genre. Gayden and Browning's fundamental question and challenge in creating the magazine was *generic*. As they put it, "What should the negro *story* be?" (emphasis mine). In their study and selection of the genre, Gayden and Browning had singled out a site for oppositional cultural practice they viewed as both under-utilized by black writers and controlled by a resistant (and racist) white commercial press. Jack Conroy's answer to their question, likewise, comparing the political burden of the short story to the work of white Left writers of the "proletarian moment," was a reminder that readers of *Negro Story*'s stories, like earlier readers of poems in Left little magazines discussed by Nelson, were agents capable of translating the written artifact into "communal" social change for black Americans.

As with 1930s proletarian poetry, this self-conscious articulation of a revised cultural politics tied to generic reform was a culmination of previous like-minded experiments. Just after the turn of the century *The Crisis* and *Opportunity* had both been created in part as periodicals for short fiction by black writers who couldn't publish elsewhere. Inspired by the successes in the genre of Alice Dunbar-Nelson and Pauline Hopkins, the magazines routinely devoted large space to black short fiction, much of it representing black middle-class experience.[8] In 1919, a young Jessie Redmon Fauset, an accomplished short story writer in the black press long before her success as a novelist, became literary editor of *The Crisis* and immediately inaugurated a short story contest to fuel competition with *Opportunity*. Chicago's most prolific 1930s short story writer, Marita Bonner, published many of her Frye Street Stories in both magazines, tales whose focus on black poverty and working-class life in Chicago anticipated many of the themes of *Negro Story* work.[9] During the Harlem Renaissance, the short story was also a staple genre of vanguard black writing: *Fire!!!*, the short-lived Harlem Renaissance magazine featured short stories by a young Gwendolyn Bennett and Zora Neale Hurston, who with Hughes was one of its founders.

Yet these examples were both temporally and philosophically less influential on *Negro Story* than those of the 1930s Left and black popular presses from which it coalesced its Popular Front-style politics. As early as the 1920s, black newspapers like the *Baltimore Afro-American* and the *Defender* began to seek out and publish black short story writers. Both, like *Negro Story* later, regularly featured rank amateurs representing through "plotless realism" images of black life meant to counter and combat stereotypical samples from the white literary, and commercial, presses. Describing the nearly one thousand short stories published in the *Afro-American* between 1925 and 1950, for example, Nick Aaron Ford and H. L. Faggett noted how black authors presented in them "Negro characters outside the familiar stereotypes. They portray them in their normal activities as American citizens, neither as paragons of virtue nor as personifications of ignorance, laziness, stupidity, and vice." Using language reminiscent of both *Negro Story*'s editors and Langston Hughes's Harlem Renaissance manifesto, "The Negro Artist and the Racial Mountain," Ford and Faggett insisted that black newspaper short fiction presented "the darker American laughing, weeping, singing, struggling, achieving, failing, praying, singing, and dreaming, dreaming of things his whiter brothers have dared to dream also."[10] Afro-American Newspapers president Carl Murphy, meanwhile, explained the newspaper's inclusion of short fiction as a balm for black readers beset with daily struggles the "news" sections couldn't help but remind them of. Comparing the function of short fiction in black newspapers to the serial publication of *Uncle Tom's Cabin* in Harriet Beecher Stowe's hometown paper, Murphy argued that "Everybody has his own daily problems, and the newspaper which must carry the news can, through the means of fiction, turn its readers' minds away from the real to the imaginative. The writer of a clean, well-written 'boy meets girl' short story," continued Murphy, "is one of the most important contributors to any newspaper. He probably has cured more indigestion than all the stomach specialists combined."[11]

This ratcheting out of "literary" context of the short story into accessible mass circulation newspapers keyed black writers and readers into the affinities between the genres and began to normalize the role of the short story in everyday black reading. Their proliferation in black newspapers amounted to a widening literary "submarket" within American and African-American culture in which amateur (i.e., "worker") black writers and working *readers* found common cause. Indeed, the short story's unique potential for publication in progressive or mass circulation periodicals arguably inspired the two most notable collections of African-American short fiction published during the 1930s: Langston Hughes's *The Ways of White Folks* and Richard Wright's *Uncle Tom's Children*. Hughes had dabbled in short fiction early in his career, turning out what he called "commercial" short stories written in 1927 for *The Messenger*, Wallace Thurman and George Schuyler's journal in which three early Hughes stories first appeared.[12] Yet Hughes's impulse to write the stories for *Ways* came after his contacts with John Reed Clubs and his 1931 trip to the Soviet Union to work on the never-completed film project *Black and White*.[13] Stories published there like "Cora Unashamed" were encoded turns on the light romantic "formula" described by Murphy, stressing, in Arnold Rampersad's words, "the volatile mixture of race, class and sexuality behind . . . the rituals of liberal race relations in the United States."[14] With rare exception, the stories were published in Left newspapers like *New Masses* or "mainstream" papers like the *Brooklyn Daily Eagle*. In turn, as Michael Denning has shown, *The Ways of White Folks* became central to both James Farrell's and Eugene Clay's address on the "Negro in American literature" at the 1935 American Writers' Congress,[15] evidence that Hughes had officially added the short story to the agenda of the Left's interracial cultural front. Wright's breakthrough short story collection *Uncle Tom's Children* was likewise a seminal Popular Front moment of the merger of black proletarian radicalism and mass market appeal deeply influential of Browning and Gayden's decision to start *Negro Story*. Like Hughes, Wright began writing short stories for commercial markets: his early story "Superstition," published in the April 1931 Robert Abbott's *Abbott's Monthly Magazine*, was his first Chicago publication. After his own leftward turn inspired by the Reed Club experience Wright wrote the stories for *Uncle Tom's Children*, including "Bright and Morning Star," published in 1938 in *New Masses*, and "Fire and Cloud," which won *Story* magazine's short fiction prize.

In Chicago the collapse of *Abbott's Monthly Magazine* and the success of both Hughes and Wright in the genre inspired the *Defender*'s own decision to begin serial weekly publication in May 1939 of short stories by erstwhile anonymous contributor and staff member Bruce Reynolds. Reynolds's stories were straightforward, almost literal transcriptions of black life on Chicago's South Side. The stories were a serial hit, and the *Defender* tried to advertise and promote Reynolds as a kind of "in-house" Langston Hughes.[16] In 1943, Hughes himself began publishing his now famous "Simple" sketches in the *Defender*. These vernacular vignettes featuring the voice of arch black working-class narrator Jesse B. Semple cumulatively constitute, as Michael Denning has suggested, Hughes's only "proletarian novel."[17] Indeed Hughes's "Simple" stories may be seen as the culmination of an early era in black literature in which the short story and black periodicals stretched each other's markets and conventions as a means of reaching and shaping a black mass readership.

It is not surprising then that a wider review of black short fiction published in the 1930s and 1940s reveals numerous other stories that supplement the traditional parameters of "proletarian" or radical U.S. literature by focusing on and targeting a specifically black working-class or mass readership. This chapter will demonstrate how by exploiting the short story's distinctive generic conventions such as its spatial economy, its accessibility to "amateurs," its comparability to popular forms like newspaper articles, and its untapped potential for both creating and shaping "mass" literary markets of black writers and readers, the genre helped to forge a new (black) market for the production and consumption of periodic protest culture. Concurrent with revisions in the cultural politics of black painting, newspapers, and magazine culture in Chicago, the short story underwent a radical metamorphosis during the Negro People's Front, coming out the other end a well-established genre for black literary experiment and radical voicing. Failure of critics of both the African-American literary tradition and the tradition of U.S. radical literature to recognize this evolution most likely reflects a conventional generic bias toward the novel and poetry. This bias in turn has helped to diminish critical understanding of the larger role of periodicals like *Negro Story* in the creation of black oppositional cultural politics. Yet the short story's recurring centrality to Chicago's black radical "renaissance" provides compelling evidence of the material struggle over the production and consumption of African-American culture—even at the level of generic reform—with which the Negro People's Front itself was ultimately most concerned.

More than any other, the short story was at the time of Browning's 1940 rejection from *Esquire,* which helped prompt the idea for *Negro Story,* the arbitrating genre of American literary and racial "value" in the periodical market to which she and Gayden sought access. Annually throughout the 1930s, for example, Edward O'Brien in collaboration with Whit Burnett published their *Best American Short Stories* collections, a gathering of stories selected by the editors as representative of the best American magazine fiction—no other genre was so cataloged. O'Brien, a donnish literary critic with New England roots, had inaugurated the annual collections in 1915; Burnett had started *Story* magazine in 1933 as the first American magazine dedicated to publishing short fiction exclusively. By the early 1930s the book included a

"Magazine Averages" index published in a "Yearbook" section supplemental to the text displaying statistical tables rating all American magazines according to what the editors deemed the number of "outstanding" stories published there during the year. Something like a stock market index to the American short story and periodical, the magazine averages consistently listed liberal commercial literary magazines like *Atlantic Monthly* and *Esquire* near the top, while only occasionally noting stories of merit published in the only two periodicals regularly publishing black short fiction, *Crisis* and *Opportunity*. (Left-wing little magazines that also published black short fiction were rarely cited).

The cultural logic of O'Brien and Burnett's genre project was aptly represented in O'Brien's 1938 "Introduction" to *Best American Short Stories*. Noting the book's publication in "a time of transition in which every value is questioned," O'Brien described the 1938 collection as representative of a shift of cultural supremacy westward linked to a changing balance of world power. "We have come a long way with the American short story during the past twenty-five years," O'Brien noted. "We have come so far, in fact, that a great deal more is expected of us as writers than was expected of us in 1914." O'Brien argued that a "special American way of looking at things" had arisen concurrent with a sudden make-over of culture globally:

> Several European cultures have died in the past few years. There is no longer an Austrian culture in Austria. There is no longer a German culture in Germany. There are no longer Czech and Slovak cultures in Czechoslovakia. I am aware of very little creative acitivty in Spain and Italy. Hungarian culture is beginning to contemplate its end. . . . Fragments of all these cultures still survive, pitiably destitute, in London, Paris, and New York. . . .
> It looks as if it were our turn now.[18]

O'Brien's ethnocentric manifesto, his own wartime "defense of culture," was published one year after Wright's and the South Side Writers' Group's own "Blueprint for Negro Writing," and in the same year as Wright's *Uncle Tom's Children*. Unsurprisingly, it payed no attention to the contribution of black artists to his favored genre. O'Brien's adjoining aesthetic criteria for the successful story of 1938—"No substance is of importance in fiction unless it is organic substance"; "The true artist will seek to shape this living substance into the most beautiful and satisfying form by skillful selection and arrangement of his material, and by the most direct and appealing presentation of it in portrayal and characterization"[19]—provides further evidence of a formally traditional, politically deracinated institutional consensus on the genre progressive black writers and editors of the late 1930s would have squarely faced in any attempt to revise it. Indeed, with rare exceptions up to the time of O'Brien's manifesto, black writers, progressive or otherwise, were routinely excluded from inclusion in *Best American Short Stories*.[20] Also characteristic of stories about blacks by white writers published in *Story* and collected by O'Brien and Burnett into the *Best American Short Stories* collection was a species of period racism encompassing a range of retrograde images. In *Best American Short Stories* of 1935, for example, O'Brien selected Elma Godchaux's "Wild Nigger," reprinted from *The Frontier and Midland,* a journal regularly praised and excerpted by the editors. The story's protagonist, Zula, "the little humpback nigger girl," is a razor-toting, wild-haired river rat invested with the spirit of the devil and hoodoo powers she deploys in pursuit of a man.[21] Replete with "coon" dialect and a brutally regressive caricature of black female lust, the story qualifies as a white gothic projection of racial and sexual stereotypes dating at least to the antebellum period. In 1938 O'Brien included in *Best American Short Stories* Richard Paulett Creyke's "Niggers Are Such Liars," reprinted from *Story* magazine. Set at a summer camp, the story concerns two boys, Jeb and Everett, who suspect that Anderson, "the nigger that cooked for the camp," goes swimming in the lake at night after the boys go to bed. Jeb and Everett test their speculations by rowing Anderson out to the middle of the river and tipping over the boat. Anderson drowns. Jeb's father arrives and members of the camp debate whether Anderson could ever swim. Jeb assuages his son's conscience by blaming the drowning on Anderson. The intended irony of the story literally drowns under the weight of its elimination of black character and agency in the story: "But Anderson could swim. He was just lying to you when he said he couldn't. All niggers lie. They're born that way. Now when we get home I'll tell you exactly what to say about this. Meanwhile, keep quiet."[22]

In 1939 O'Brien included David L. Cohn's "Black Troubadour," reprinted from the *Atlantic Monthly,* about Joe Moss, a "rambling, rolling, train-riding, harp-blowing" black man. The story's narrative voice slips quixotically from third to first person, producing a literary version of the theatrical minstrel projections Eric Lott has diagnosed in *Love and Theft*:[23] "Winter and summer, fall and spring, Joe rambles the land, a sweat shirt and red corduroy trousers covering his nakedness, and a ragged hat on his nappy head. It ain't no need to work. It ain't no need to have no one woman and no one home. A man with music in his body can win hisself a woman and a home wherever he lights. A nigger ain't gonna have nothin' nohow, so it ain't no need to try to have nothin'."[24]

Recounting the varying degrees of offensiveness and the aesthetic program for celebrated short stories of the late 1930s is meant not to feign or
incite naive shock, but to begin to illuminate the cultural position of the black
short story and periodical in the period preceding the start-up of *Negro Story*
magazine. The necessity of Alice Browning, an African-American woman,
becoming the WASPish and masculine "Richard Bentley" in order to publish a story about white soldier rape was, this sampling of magazine fiction
suggests, paralleled by the necessity of Browning creating *Negro Story*, in her
own words, as the Negro *Story.* The "intertextual" or dialogic logic of these
transformative strategies was articulated by the editors in their second issue
of the magazine published in June 1944:

> That the Negro writer should propagandize and reflect bitterness of atti-
> tudes is understandable, but he must try to study the techniques of writing
> and portray his material as artistically as possible. We feel that we can say,
> with justification, that the theme of the virtuous negro victim and the sav-
> age white tyrant may be overworked, when the Eleanor Roosevelts, Lillian
> Smiths, and other courageous leaders are destroying their "demons" in
> America, and many whites and blacks are striving to solve their common
> problems. These stories have their place, but we do not intend to show only
> the "rosy" side of Negro life with the sentimentalized heroine and hero. We
> want to present real live [*sic*] characters. . . . Our main desire is for a good
> story. It may be realism, romanticism, naturalism or phantasy, as long as it
> is good. We are urging young writers to study story techniques in order to
> present effectively the wealth of dramatic material at hand. There is a wide
> change in conditions. The Negro is achieving status and consciousness in all
> phases of life.
>
> Summing it up, we are trying to say that the writer who chooses Negro life
> for his theme is confronted by a huge task. It is his responsibility to widen
> his horizon, examine the facts and to give truthful and honest interpretations
> of life. We would like to have humor and entertainment. We want some ex-
> citing love stories, stories of psychological conflicts—anything that lends
> itself to a good plot. The writers should carry these stories to the climax with
> adequate suspense and then effect the denouement without an anti-climax.[25]

Gayden and Browning's formula for a "well wrought" protest story was
a racial turn on the generic conventions celebrated in the American "slicks"
and their anthologies. It also alluded to the insurgency of a generation of new
black writers who had convinced them of the magazine's political necessity
and potential commercial success. Among the young, black (and Left) Chicago writers with short story publications by 1944 were Willard Motley, Rich-

ard Wright, Frank Yerby, Gwendolyn Brooks, Margaret Taylor Goss Burroughs, and Browning and Gayden themselves; among non-Chicago short story writers who were already published and would find their way into *Negro Story*'s pages were Ralph Ellison, Chester Himes, and Langston Hughes. It is worth noting that as of 1944 none of these writers with the exception of Wright had yet published a novel. Savvy entrepreneurs, Gayden and Browning would have known of the short story's role as a stepping stone toward that end (indeed within six years after *Negro Story*'s demise Motley, Brooks, Yerby, Ellison, and Himes would publish novels). In addition, the contributing role of the short story in the development of a proletarian and radical literature sympathetic to interracial struggle was emblematized for the editors by the supportive and congenial influence of white Chicago short story writers like James Light, Nelson Algren, and Jack Conroy. The conjunction of these Left-influenced black and white writers with the steadfastly regressive racial judgments of white commercial magazines thus made the genre, Browning and Gayden were prescient to realize, not an incidental but an *inevitable* and necessary nexus for reform of black cultural politics and political culture.[26]

For an example the editors could have looked to the strange career of Willard Motley. His unique place at the margins of Chicago's "renaissance" of black radicalism is best illustrated and foretold by Motley's long engagement with short fiction preceding publication of his 1947 breakthrough novel *Knock on Any Door*. The latter, described by Walter Rideout as one of the ten "radical" novels of the 1940s with "permanent literary value,"[27] is best understood as an "intertext" of Motley's earlier experiments and failures in the short story in his own evolution from bourgeois refugee to proletarian tourist among the black and white poor and working classes of the Depression. Born and raised in a nearly all-white Chicago neighborhood, son of a Pullman porter on the "Wolverine" train from Chicago to New York,[28] Motley entered professional writing around the age of thirteen when he became editor of "Dollar Ideas" in the *Evening Post*, a column to instruct children on how to save money. Motley's qualifications included precocious writing ability and a "reasonably comfortable, middle-class background."[29] For the same publication he edited a column called "The Weekly Short Story," in which readers were invited to complete unfinished short stories by adding an appropriately melodramatic denouement. In 1922 Motley published his own first short story, "Sister and Brother," in the *Defender*. The story, about two orphans taken into the home of a well-to-do elderly couple where they lead what Robert Fleming calls a "Cinderella style life," crudely foreshadowed Motley's

lifelong obsession with class mobility and his literary attempts at resolution
of the lives of the urban poor.[30]

In 1922 Motley became editor of a weekly column on the new children's
page of the *Chicago Defender,* the "Defender Junior." The column, called "Bud
Says," included Motley's by-line and pen name "Bud Billiken," his self-
selected moniker derived from "billiken," the Chinese god of things "as they
ought to be."[31] Motley's column also bore the entrepreneurial stamp of publisher Abbott: it sponsored "Billiken Club" chapters in different neighborhoods and contests for drawings, poems, and letters from children readers.
Young Motley's literary ambitions likewise reflected an entrepreneurial drive
toward assimilation into the conventions of the predominantly white commercial short story market. Through high school he repeatedly sent stories
to *Boy's Life* and other adolescent magazines; influenced by the work of
O. Henry, he experimented with "romantic tales with 'twist' endings" and
shipped them to white mainstream magazines like *Esquire, Colliers* and *Liberty,* publishing none.[32]

The recipe for Motley's "formula fiction" and literary ambitions was
permanently altered around 1936. Influenced by the Depression-era road
reportage and fiction of writers like Algren and Farrell and even the personal
journalism of George Orwell, Motley set off on a cross-country journey to
the West.[33] Eager to document the conditions of the Depression poor, Motley merged his fledgling short story techniques with reportage to turn out
romanticized nonfiction accounts of his travels. "In All the World No Trip
Like This!" described his experience in a Laramie, Wyoming, county jail after siphoning gas; shortly thereafter he published "Religion and the Hand-
out" in *Commonweal,* describing his experiences in a soup kitchen.[34] In 1938
and 1939 he published "The Boy" and "The Boy Grows Up," in *The Ohio
Motorist,* nonfiction accounts of his encounters with Joe, a young Mexican
American who was the inspiration for Nick Romano, Italian-American protagonist of *Knock on Any Door.*[35] As Robert Fleming has observed, Motley's
role in telling these stories anticipated the narrator role of Grant Holloway
in his debut novel.[36] Tormented by what Meridel Le Sueur called "The Fetish of Being Outside," or what Parksian sociologists called "participant
observer status," Motley attempted to use short prose pieces to delineate his
role as voyeur/author/reporter in his documentation of the Depression.[37]

By 1938 Motley had moved to the Maxwell Street and Skid Row neighborhoods of Chicago, where he hoped for closer documentation of the poor
and working class. In the fall of 1939 he visited Hull House at 800 S. Halsted
Street. Founded by Jane Addams and Ellen Starr in 1899, Hull House was by

the time of his arrival also a center for white radicals. There Motley met William P. Schenk and the later Communist writer and publisher Alexander Saxton. Together, the three founded *Hull-House Magazine*. For it, Motley wrote "realistic, plotless" sketches of South Side neighborhoods—proletariat vignettes or "plotless realism" as described in 1944 by Gayden and Browning.[38] In 1940, while working for the WPA, Motley sent "The Beer Drinkers," a short story, to *The Anvil*. The story about a woman and her proletarian lover—another interclass fantasy—was likely rejected by editor Jack Conroy, who encouraged him to submit to more commercial markets like *Esquire*.[39] Their encounter was portentous of the revision of the "radical" novel tradition Motley would undertake in 1947. *Knock on Any Door* reconstituted the "naturalism" and Marxian class analysis of many preceding novels into a fable of "racelessness" and bourgeois irony. Nick Romano's fall from a middle-class Italian family into murder tweaked the trajectory and focus of the proletarian novel to describe Motley's own attempted transgressions downward into the slums of Little Sicily. Obviously inspired in part by Wright's *Native Son*, Motley's novel was likewise shot through with a brand of "popular front" anxiety, not about communism's relationship to American liberalism and liberal capitalism but of the black bourgeois novelist's relationship to radical or revolutionary literature itself. Walter Rideout's claim for the book's "literary value" as a radical novel is thus apt insofar as it describes the novel's attempt to master what had become after Dreiser and Wright a formula for readers of popular American class mobility tales—the naturalistic tragedy. Such could be seen as the inevitable legacy of a writer whose early career was beholden to the principles of "craft" and design in the American short story and its commercial market mechanisms. Yet Motley's book was also a singular contribution to a national reconsideration of the African-American novelist as *in* a radical literary tradition (naturalistic protest fiction). Indeed, *Knock on Any Door* was yet another example of Chicago's radical "renaissance" sustaining a tradition of radical political experiment while revising it, just as Motley himself had consistently reconfigured the nature and role of the short story to reflect the increasingly progressive direction of his writing career.

The short story's role in the shifting political position of the black literary market is even more tellingly evident in the career of Chester Himes. Though he never lived or worked in Chicago, Himes was according to Browning and Gayden *Negro Story*'s most popular contributor among the magazine's Chicago readers. His role as a chronicler of black proletariat life in wartime Los Angeles, where he wrote his stories for the magazine, provides uncanny evidence of the dialogic means by which both short fiction and the short fiction market coalesced oppositional culture and politics during the Negro People's Front.

Himes's first short story, "To What Red Hell," was published by *Esquire* in 1934. Written from an Ohio prison, where he was doing twenty years for armed robbery, the story was based on the Easter 1931 fire and riot at the state penitentiary. One year before, Himes had published his first short story, also written in jail, on a typewriter purchased after inspiration from reading Dashiell Hammett stories in *Black Mask,* a pulp detective magazine.[40] Himes's "His Last Day" appeared in Robert Abbott's *Abbott's Monthly* in 1933, as did "Prison Mass," another prison tale. In 1933 Himes also published "The Meanest Cop in the World" and "A Modern Marriage" in the *Atlanta Daily World.* These pulp influenced "slick" stories in black newspapers anticipated his success in the mid-1930s during which he published four stories in *Esquire*— the only black author to crack that prestigious white market: "To What Red Hell," "The Visiting Hour" (1936), "Every Opportunity" (1937), and "The Night's for Cryin'" (1937). Himes's *Esquire* stories on black prison lumpen-prol were, by his own later admission, calculated attempts to fit white commercial magazine readers' conceptions of black suffering and devoid of "race consciousness."[41]

In 1935, Himes took a job as a laborer on the WPA. After a clash with a WPA executive, Himes moved into contact with the Cleveland CIO, where "I developed a hatred of the ruling class of whites. I identified myself with labor."[42] When the WPA ceased, Himes queued for jobs at American Steel and Wire and other industries in Ohio's Cuyahoga Valley, where "I learned what racial prejudice is like."[43] In 1941, Himes moved to Los Angeles, where he worked for a year on the Federal Writers' Project. When the war broke out, he took a job at Kaiser Shipyards as a shipfitter, where, in the American Federation of Labor union to which he belonged, he encountered even more severe racial discrimination. In his memoir *The Quality of Hurt,* Himes summarizes the Los Angeles years that jump-started and reversed the direction of his writing career:

> Los Angeles hurt me racially as much as any city I have ever known—much more than any city I remember from the South. It was the lying hypocrisy that hurt me. Black people were treated much the same as they were in an industrial city of the South. They were Jim-Crowed in housing, in employment, in public accommodations, such as hotels and restaurants. During the filming of *Cabin in the Sky,* starring Ethel Waters, Bill "Bojangles" Robinson

and Lena Horne, the black actors and actresses were refused service in the MGM commissary where everyone ate. The difference was that the white people of Los Angeles seemed to be saying, "Nigger, ain't we good to you?"[44]

The dimensions of Himes's wartime conversion to "race consciousness" resulting from these hostile experiences are evident in the radically transformed writings they immediately produced. In 1944, Himes published "Negro Martyrs Are Needed" in *The Crisis*. The essay's opening lines indicated the clear direction of Himes's new outlook: *"Martyrs are needed to create incidents. Incidents are needed to create revolutions. Revolutions are needed to create progress."*[45] The essay was an intensely personal application through Himes's charged emotional lens of the message of Left and Communist organizers in the Los Angeles shipyard milieu to the state of black America:

> There can be only one (I repeat: *Only one*) aim of a revolution by Negro Americans: *That is the enforcement of the Constitution of the United States.* At this writing no one has yet devised a better way for existence than contained in the Constitution. *Therefore Negro Americans could not revolt for any other reason.* This is what a Negro American revolution will be: A revolution by a racial minority for the enforcement of the democratic laws already in existence.
>
> What will a revolution by Negro Americans do: (1) Bring about the overthrow of our present form of government and the creation of a communistic state. A communist organization of immense proportions already exists in this nation.[46]

Citing Engels, Himes called for a proletariat uprising that would bring the United States closer to the ideal "Wherein every one is free" to which citizens of the "social state of the U.S.S.R." had come closest.[47] Though his sentiments could hardly have been original to readers then or now of Left doctrine, I quote Himes at length for several reasons. First, Himes's revolutionary "program" published in *Crisis,* the country's leading black intellectual journal, could not have been missed by the avowedly "non-political" editors of *Negro Story* in Chicago, where Himes's "A Night of New Roses" debuted him in the magazine in the December–January 1944 issue and where, as documented in previous chapters, black absorption and revision of Leftist influence was at fever pitch. In addition, Himes's "Americanization" of twentieth-century communism as a restoration of black Constitutional rights placed him squarely in the ideological mainstream of the Negro People's Front. Yet more importantly here, Himes's "Negro Martrys Are Needed" functioned as a dialogic intertext for the stories Himes wrote and published in its wake. Stories like "One More Way To Die," discussed earlier, and "Let me at the Enemy—an' George Brown," both originally published in *Negro Story*, portrayed failed black proletarian "martyrs" ground under by brutally repressive and racist state apparatuses. In the former, the death of a black worker at the hands of Los Angeles cops for approaching a white woman in a bar was a reenactment of racial violence against Los Angeles minorities and white fears of miscegenation Himes had both witnessed and experienced during the summer of 1943 "Zoot Suit" riots in Los Angeles. In a 1943 issue of *Crisis*, Himes's essay/reportage "Zoot Riots Are Race Riots" had traced the lineage of the zoot suit from white designer to black and Mexican "pachuco," both of whom were marked as "race rebels" and violently singled out by police in the riots. Himes compared Los Angeles police during the riots to "storm troopers" abolishing civil rights and wrote: "what should any Mexican or Negro youth do when walking down the public streets of Los Angeles with his wife or sweetheart to have a group of white servicemen look her over and wink or say, 'Boy, Ah ought to change mah luck.' Should he go back and hit them in the mouth? The best he could expect from such a procedure, attempted alone, would be a whipping by the gang of servicemen, a whipping by the Los Angeles police, and then a charge in the Los Angeles courts of inciting a riot."[48]

Himes's simultaneous role as essayist/reporter from the Los Angeles front and contributor of autobiographical stories to *Negro Story* in Chicago—where the *Defender* paid careful attention to the Los Angeles riots[49]—made them concurrent dialogic sites of black oppositional cultural practices. Himes's literary praxis and the mechanism of his publication paralleled that a decade earlier of Tillie Olsen, whose poetic "reportage" of San Francisco dockworkers strikes published in *New Masses* in 1934 made a symbolic "intertext" in Nelson's words, of the event, the poem, journalistic accounts of the event, and their publication. Himes's first two novels evolved precisely from this dialogic logic. One of the most important pretexts for both *If He Hollers Let Him Go* (1945) and *Lonely Crusade* (1946) was another *Negro Story* story, "Make With the Shape," published as the lead piece in the August–September 1945 *Negro Story*.

In "Make With the Shape," Sergeant Johnny Jones has been honorably discharged from three years in the service. He returns to Los Angeles looking forward to reuniting with his wife Jessie May, whose "fine, round gams" and "everloving peepers" have been on his mind throughout the war. Jones arrives at her apartment one night when she is out and is startled to see "overalls, leather gloves, and logger's boots" lying about. Suddenly fearing he has "lost his happy home," he remembers that she had written him about giving up her office job and going to work on the swing shift in a pipe factory. He lays down on the couch to await her return. The door opens slowly, and "then something blew in like commandoes on D-day. He was yanked off of his feet, tied in a knot, and slammed against the floor with such vigor he went out like a light."[50] He wakes up to kisses from Jessie May, who, thinking he is an intruder, has layed him out with her judo instruction in the class for self-protection offered at the shop. Rubbing the lumps on his conk, Jones admits that the judo works alright, then muses, "But he didn't like it. In all those foxholes in Italy he had thought of her as strictly the clinging-vine type that will shy from a shadow, sweet and demure and soft as drugstore cotton, and to say he was disappointed in finding her so industrialized and athletic and self-reliant is an understatement. However, now that he was home, he figured she would fall back in the groove and become his little kitten again."[51]

Johnny's dream that Jessie will "make with the shape in satin and lace" and give up her job is corollary to his own certainty that he can translate his skills as a "good greasemonkey" in the service into work. But she refuses to let him work on her car, having learned to fix it herself, and when he proposes that both of them shouldn't have to work, thinking she will quit her job (and perhaps he can take it), she backs off. Insult is added to injury when Jessie May saves them both from an attacking dog by kicking it in the teeth. Disemployed, displaced, and second class to his working wife, Johnson resorts to "scouting about for a soft, clinging chick with big adoring eyes" to make Jessie May jealous. It works. She discovers him with the woman, the women fight, and Jessie decides to come home to be his "sweet little wife" and make with the shape once more.[52]

Johnson's dilemma is to be a "negro martyr" to what Himes perceived as the triple trap of black proletariat masculinity during and after the war. Ultimately Johnson is a "slave"—a prospective industrial worker, in street idiom; a subject to a suddenly empowered female worker, and a veteran whose credentials, including his medals, are not refundable on his manhood in a racist postwar economy; they are "only for valor" laments Johnny. Himes's retrograde conception of the war's effects on black gender dynamics was consistent with his masculinist calls for black revolutionary warriors cut from the same cloth of black nationalist romanticism later embodied by Eldridge Cleaver. Yet "Make With the Shape" was also as nearly an autobiographical piece of fictional reportage as Himes had yet attempted. In his autobiography he recounts his first marriage in Los Angeles to a woman serving as co-director of women's activities for the Los Angeles area USOs while he was bouncing among twenty-three different jobs during the first three years of the war, nearly all unskilled. "It hurt me for my wife to have a better job than I did and be respected and included by her white co-workers, besides rubbing elbows with many well-to-do blacks of the Los Angeles middle class who wouldn't touch me with a ten-foot pole. . . . I found that I was no longer a husband to my wife; I was her pimp. She didn't mind, and that hurt all the more."[53]

Directly from this experience, according to Himes, he wrote his "bitter novel of protest" *If He Hollers Let Him Go*.[54] It is also clear that Himes rewrote and revised the bulk of his *Negro Story* stories and themes into the larger work. The novel's protagonist Bob Jones is a Los Angeles shipyard worker caught between racist white industry, union organizers and workers, and a lustful white woman named Madge. The novel replays the satiric tensions of Himes's comical wartime stories as straight proletarian protest fiction while extrapolating Himes's gender and sexual psychoses into novel-length drama. In *Lonely Crusade*, to be discussed again in chapter 7, Johnny Jones becomes Lee Gordon, a black union organizer confronted with racial, sexual, and class antagonisms that doom black and interracial solidarity. The commercial appeal to black readers of both books was predictable given the popularity of Himes's wartime stories in *Negro Story* and *Crisis*, the two magazines in which he almost exclusively published after 1940, consciously turning away from the commercial white magazine market. Likewise, Himes's Rosenwald Fellowship that financed his writing of *If He Hollers* had been made possible largely due to his *Negro Story* notoriety. The publication of *If He Hollers* in 1945 thus encapsulated the aspirations Gayden and Browning had laid out for a shift in both the "status" and "consciousness" of both writers and readers of black short fiction. The book culminated not only Himes's shift in political awareness during the war, but his longer race and class conscious revision of the short story. In this sense *If He Hollers* was an "intertext" representative of both the local and national fronts of the "defense of culture" to which Chicago and *Negro Story* were central. Racial and economic woes and the response of black and white militants, literary and otherwise, from Los Angeles to Cleveland to Chicago sustained Himes's writing and his reading audience long enough to result in his appearance as the most popular and vanguard novelist of the national black urban proletariat in 1945.

⚜

Fern Gayden and Alice Browning's 1944 call for a commercially viable black protest story also evoked Richard Wright's one certain legacy to black Chicago's upsurge of cultural radicalism. Wright's breakthrough as a fiction writer was, of course, his short story "Big Boy Leaves Home," published in the momentous *The New Caravan* anthology in November 1936. In April of that year he had already summoned the first meeting of the South Side Writers' Group, where according to Fern Gayden, Wright's own short stories—and those of others like herself—took center stage. In addition to "Big Boy Leaves Home," Wright's "Fire and Cloud" and "Bright and Morning Star" were presented as fictional "case studies" demonstrating the radical folk/proletarian aesthetic articulated in the Writers' Group's "A Blueprint for Negro Writing" published in 1937. The cadre of radical amateur writers attempting to embody this ethos portended the communal insurgency and strong Leftist cast of *Negro Story.* So too did Wright's startling commercial success foretell the entrepreneurial zeal with which the magazine marketed black short fiction ranging from liberal to revolutionary. "Fire and Cloud" won Wright first prize of $600 in *Story* magazine's annual contest—the first story by a black writer so honored and a previously unthinkable moment of rapprochement between the conservative cultural capitalist Whit Burnett and Wright's openly Marxist fiction. In 1938 "Fire and Cloud" won second prize of $200 in the O. Henry Memorial Award competition. "Bright and Morning Star," arguably the most incendiary—and didactic—of the tales in *Uncle Tom's Children,* traveled from first publication in the May 1938 *New Masses,* to dramatization by Wright's close friend Ted Ward, to inclusion in O'Brien's *Best American Short Stories, 1939* and *Fifty Best American Short Stories (1914–1939).*

Gayden, who had been there, would have thus known even better than Browning the potential for reforming the status and marketability of black protest culture through vanguard communal literary production embodied by the South Side Writers' Group. *Negro Story* might be read as an intertextual and interhistorical echo of that important moment in Chicago—and national—black radicalism, one intended to produce new "blueprints" for Negro writing and publishing that included attention to generic reform. The magazine created something akin to a national and international "circle" of writers coming together *in print* on a bimonthly basis to diagnose and protest pressing crises in black America. The May–June 1945 "Anniversary Issue" is perhaps the best case in point. Lead piece for the issue was Langston Hughes's "Private Jim Crow," a one-act play in which a black soldier on a southern train car is exposed to Jim Crow taunts and "Fifth columnist" racism.[55] Two other stories and several poems in the issue presented black soldiers facing racist threats: the stories "A Message of Promise" by Lieutenant Howard Peeks and "Harlem Hammer" by Private Rufus Wells; and the poems "The Mistake" by Roma Jones, an ex-Chicago teacher; "Interment" by Lieutenant William Couch Jr., graduate of Inez Cunningham Stark's South Side Art Center poetry class; and "The Decision" by Owen Dodson, reprinted from *Common Ground.* The soldier-writer status of some contributors to the issue evoked the commonality and communality of interest and occupation of short story writers and poets addressing issues of war. Meanwhile, no less than three other stories in the issue concerned the ongoing lynching of black males: Ralph Ellison's "The Birthmark," about the beating and castration of a black man by white state troopers; "Alabama Evening" by Earl Conrad; and Columbia professor Dr. Vernon Loggins's "Neber Said a Mumblin' Word," whose title derived from the popular spiritual about Christ's stoicism at the crucifixion.

Indeed, Ellison's brief interlude as a short story writer and contributor to *Negro Story* is emblematic of the overlooked role the genre played in the creation of a radical black literary culture of the 1940s. Ellison's only overtly Left and proletarian-influenced fiction was his 1940s short stories published in *Negro Story* and elsewhere. Similar to Himes's own *Negro Story* stories, "The Birthmark" was a faithful political intertext of Ellison's other writings for *New Masses,* inspired by his contacts with the New York Communist Party and his reports on the Harlem riots of 1943 for the New York *Post.* As Barbara Foley has demonstrated, Ellison was receptive to much of the CP's Popular Front program during his short story writing years and worked hard to eliminate it, with some success, from his literary record after publication of *Invisible Man* in 1952.[56] The relative ease of this erasure, like the delay in collection and publication of Himes's own stories and the disappearance of *Negro Story* from critical view, speaks as much to the traditional ephemerality and obsolescence of the genre in relation to the novel as it does to critical disengagement with African-American radicalism in many cultural histories of the United States.

Frank Yerby is yet another case in point. In 1944 Yerby won special prize of $100 for best first-published story for "Health Card," published in *Harper's.* Yerby, a veteran of the Illinois Writers Project, poured the racial radicalism of his early years described by his close friends and colleagues Frank Marshall

Davis and Jack Conroy[57] into a brief, harrowing tale about a black soldier in a southern town who is hassled by police when his wife comes to visit. In the story, a virtual carbon of the themes of Himes's wartime stories, the black soldier is threatened with symbolic "emasculation" by white MPs who think his wife is a prostitute. "I ain't no man! I ain't no man," laments the soldier, who is ultimately comforted by a preacher and his wife, who steadfastly stands by him.[58] In 1946 Yerby published his first novel, *The Foxes of the Harrow*. Yerby's abandonment of a protest voice in that novel and subsequently merely underscores the short story's importance during Chicago's radical front years as the prevailing genre for its most militant voices. Inclusion of Yerby's story in *Prize Stories of 1944*, edited by Herschell Brickell, and its designation as an O. Henry Memorial Award winner for that year further suggests how revisions by Left-influenced black and white writers altered the content and market standing of the genre by the mid-1940s.

Indeed, in the same year Martha Foley's edition of *The Best American Short Stories* (Foley had replaced the recently deceased O'Neill as annual editor) became a critical lightning rod of the genre's newly racialized and politicized status. Ben Burns, in his September 30, 1944, review of the edition, noted that the book's publication had been "preceded by a heated controversy over the source of the contents." Burns reported that the liberal Bennett Cerf of Random House and other critics had deemed the choices of stories in the collection "narrow-minded, partisan and super-intellectual."[59] Burns singled out for criticism in his review two stories by white writers about blacks, Sidney Alexander's "The White Boat," about a black domestic's death during a rare off-day outing, and "The Mohammedans" by H. J. Kaplan. The latter, first published in *Partisan Review,* would have been of particular interest to Burns and black Chicago readers. It was a loosely veiled fictional account of several notorious sedition trials held in Chicago in the early years of the war in which black separatist cult leaders had been indicted and charged with attempted sabotage of the war effort. Their actions and rivalry—which resulted in a fatal shooting—were all reported with acrimonious disdain by the *Defender,* which accurately described the cults as marginalized nationalists to whom few white or black wartime radicals—nor certainly liberals —were sympathetic. Kaplan's story concerned a white protagonist named Charles Rodney Simon, a middle-aged aspiring poet living in an aging, decrepit family home in an increasingly black neighborhood somewhere on Chicago's South Side. Simon, a "man who had lived abroad and seen T. S. Eliot" close up, is in something of a Prufrockian crisis over his close contacts with his black neighbors. To make ends meet he takes in a boarder, a black Mohammedan named Wiley Bey, who is on the run from the draft board for refusing to register for the war. Bey reminds Simon that, to him, blacks are "creatures of music and dream who formed a world apart in America." Yet Simon also finds spiritual affiliations with Bey because of his own financial dispossession and racial displacement. He thus accepts Bey's argument that the war is a "white man's war . . . a war of the dynasts" and attempts to convince the draft board that Bey should be exempted. The board refuses despite Simon's pleas that "Simon is guilty—I mean Wiley Bey is guilty. We are all guilty!" When he returns home, Bey is beaten and arrested by police for failure to register. Simon interprets Bey's bloodied, principled stance as giving off "a quite repulsive air of triumph and self-satisfaction." The story ends with Simon musing on the futility of meaning of Bey's resistance: "But there's nothing, he said to himself bitterly, nothing you can make of it."[60]

Burns's review, preserving the spirit of an earlier decade's Marxian attacks on literary subjectivism, dismissed "The Mohammedans" as a "confused hash of trick impressionistic prose."[61] The larger attack on Foley, Kaplan, and *Partisan Review* for their tendentious representations and appropriations of black protest was also another indelible sign of the shifting trajectory of political and literary value in the short story.

Evidence that the publishing world took note of this shift was evident as early as Foley's *Best American Short Stories of 1946:* no fewer than seven stories from 1945 editions of *Negro Story* were listed in the book's "Distinctive Short Stories in American Magazines, 1945" index—the only stories by African-American writers so designated for that year. Included were Ellison's "The Birthmark," Himes's "The Song Says 'Keep on Smilin'," and "My But the Rats Are Terrible," Random House editor Bucklin Moon's "Slack's Blues," Charles Neider's "The Outcast," and two pseudonymous stories by Alice Browning, "The Slave" and "Tomorrow." Further evidence still of black short fiction's shifting cultural cache was provided in more progressive collections published in the same year like Edwin Seaver's *Cross-Section,* which included five short stories, a play, and several poems on black life. The most significant stories were Ellison's now classic "Flying Home," about a black flier's experience in Dixie, and Wright's "The Man Who Lived Underground." In addition to noting Ellison's obvious brilliance, Burns's review of Seaver's collection anticipated his skeptical reading of Wright's retreat from Left-influenced writing in *Black Boy* a year later, accusing the story of suffering from "the persecution complex inherent in too much of Wright's work," of unremitting gloominess, and of "incomplete, meaningless writing, even if superlative prose."[62] For Burns and other Chicago radicals, the appearance of Wright's story coincident with the popularity of *Negro Story* was a logical moment in which to reconsider the role of the short story in a black cultural front that Wright's own *Uncle Tom's Children* had seemed to announce, even if Wright had to their eyes abandoned the project.

A final measure of the short story's revised status in the shifting national literary discourse on race and racial politics appeared just six months after *Negro Story*'s debut issue. In January 1945, the Writers' War Board issued a pamphlet titled "How Writers Perpetuate Stereotypes." Chaired by Rex Stout, a white man, the board had come together at the urging of black and white liberals to survey representations of race and ethnicity in various popular American media including theater, film, and radio. The survey's findings targeted the short story as the *worst* offender of racial sensibility. After reviewing 185 short stories published in popular magazines, it noted that "In magazine stories, Anglo-Saxons received better treatment than minority and foreign groups: in frequency of appearance, importance in story, approval and disapproval, status and occupation, and in traits."[63]

While the widely distributed report might have been small consolation to black and white radicals whose work dating back nearly ten years had anticipated these findings, it undoubtedly functioned as an "official" moment of generic insurgency. The dialogic voices and voicings in the black short story beginning with Langston Hughes's *Ways of White Folks* and the experiment in Chicago literary radicalism of the South Side Writers' Group and ending in *Negro Story* could at least proclaim an "echo" in mainstream and liberal assent to new marks and marketings of race in the genre. As the Writers' War Board report confirmed, the Negro "story" of the post-1935 era was implicitly about the shift away from one set of evaluative criteria for creating and assessing black expressive culture and toward another. With the help of Browning and Gayden, the short story had reinvented itself as a generic symbol of these reforms. As this chapter has shown, neither was imaginable without the conscious and conscientious work of black literary radicals. For critics of our time, reconsidering the role of the short story in African-American political culture of the 1930s and 1940s at the very least allows us to rethink the careers of important figures like Motley, Himes, Ellison, and Yerby, while filling gaps in the wartime and postwar shape of African-American letters and the marketplace for African-American culture the short story did much to alter.

# 6 Engendering the Cultural Front: Gwendolyn Brooks, Black Women, and Class Struggle in Poetry

*Still in need of refinement is our understanding of the connection between migration and black social-class formation and between migration and the rise of protest ideologies which shaped the consciousness of the "New Negro," not only in Harlem, but also in midwestern cities.*
    —Darlene Clark Hine, *HineSight: Black Women and the Re-Construction of American History*

*People are so in need, in need of help.*
*People want so much that they do not know.*
    —Gwendolyn Brooks, "The Sundays of Satin-Legs Smith"

Darlene Clark Hine's *HineSight: Black Women and the Re-Construction of American History* documents the economic hardship of black women before and during the Great African-American Migration and their role in social class formation in new black northern urban centers like Chicago. Clark Hine views black women as links in the "migration chain" for whom the mission of moving friends and family up north, often after men had gone ahead to find work, was the beast-like burden of their sex. Once there, black women compensated for their persisting economic marginalization (as domestic workers, unskilled factory workers, or unpaid housewives, for example), by "domesticating" the disorder of black urban public space. Black women were primary initiators of and participants in what Clark Hine calls the "institutional infrastructure" of new northern urban black communities in the form of sororities, church groups, social clubs, and charity organizations. These public networks functioned as symbolic arenas for social class formation, stressing "status" rather than material wealth and "values and attitudes traditionally associated with the middling classes."[1] In *Black Metropolis,* Cayton and Drake explained the historical roots of these social networks as follows:

For thousands of Negro migrants from the South, merely arriving in Bronzeville represented "getting ahead." Yet Negroes, like other Americans, share the general interest in getting ahead in more conventional terms. The Job Ceiling and the Black Ghetto limit free competition for the money and for residential symbols of success. Partly because of these limitations . . . it has become customary among the masses of Negroes in America to center their interest upon living in the immediate present or upon going to heaven—upon "having a good time" or "praising the Lord." Though some derive their prestige from the respect accorded them by the white world, or by the professional and business segments of the Negro world, most Negroes seem to adopt a pattern of conspicuous behavior and conspicuous consumption. Maintaining a "front" and "showing off" become very important substitutes for getting ahead in the economic sense.[2]

Cayton and Drake credited Bronzeville's largely female-created social networks with delineating what the authors called the "respectable," the "refined," and "riffraff" on the South Side.[3] The terms belied the ease with which many South Siders could repress and displace material economic hardship and the animus of class division through "fronting" strategies. In Chicago, church happenings, sorority meetings, "pay dances," fashion shows, artists and models balls, social club teas, book clubs, and beauty contests were events created primarily by and open to "strainers and strivers" from the working- and lower-middle-classes as a place where leisure could replace work and sorority displace male-female, black-white, and rich-poor antinomies under a benign, if illusory, middle-class consensus.[4]

This gendered public space extended a domestic economy in which black female social empowerment and wish-fulfillment were increasingly measurable as symbolic material acquisition. Newspaper and magazine ads in the black press for skin lighteners, dream books, clothiers, beauty salons; well-publicized celebrations of the graduations and accomplishments of South Side beauty schools like the Poro College, trainer of hundreds of South Side women; the targeted marketing in the black press of products like "Brown Bomber Enriched Flour" featuring photographs of Joe Louis's mother pitched with the slogan "What Every Negro Housewife Should Know"; the public lionization of black "race women" such as Mary McLeod Bethune and Rebecca Stiles Taylor, editor of the "For Women Only" column in the *Defender* and in 1943 coeditor (with Bethune and Jessie Fauset Harris) of *Aframerican Woman's Journal,* official organ of the National Council of Negro Women, the national apotheosis of black women's striving for middle-class sorority: these images and processes delineated a range of strategies reinforcing the idea that black women were "getting ahead" in Bronzeville even if there was little or no significant change in the material conditions of the majority of their lives.[5]

This social, economic, and historical context helps to frame and illuminate Gwendolyn Brooks's complex position in and contribution to Chicago's Negro People's Front. Brooks's early life and writings, often celebrated as isolated artifacts of mid-century black modernism, or quaint but marginalized aspects of Chicago's literary "renaissance,"[6] are also powerfully encoded texts revealing many of the socializing traumas, class tensions, and ideological turmoil of both the Great Migration and the black cultural front it helped to produce. Like her friend and publisher Fern Gayden, Brooks came to Chicago from Kansas. *Report from Part One*, the first part of her autobiography, testifies to the overdetermining of her own migrant class consciousness in Chicago. Her mother's prior standing as a schoolteacher in Kansas and her father's ambitions to be a doctor (he had studied for a year at Fisk) were psychological buffers against the intrusive psychic effects of the latter's janitor's income, buffers her parents preserved by marking their daughter's body with emblems of "respectability." "Among the Lesser Blacks my decent dresses were hinders to my advance," writes Brooks of those years. "The girls who did not have them loathed me for having them. When they bothered to remember that I was alive, that is. When they bothered to remember that I was alive, they called me 'ol' stuck-up heifer'; and they informed me that they wanted 'nothin' t' do with no rich people's sp'illed chirren.'"[7] As a result, "All I could hope for was achievement of reverence among the Lesser Blacks."[8] In *Maud Martha*, her 1952 novel, Brooks reiterates the imposition of black female class-conscious self-consciousness through her febrile protagonist's reaction to a Hollywood film:

> But you felt good sitting there, yes, good, and as if, when you left it, you would be going home to a sweet-smelling apartment with flowers on little gleaming tables; and wonderful silver on night-blue velvet, in chests; and crackly sheets; and lace spreads on such beds as you saw at Marshall Field's. Instead of going back to your kit'n't ap.t, with the garbage of your floor's families in a big can just outside your door, and the gray sound of little gray feet scratching away from it as you drag up those flights of narrow complaining stairs.[9]

After they move into a new kitchenette apartment, a sign of her aspiring upward mobility, her husband Paul tells Maud Martha "Your apartment, eventually, will be a dream. The *Defender* will come and photograph it."[10] The remark, coupled with the appeal of mass media and mass market emblems of class propriety marks Maud Martha as a vehicle of mass cultural double consciousness. Not surprisingly given her own social connections to the early 1940s Chicago Left, the intersection of that consciousness with "progressive" or resistant notions of self is also a subject of Brooks's book. In *Maud Martha,* Brooks literally and figuratively encrypts the (in her time) politically and rhetorically explosive idea of "racial equality" within a psychic discourse of black female domestic dis-ease. The associative logic of Maud Martha's consideration of a spot of impoverishment in her apartment ("a sad hole") followed by the malodor of racial stereotyping ("it was said that colored people's houses necessarily had a certain heavy, unpleasant smell") followed by racist self-abnegation ("she opened every window"), is a tortured inversion of what Brooks would have known firsthand to be the "theory and practice" of radical race and class consciousness among the cast of progressives surrounding her formative years as a writer at the South Side Community Art Center.

The apparent displacement of radical consciousness in Brooks's early creative work mirrors her quietude about Chicago's Negro People's Front. Though identified by Franklin Folsom as a member of the Popular Front League of American Writers and a participant in the 1944 Interracial Conference on the Arts, Brooks has escaped identification as a writer under immediate or adjunct Left political and cultural influence.[11] Yet Brooks's own subtle and nuanced observations of social class formation and protest ideology in her early work and *A Street in Bronzeville* reveal discursive marks of both the influence of Left cultural and political thought as well as their highly self-conscious and coded revision. This influence and revisionary process may be aptly described as Brooks's "radical irony." Her poetic "slippage" in voice, persona, point of view, and even subject matter in the poems from *Bronzeville,* what Maria Mootry calls their "indeterminacy, fragmentation, multi-locused meaning, and difficulty of interpretation,"[12] can be read as emblematic of the slippages and contradictions of Negro People's Front cultural politics. The paradox of black desire for participation in and resistance to American democratic capitalism during Chicago's Negro People's Front arguably reaches its ironic epitome in Brooks's 1945 book of poems. The collection moves from a misleadingly "unifying" first section, "A Street in Bronzeville," where through shifting voices and personae Brooks measures the South Side's collective potential resistance to its own material subordination, particularly as it is encumbered by strategies of economic and social "fronting"; to a second section where proletarianized black women speak in counter-voice to this same question from a lower place in the economic order; to a transgressive third section, the war sonnets, where Brooks collapses

and deconstructs dialectical modes of inquiry and analysis in order to declare radical black resistance in apocalyptic suspension. Both deploying and
signifying on the revolutionary aspirations of protest writing practiced by
an earlier generation of white Left poets and her own black contemporaries
(including Langston Hughes, Margaret Walker, Margaret Burroughs, and
Frank Marshall Davis, for example), Brooks shuns these as inadequate to the
resolution of old and new forms of social oppression, particularly for black
women. In addition, Brooks's first book challenges the primarily masculine
radical protest tradition in American poetry and finds it wanting for its exclusion of black female voices and selves, revising and reinscribing classic
moments in American protest literature (like the Scottsboro Boys case) with
a proto-modern black feminist sensibility.

That all of these things are accomplished by a poet who was by no means
a Communist or public political figure and whose work can hardly be reduced to singular interpretations is a mark in part of black women's subtle
reconfiguration of radical political discourse during the Chicago Negro
People's Front. Darlene Clark Hine's call for attention to the appeal of "protest ideologies" among midwestern migrants finds answer in the cultural
work of black Chicago women who were Brooks's contemporaries during the
late 1930s and early 1940s: Margaret Burroughs, Fern Gayden, Margaret
Walker, Grace Tompkins, Alice Browning. Their non-programmatic rendering of Left theory and practice bespeaks not only the influence of the organized Left's progressive articulations on the "woman question" never far from
its discussions of race, as well as a class-conscious determination to avoid the
tendencies toward class acculturation for black women described by Clark
Hine. Both a product of and a challenge to the Left milieu that surrounded
its creation, *A Street in Bronzeville* is a skeptical interrogation of the possibility of a modern poetic vocabulary describing and resolving the particular class, racial, and gender traumas of mid-twentieth-century black women.
As Barbara Johnson has argued in her poststructuralist reading of Brooks's
"the mother," her famous abortion poem from *A Street in Bronzeville,* the
slippage of speaker between "I" and "you" in the mother's lament—a slippage of speakers characteristic of the entire collection, as I will show—is in
part the text's admission that it "attempts the impossible task of humaniz-
ing both the mother and the aborted children while presenting the inadequacy of language to resolve the dilemma without violence."[13] Johnson
suggests an essential tension in Brooks's poem between *material* resistance
to patriarchal, economic, and racist norms, and the *idealistic* realm of lan-

guage where, at least in literary texts, class, racial, and gender struggle must be carried out. Hence, as with her protagonist Maud Martha, the question of Brooks's being "up to the task" of purporting racial equality, or the "equalizing" of social and political injustice as she teasingly describes it in Bronzeville's most representative political text, "The Sundays of Satin-Legs Smith," is one her poems can only ask, not answer. *A Street in Bronzeville* may thus be read as a black woman's poetic revolution without antecedents or correspondence in the progressive literature of Negro People's Front Bronzeville. The book is a fellow traveler to a future generation of black feminist writing Brooks could in 1945 only limn. At the same time, Brooks's revision of black women's poetry as resistive to oppressive class, racial, and gender norms puts her work in sorority with that of female cultural workers of South Side Chicago whose contemporary work and struggles help give dimension to the events about which she writes.

Both the ironic distance and the anxious affiliation between Brooks's first book of poems and the most radical utopian aspirations of her Left contemporaries is suggested in its eponymous first section. "A Street in Bronzeville," under the auspices of a unifying geography and commonality of experience ("a street" ought to be "any street"; Bronzeville is by implication a municipality united by racial experience), instead delineates lines of caste, race, gender, and class difference on the South Side. In stark and immediate contrast to, for example, her contemporary Margaret Walker's stirring revolutionary poem and book "For My People," or the communal urgency of Chicago colleague Frank Marshall Davis's "For All Common People," described earlier, Brooks implodes the idea of black unity as a casualty of uncritical black participation in, and passive subordination to, black and white democratic capitalism.

Brooks's variegated play of pronouns foregrounds this theme. In "the old-marrieds," the section's first poem, the potentially idealizing description of a married couple is undermined by their emphatic anonymity and segregation.

> But in the crowding darkness not a word did they say.
> Though the pretty-coated birds had piped so lightly all the day.
> And he had seen the lovers in the little side-streets.
> And she had heard the morning stories clogged with sweets.
> It was quite a time for loving. It was midnight. It was May.
> But in the crowding darkness not a word did they say.[14]

The unnamed "he" and "she" literally sit apart in separated lines in the poem (numbers four and five), attentive to others, not each other. "They" come together only to reinforce each other's isolation, a point stressed by the use of the pronoun only in the poem's first and last lines. This spatial/emotional distancing evokes the effects of "clogged streets" and "crowding darkness" surrounding them, emblematic of the overcrowding, restrictive covenants, and alienating Jim Crowism of public space in Bronzeville. The mock lyricism and faux carpe diem in images of piping birds and May midnights suggest a temporal imprisonment corollary to the spatial one: the couple is seized *by* the day, the historical complex of social conditions in Bronzeville. Anticipating a theme of the entire collection, stasis, not "the progress"; imprisonment, not liberation; isolation, not unity are symptomatic of Bronzeville daily life.

The spatial and temporal thematics of "the old-marrieds" foreshadow the next poem, "kitchenette building," literally and figuratively next door in Brooks's overcrowded and subdivided cityscape. The "we" of "We are things of dry hours and the involuntary plan" is the distracted collective consciousness of Brooks's Maud Martha, and by extension the South Side, for whom any movement toward agency (volunteerism) is preempted by physical, temporal ("dry hours"), and psychic separation. Brooks's invocation of black "Dream" as a giddy sound, pale next to "rent" and "feeding a wife," is intertextually equivalent to the "clear delirium" from which Brooks's Satin-Legs Smith emerges each day in order to repress all thought beyond the goal of survival. The urgent closing line, "We think of lukewarm water, hope to get in it," with its cute mock rhyme to "minute," underscores the material logic of the kitchenette's partitionings of time and space, a kind of Fordist or Taylorist "efficiency" (the pun is resonant again of real estate) that makes competition to live the all against the dream of self-sustained cooperative action. The gentle sarcasm and wit in "minute/in it" likewise mocks the contrast between "play" and the iron work of survival. Put another way, Brooks's irony derives from a critique of any progressive evaluation or idealization (including a "literary" one) of the material ground of the poem.[15]

Indeed, consistently in part one Brooks deploys a classic materialist interpretation of Bronzeville life only to refuse to admit any analysis, or position, that would transcend its suffocating material parameters. As if haunted by the dystopian side of her radical milieu, Brooks delineates the restrictions on black agency and autonomy Margaret Walker had included as a cautionary stanza in "For My People": "For my people blundering and groping and floundering in the dark of churches and schools and clubs and societies, associations and councils and committees and conventions, distressed and disturbed and deceived and devoured by money-hungry glory-craving leeches, preyed on by facile force of state and fad and novelty, by false prophet and holy believer."[16] Likewise, Brooks demonstrates how cravings for respectability, decency, self-sufficiency, middle-class morality, blind religiosity, and vulgar materialism are "fronting" strategies in Bronzeville that displace a progressive or radical consciousness.

In "the funeral" and "obituary for a living lady," for example, Brooks offers ironic portraits of religious respectability as the opiate of a divided and suffering community. In "the funeral," a preacher is advised by a supremely disinterested speaker to handle the delicacies of consolation "with a dishonesty of deft tact." The "dainty horror" at the death of a person significantly unnamed, without specific relation to those who mourn, suggests the displacement of solidarity and compassion enacted in the self-distancing strategies of the congregation: "They glance at each other, want love from each other: / Or they do not glance but out of tight eyes vaguely pray." These glances are furtive, apprehensive, eagerly awaiting the "blindfold" of the sermon: "Heaven is Good denied. / Rich are the men who have died." The note of lack overcompensated is embedded in earlier lines denoting the many unnamed "friends" who have sent flowers, and the "clubs . . . kind with sprays, Wreaths." The sick heat of this aromatic is the perfume of benign social ritual—clubs, decorative displays, "dainty horrors"—metaphorically the sensory perfumes that cover both the congregational body and its this-worldly discontents. The church itself is an ornamental extension of the club logic, a theatrical showcase for its taste and decorum. In totality the poem conceives the church as something of an expensive casket for the congregation, whose self-aggrandizement is a costly death-in-life ritual.[17]

In "obituary for a living lady," Brooks engenders this theme by inscribing it onto the body of a single black female. The speaker describes a friend "decently wild," a young girl whose sexual modesty with men leaves her morally upright but jilted and alone. After long mourning, the friend discovers the "country of God. Now she will not dance / And she thinks not the thinnest thought of any type of romance." Yet as in "the funeral," Brooks's target is the socially constructed propriety that disengages black unity. The speaker, for example, is configured as a slave to material fashion insensitive and cynical toward the living lady's dilemma: she describes her friend's grieving as "a hundred weeks or so wishing she were dead," and laments that she "can't get her to take a touch of the best cream cologne" after the latter's conversion to chastity. The companion's shallow disinterest is summoned in the oxymoronic description of her friend as "*decently* wild" (emphasis mine).[18] The word "decent" is a coded and loaded one in Brooks's vocabulary: she used it to describe the dresses she wore as a girl that estranged her from her poorer companions; it is also used by Mrs. Martin in "when Mrs. Martin's Booker T." When her son "ruins" Rosa Brown by getting her pregnant, Mrs. Martin moves to the low West Side until she hears he has gotten her "decent wed."[19] In "The Sundays of Satin-Legs Smith," the protagonist strolls the South Side oblivious to the street whose broken windows are

> Hiding their shame with newsprint; little girl
> With ribbons decking wornness, little boy
> Wearing the trousers with the decentest patch,
> To honor Sunday. . . .[20]

The stopgap measure of each of these gestures connotes poverty or disgrace *not* as understood social distortions but as occasions for "fronting." All of this is embedded in the frailty of Brooks's "decent." Thus the speaker's apprehension of her friend's calculatedly "decent" wildness reveals a shared code of consciousness bounded by the church's moralizing version of black respectability on one hand, and the fashionable accessories of commercial taste on the other. Beyond either resides no critical consciousness in the poem with which to apprehend individual or collective sufferings in Bronzeville.

Indeed, many of the subjects for poems in part one (churches, beauty schools, funeral parlors, undertakers) were a common domain and points of entry for the development of black capitalism in Brooks's time.[21] Brooks repeatedly directs her attention to spheres where some Bronzevillians could invest their aspirations for "improving the race" only to tweak this vehicle of hope. Black capitalism itself is held accountable for the reifying and reductive construction of gender roles and social class formation in Bronzeville in poems like "southeast corner" and "patent leather." The first is arguably a seminal poem for understanding Brooks's critique of these processes. I quote it in its entirety:

> The School of Beauty's a tavern now.
> The Madam is underground.
> Out at Lincoln, among the graves
> Her own is early found.
> Where the thickest, tallest monument
> Cuts grandly into the air
> The Madam lies, contentedly.

Her fortune, too, lies there,
Converted into cool hard steel
And right red velvet lining;
While over her tan impassivity
Shot silk is shining.[22]

The implied imagination of the death of the most famous American "Madame," cosmetics titan C. J. Walker, marks "southeast corner" as a poem about an era of black proprietary capitalism also emblematized in the life and times of Chicago newspaper magnates Robert S. Abbott and Claude Barnett. Yet rather than celebrate Walker's transgressive success as a woman, Brooks offers the priapic figure of the Madame's grave as ironic comment on its profitability. More lingering irony lies in the dead-end utility of the wealth of the Madame, whose crypt is simultaneously a bank vault and a funereal gown: its "cool hard steel" and "shot silk" are the external show fit for her lying self, a "fortune" literally embodied. The Madame's "tan" aspect is the final ornament, the caste chip cashed in by racist beauty standards in the black cosmetic industry of lighteners, brighteners, and straighteners. The disturbing addition of "contentedly" in the description of the corpse revives the "death-in-life" specter of the living, breathing dead children of "the mother" and the necromantic undertones of "obituary for a living lady" and even "the funeral." Pace Marx and Engels, no "gravediggers" of black or white capitalism are likely to emerge from such graves.

That black women are both the lure and target of what Brooks views as a cosmetic blackface version of the production/consumption cycle is further suggested in "patent leather." The title, describing a man's pomaded hair, suggests the same transposition of self and product as "southeast corner":

That cool chick down on Calumet
Has got herself a brand new cat,
With pretty patent-leather hair.
And he is man enough for her.

Us other guys don't think he's such
A much.
His voice is shrill.
His muscle is pitiful.

That cool chick down on Calumet,
Though, says he's really "it."
And strokes the patent-leather hair
That makes him man enough for her.[23]

As James Smethurst has noted, the diction and form of "patent leather" suggests the commercial "process" of hair processing it describes. The poem's irregular rhythms and rhyming couplets in full stop resemble a "hip" jingle for patent-leather hair.[24] Thus the construction of black masculinity is rendered a by-product of what might be called customer satisfaction: "the patent-leather hair / That makes him man enough for her." As with "southeast corner," "patent leather" offers a semiotics of commodification under black capitalism, whose effects are rendered at best comically deleterious, at worst pathetic or tragic.

These tendencies culminate in "The Sundays of Satin-Legs Smith," whose history suggests its status as a punctuation mark to Brooks's themes in part one. The poem was written and included late after Brooks had received a copy of Richard Wright's letter appraising the original manuscript for Harper and Row. Wright had praised the collection generally but noted the lack of "one real long fine" poem around which others are grouped characteristic of many modern collections.[25] Wright had also derided "the mother" as a weak poem because abortion was, he said, not a fit subject for poetry. The narrow masculinist bias of Wright's assessment was consistent with his definitions of cultural politics in 1944 as some combination of social realism, naturalism, and, most often, concentration on black male urban proletariat life. These aspects of the "political" also help comprise "Sundays," yet with the addition of radical Brooksian irony. The poem adds to Wright's caveat (and his own work) an elided feminist consciousness that both enacts and complicates the poem's status as a "unifying" text for part one.

### "THE SUNDAYS OF SATIN-LEGS SMITH"

Inamoratas, with an approbation,
Bestowed his title. Blessed his inclination.

He wakes, unwinds, elaborately: a cat
Tawny, reluctant, royal. He is fat
And fine this morning. Definite. Reimbursed.

He waits a moment, he designs his reign,
That no performance may be plain or vain.
Then rises in a clear delirium.

He sheds, with his pajamas, shabby days.
And his desertedness, his intricate fear, the
Postponed resentments and the prim precautions.

Now, at his bath, would you deny him lavender
Or take away the power of his pine?
What smelly substitute, heady as wine,
Would you provide? life must be aromatic.
There must be scent, somehow there must be some.
Would you have flowers in his life? suggest
Asters? a Really Good geranium?
A white carnation? would you prescribe a Show
With the cold lilies, formal chrysanthemum
Magnificence, poinsettias, and emphatic
Red of prize roses? might his happiest
Alternative (you muse) be, after all,
A bit of gentle garden in the best
Of taste and straight tradition? Maybe so.
But you forget, or did you ever know,
His heritage of cabbage and pigtails,
Old intimacy with alleys, garbage pails,
Down in the deep (but always beautiful) South
Where roses blush their blithest (it is said)
And sweet magnolias put Chanel to shame.

No! He has not a flower to his name.
Except a feather one, for his lapel.
Apart from that, if he should think of flowers
It is in terms of dandelions or death.
Ah, there is little hope. You might as well—
Unless you care to set the world a-boil
And do a lot of equalizing things,
Remove a little ermine, say, from kings,
Shake hands with paupers and appoint them men,
For instance—certainly you might as well
Leave him his lotion, lavender and oil.

Let us proceed. Let us inspect, together
With his meticulous and serious love,
The innards of this closet. Which is a vault
Whose glory is not diamonds, not pearls,
Not silver plate with just enough dull shine.
But wonder-suits in yellow and in wine,
Sarcastic green and zebra-striped cobalt.
All drapes. With shoulder padding that is wide
And cocky and determined as his pride;

Ballooning pants that taper off to ends
Scheduled to choke precisely.
                              Here are hats
Like bright umbrellas; and hysterical ties
Like narrow banners for some gathering war.

People are so in need, in need of help.
People want so much that they do not know.

Below the tinkling trade of little coins
The gold impulse not possible to show
Or spend. Promise piled over and betrayed.

These kneaded limbs receive the kiss of silk.
Then they receive the brave and beautiful
Embrace of some of that equivocal wool.
He looks into his mirror, loves himself—
The neat curve here; the angularity
That is appropriate at just its place;
The technique of a variegated grace.

Here is all his sculpture and his art
And all his architectural design.
Perhaps you would prefer to this a fine
Value of marble, complicated stone.
Would have him think with horror of baroque,
Rococo. You forget and you forget.

He dances down the hotel steps that keep
Remnants of last night's high life and distress.
As spat-out purchased kisses and spilled beer.
He swallows sunshine with a secret yelp.
Passes to coffee and a roll or two.
Has breakfasted.
                              Out. Sounds about him smear,
Become a unit. He hears and does not hear
The alarm clock meddling in somebody's sleep;
Children's governed Sunday happiness;
The dry tone of a plane; a woman's oath;
Consumption's spiritless expectoration;
An indignant robin's resolute donation
Pinching a track through apathy and din;
Restaurant vendors weeping; and the L
That comes on like a slightly horrible thought.

Pictures, too, as usual, are blurred.
He sees and does not see the broken windows
Hiding their shame with newsprint; little girl
With ribbons decking wornness, little boy
Wearing the trousers with the decentest patch,
To honor Sunday; women on their way
From "service," temperate holiness arranged
Ably on asking faces; men estranged
From music and from wonder and from joy
But far familiar with the guiding awe
Of foodlessness.
              He loiters.
                      Restaurant vendors
Weep, or out of them rolls a restless glee.
The Lonesome Blues, the Long-lost Blues, I Want A
Big Fat Mama. Down these sore avenues
Comes no Saint-Saëns, no piquant elusive Grieg,
And not Tschaikovsky's wayward eloquence
And not the shapely tender drift of Brahms.
But could he love them? Since a man must bring
To music what his mother spanked him for
When he was two: bits of forgotten hate,
Devotion: whether or not his mattress hurts:
The little dream his father humored: the thing
His sister did for money: what he ate
For breakfast—and for dinner twenty years
Ago last autumn: all his skipped desserts.

The pasts of his ancestors lean against
Him. Crowd him. Fog out his identity.
Hundreds of hungers mingle with his own,
Hundreds of voices advise so dexterously
He quite considers his reactions his,
Judges he walks most powerfully alone,
That everything is—simply what it is.

But movie-time approaches, time to boo
The hero's kiss, and boo the heroine
Whose ivory and yellow it is sin
For his eye to eat of. The Mickey Mouse,
However, is for everyone in the house.

Squires his lady to dinner at Joe's Eats.
His lady alters as to leg and eye,
Thickness and height, such minor points as these,
From Sunday to Sunday. But no matter what
Her name or body positively she's
In Queen Lace stockings with ambitious heels
That strain to kiss the calves, and vivid shoes
Frontless and backless, Chinese fingernails,
Earrings, three layers of lipstick, intense hat
Dripping with the most voluble of veils.
Her affable extremes are like sweet bombs
About him, whom no middle grace or good
Could gratify. He had no education
In quiet arts of compromise. He would
Not understand your counsels on control, nor
Thank you for your late trouble.

                    At Joe's Eats
You get your fish or chicken on meat platters.
With coleslaw, macaroni, candied sweets,
Coffee and apple pie. You go out full.
(The end is—isn't it?—all that really matters.)

        And even and intrepid come
        The tender boots of night to home.

        *Her body is like new brown bread*
        *Under the Woolworth mignonette.*
        *Her body is a honey bowl*
        *Whose waiting honey is deep and hot.*
        *Her body is like summer earth,*
        *Receptive, soft, and absolute . . .*[26]

Brooks's protagonist in "Satin-Legs Smith" is rendered as a gendered by-product of the economically driven black masculine and feminine identities in Bronzeville portended in "patent leather." His "titles" and "approbation," his imaginary "reign" as king of the South Side streets is, after all, the bequest of his female paramours, "inamoratas" who would be, and are, his queens. Brooks's mock chivalric jargon suggests that while the class locus in the poem has shifted from a predominantly domesticated petit bourgeoisie world of the earlier "A Street in Bronzeville" poems, "fronting" strategies still obtain as all that separates the "respectable" and "riffraff" in Bronzeville.

Brooks suggests this by exposing the earlier ostentatious displays in the religious world of Bronzeville as mirrors to the secular preening of the lumpenprol. Smith's "Sunday" self-ornamentation, his dress, style, even fragrance are the gaudy but complementary versions of religious "decency"'s more aromatic compensatory gestures. The sacred innards of his closet are his "vault" whose "glory" is not diamonds or pearls but "wonder-suits in yellow and in wine, / Sarcastic green and zebra-striped cobalt. / All drapes." Brooks's seizure of the slang for hip dress in application to interior decoration underscores their common cause. Smith's zoot is his domicile just as the street is his domain. His clothes are psychic projections, "cocky and determined as his pride," a pride in "performance" for which he is "reimbursed" by the spectatorship of the streets. Yet Brooks directs much of her satire at the "strainers and strivers" above him, leveling their pretensions to better or higher taste: "Now, at this bath, would you deny him lavender / Or take away the power of his pine? / What smelly substitute, heady as wine, / Would you provide? life must be aromatic." The latter phrase, resonant of a commercial jingle, is the consumer absolute that links Smith's method of erasure of the marks of poverty to that of an unnamed "you" above him still straining to escape its mark, too:

> might his happiest
> Alternative (you muse) be, after all,
> A bit of gentle garden in the best
> Of taste and straight tradition? Maybe so.
> But you forget, or did you ever know,
> His heritage of cabbage and pigtails,
> Old intimacy with alleys, garbage pails,
> Down in the deep (but always beautiful) South
> Where roses blush their blithest (it is said)
> And sweet magnolias put Chanel to shame.

Brooks unmasks black bourgeois shame at Smith's "nigger" flashiness in the perverse ascription of white Dixiecrat nostalgia to commodified black tastes. Fetishized consumption perfumes consciousness and memory, transforming the horrors of both northern and southern Jim Crow into the imagined "sweet magnolias" of Tara. Hence Smith's wardrobe becomes Brooks's best ironic metaphor for both the traumatic markings of black social class formation and the dismal potentiality of protest ideologies for those beholden to a "front," or by now a parodic "false" consciousness:

No! He has not a flower to his name.
Except a feather one, for his lapel.
Apart from that, if he should think of flowers
It is in terms of dandelions or death.
Ah, there is little hope. You might as well—
Unless you care to set the world a-boil
And do a lot of equalizing things,
Remove a little ermine, say, from kings,
Shake hands with paupers and appoint them men,
For instance—certainly you might as well
Leave him his lotion, lavender and oil.

The "choice" of race rebellion is here reduced to consumer preference. The leveling of revolutionary aspiration is heard in the mocking music of "equalizing," a hipster's throwaway rendition in which social class and clothing are themselves inter-changeable. Identifying no viable audience in the poem beyond the dialectic of consumer desire and its popular fronts, Brooks ridicules not the human "need" for help, actualization, agency, "so much that they do not know," but its seemingly permanent displacement into instant gratification.

In this version of Marx's modernity in which "All that is solid melts into air," discord and contradiction resolve not in Smith's facing the "real conditions" of his life or his "relations with" his fellow man[27] but in the elimination of knowing. Out on the streets, "Sounds about him smear, / become a unit. He hears and does not hear" alarm clocks, children's "governed" Sunday happiness, the dry tone of a plane, random sounds, weeping vendors, and the L "that comes on like a slightly horrible thought." Of what? Brooks never says since Smith can never know. Pictures, too, are

blurred.
He sees and does not see the broken windows
Hiding their shame with newsprint; little girl
With ribbons decking wornness, little boy
Wearing the trousers with the decentest patch,
To honor Sunday; women on their way
From "service," temperate holiness arranged
Ably on asking faces.

This delirium is rendered a logical outcome of the displacement of historical consciousness onto the flat surface of the material now:

The pasts of his ancestors lean against
Him. Crowd him. Fog out his identity.
Hundreds of hungers mingle with his own,
Hundreds of voices advise so dexterously
He quite considers his reactions his,
Judges he walks most powerfully alone,
That everything is—simply what it is.

James Smethurst and other critics have noted here Smith's similarity to
Bigger Thomas, a similarly beclouded consciousness most himself when in
isolation.[28] Indeed the distinctive brand of "American hunger" Brooks foists
upon her creation is a literal and ultimately sexualized one that insists on
black urban masculinity as part of a larger network of predatory consumer
strategies. After tripping Bigger-like through a movie where he boos "the
heroine / Whose ivory and yellow it is sin / For his eye to eat of," Smith sati-
ates himself on the only product within reach—what jive crooners called
"meat"—a term whose social and sexual ground Brooks unpacks in the
poem's culminating and consummating scene. Smith "squires his lady to
dinner at Joe's Eats," where she, too, is defined by a longing for elevation
outwardly rendered in "royal" street costume:

In Queen Lace stockings with ambitious heels
That strain to kiss the calves, and vivid shoes
Frontless and backless, Chinese fingernails,
Earrings, three layers of lipstick, intense hat
Dripping with the most voluble of veils.
Her affable extremes are like sweet bombs
About him, whom no middle grace or good
Could gratify.

Smith's lack of "good taste" is as glaring and obstinate as his literal poverty and daily hunger. The former is fed by the latter. Hence the detailed
"menu" of his date's garish accessories is followed immediately by a list of
the offerings at Joe's Eats—fish, chicken, coleslaw, macaroni, candied sweets,
coffee, apple pie—more "sweet bombs" to his appetite: "You go out full. /
(The end is—isn't it?—all that really matters.)" Brooks's interlocutory "isn't
it" taunts the reader again to imagine a different "means" for the resolution
of Smith's desires. The rhetorical question leaves as the only possible answer
the consummation of Smith's consumption:

And even and intrepid come
The tender boots of night to home.

*Her body is like new brown bread*
*Under the Woolworth mignonette.*
*Her body is a honey bowl*
*Whose waiting honey is deep and hot.*
*Her body is like summer earth,*
*Receptive, soft, and absolute . . .*

Given the preceding allusions to food, readings of these closing lines in light of Wright's "advice" to Brooks about the function of a summarizing poem for her collection bear strange fruit. Smith's girl's body in its fecund and naturalistic description bears more than passing resemblance to Wright's description of Bigger's Bessie in their lovemaking before he eventually kills her:

> He felt two soft palms holding his face tenderly and the thought and im-age of the whole blind world which had made him ashamed and afraid fell away as he felt her as a fallow field beneath him stretching out under a cloudy sky waiting for rain, and he slept in her body, rising and sinking with the ebb and flow of her blood, being willingly dragged into a warm night sea to rise renewed to the surface to face a world he hated and wanted to blot out of existence, clinging close to a foundation whose warm waters washed and cleaned his senses, cooled them, made them strong and keen again to see and smell and touch and taste and hear, cleared them to end the tiredness and to reforge in him a new sense of time and space.[29]

Brooks rewrites Bigger's sexualized fantasy of escape from the city, a shadow of his migrant roots, as a nakedly urban zeal for mass-marketed food. Smith is an acclimated and unalienated Bigger blindly and ravenously at home among the comestibles. The ironic play of elements is consistent with Brooks's imagining of Bronzeville as a modern range of black consumer choices and fronting strategies. Thus Smith's girl is even less individuated or capable of symbolic value than Wright's Bessie: she is, to him, and perhaps to herself, Woolworth's bread, nothing more or less. The ellipsis concluding the poem also provokes a completing thought for which Wright's novel is one possibility. The "even and intrepid" pace of "somebody in boots" (the title of Nelson Algren's 1935 proletarian novel whose working title gave Wright the phrase "native son") in wartime Chicago could connote a range of sug-gestive images: fascist armies, soldiers, and war, "conquerors" of a variety of stripe. About Bigger Thomas, Wright had written in "How Bigger Was Born," that he was both fascist and Communist guerilla manqué, a warrior whose violence was ultimately "tenderly" realized against white and black women.[30] In this light, the oxymoron of Smith's "tender" boots casts over "The Sundays of Satin-Legs Smith" an eerie but suggestive irresolution. Heeding Wright's advice and example in imaginative ways, Brooks brings to the homefront of a casual Sunday dinner date the suggestive iron metaphors of war, imperialism, rape, pillage. Such are the choices left open in the ellipsis to the twilight consciousness of *A Street in Bronzeville*'s most fully rendered and gendered male agent.

In keeping with her critique of the deleterious effects of "fronting," part one of Brooks's collection glosses over what might be called the question of work. The pervasive displacement of radical class (as well as race and gender) consciousness from the "straining and striving" of daily life in Bronzeville is denoted by the absence of one of daily life's most potentially disruptive experiences. It is thus important to note the distinctive shift in the final two sections of the book into poems almost exclusively about black male and female proletarianization. Ann Folwell Stanford, for example, groups "Negro Hero" and the "Gay Chaps at the Bar" sonnet sequence as a body of poems interrogating the implications of black male "service" in the armed forces during World War II.[31] Beginning with Brooks's heavily class-conscious account of galley man Dorie Miller's ascent into the ranks of anti-aircraft gunner in "Negro Hero," the war poems raise provocative and unresolved questions about black male "work" in white patriarchal capitalist warmongering. The poems between, the "Hattie Scott" sequence, "Queen of the Blues," and "Ballad of Pearl May Lee," constitute another block in which Brooks radically alters the voice, subject, and political thematic of part one in order to foreground questions about the daily working lives of black women, questions traditionally specific to the Left and progressive milieu against which she emerged but that are startlingly transformed and revised in her hands.[32]

The most prominent example is the "Hattie Scott" sequence, which begins with "the end of the day":

> It's usually from the insides of the door
> That I takes my peek at the sun
> Pullin' off his clothes and callin' it a day.
> 'Cause I'm gettin' the dishes done

About that time. Not that I couldn't
Sneak out on the back porch a bit,
But the sun and me's the same, could be:
Cap the job, then to hell with it.

No lollin' around the old work-place
But off, spite of somethin' to see.
Yes, off, until time when the sun comes back.
Then it's wearily back for me.[33]

Brooks here reveals formal and thematic affiliations with Langston Hughes's "Madame, To You" series, described earlier as Hughes's own feminization of his 1930s proletarian themes.[34] Indeed, Brooks's poem seems of a piece with earlier Left and radical aesthetics dating to the Third Period and its engagement with rural concerns of the Black Belt. The deployment of southern vernacular, the gradual, sing-songy oral rhythms, the poem's unabashed voicings of an organic first-person consciousness all mark it as a flower of the rural proletarian ground of the migration. Brooks's "Hattie" is also the first self-speaking and coherent female subject in the book: the poem is devoid of the voice and persona switching games of part one, where social distance and alienation were attributes of a fractured community and a politically ironic poetic voice.

Like "The Sundays of Satin-Legs Smith," the poem also may bear Wright's influence, though of the earlier, Third Period-influenced *Uncle Tom's Children* rather than *Native Son*. The deployment of the "sun" as the temporal measure of Hattie's workaday life recalls Wright's elaborate meditation in "Long Black Song" about the rural pastoral versus urban mechanization of black peasant life. Yet the sun's cycle is a labor cycle unavailable to the idle, dependent, and entrapped "heroine" of Wright's tale. If Hattie is a character from *Uncle Tom's Children* or descendant of the southern rural peasant, she is also one infused in part with the radicalized spirit of the women from "Bright and Morning Star." The remaining poems of the sequence document and reinforce this link. In "the date," the second poem in the sequence, Hattie begins with an assertion—

If she don't hurry up and let me out of here.
Keeps pilin' up stuff for me to do.
I ain't goin' to finish that ironin'.
She got another think comin'. Hey, you.[35]

Here, the vernacular is the source and symbol of an unabashed working-class talk-back encapsulated in the abrupt rhyme of the shouted "Hey, you." The break in poetic diction, its interruptive quality, liberates Brooks's/Hattie's torrential voice of resistance in the following lines:

> Whatcha mean talkin' about cleanin' silver?
> It's eight o'clock now, you fool.
> I'm leavin'. Got somethin' interestin' on my mind.
> Don't mean night school.[36]

The domestic's shift from thought to action is embodied in the shift in audience: the madame, not the reader, is now the target of verbal assault. Hattie's outburst is a liberatory first step precursive to "higher" education, which may or may not be within reach. Indeed, the next poem in the sequence has Hattie at the hairdresser asking for an "upsweep" that will raise the level of her hair, if not her social position, a working-class "front" strategy possibly replete with Madame C. J. Walker accessories. Yet in the next poem Hattie immediately deflates her own social pretensions. "when I die" marks the contrast between proletarian life, work, and death and the ornamental adornment of each belabored by Brooks in part one:

> No lodge with banners flappin'
> Will follow after me.
> But one lone little short man
> Dressed all shabbily.
>
> He'll have his buck-a-dozen
> He'll lay them on with care.
> And the angels will be watchin',
> And kiss him sweetly there.
>
> Then off he'll take his mournin' black,
> And wipe his tears away.
> And the girls, they will be waitin'.
> There's nothin' more to say.[37]

The contrast in diction, image, tone, and voice between "when I die" and "obituary for a living lady" might be described as the social distance between Brooks's renegade class-conscious Hattie and the black petit bourgeoisie. The empty rhetoric at poem's end—"There's nothin' more to say"—is as stern a rebuke to the idealization or evasion of working-class hardship as Brooks delivers in the collection.

If the "Hattie Jones" sequence constitutes, like Hughes's "Madam, To You" poems, an overt "proletarianization" of wartime black female domestic workers, the two succeeding poems rewrite black women's socialization as inadequately constructed by a preceding generation of black male writers and Leftists. "Queen of the Blues" on its surface most immediately recalls Sterling Brown's epic 1930s verse "Ma Rainey," Brown's most popular and arguably successful articulation of his own aesthetic program. Brown's poem famously configures the classic blues singer as an avatar of his own "Black Belt Thesis" for the emancipatory and unifying power of the rural folk tradition. Much in sympathy with Richard Wright's articulations on rural blues as the foundation of a counterhegemonic black cultural politics, Brown used "call-and-response" between singer and audience in the poem to render the transformative potential of performance for rural peasants and northern migrants.[38] Brooks's "Queen of the Blues" bluntly engenders those themes to demonstrate their inadequacy as a liberatory model for working-class black women. Shorn of the reconstructive theoretical context of Marxian Third Period influence or a fetishized black blues aesthetic, Brooks's poem is a poetic case study resisting idealization or "meta" critical awareness for reader, author, or subject.

"Mame," the poem's protagonist, has ironically just buried her own mother and is devoid of either a socially constructed or natural family. She lacks "Legal pa," "Big Brother," "small brother," "baby girl," or "baby boy," any of whom might supply a moral or communal framework in which to evaluate her isolation. Put another way, Mame is without "front," naked, stripped down, pure product as suggested by the rhetorical emptiness and immediacy of Brooks's opening stanza:

> Mame was singing
> At the Midnight Club.
> And the place was red
> With blues.
> She could shake her body
> Across the floor.
> For what did she have
> To lose?[39]*

The poem's answer is nothing, since Mame has already lost all attachment to "decency": there are no "sweet / Sonny boy lies" to distract her from the

---

*See the appendix for the complete text of "Queen of the Blues."

existential or material base of her life. This deracinated conception of the blues is arguably a challenge to earlier Left and black male configurations, Brown and Wright included. Mame's laments are specific to a black female urban migrant experience as yet irreclaimable within traditional narratives of blues/folk aesthetic circa 1944 or 1945. Her request for a man "What will love me / Till I die" is rebuked by the recognition that "Ain't a true man left / In Chi;"[40] love once given is returned only as caste insult to the dark-complected singer, like Brooks's "chocolate Mabbie," one of a number of black women stung by color and caste-conscious suitors:

> I loved my daddy.
> But what did my daddy
> Do?
> Found him a brown-skin chicken
> What's gonna be
> Black and blue.[41]

This cycle of abusive race and gender norms is grounded in the gendered domestic economy of Bronzeville's working female poor:

> I was good to my daddy.
> Gave him all my dough.
> I say, I was good to my daddy.
> I gave him all of my dough.
> Scrubbed hard in them white folks'
> Kitchens
> Till my knees was rusty
> And so'.[42]

As she does throughout the collection, Brooks creates metaphors of "use" and "exchange" to characterize social class formation and gendered identity. Mame's "giving away" of her domestic worker's income to an unreliable man both prefigures and is consummated in her giving away of the story of that loss to a largely male audience. Indeed, Brooks stresses the utter distance and detachment of the crowd to Mame's plaintive plea. The stanza after her lyrics are completed reports, "The M.C. hollered, / 'Queen of the blues! / Folks, this is strictly / The queen of the blues!'" The dissociative indifference of the promoter to the product is mimed in Brooks's next lines, given by the speaker, whose reiteration of the opening question now carries the aftertaste of Mame's revealed pain and isolation:

She snapped her fingers.
She rolled her hips.
What did she have
To lose?[43]

Brooks's concluding stanzas leave the bare ethnographic fact of Mame's existence as a problem in need of a solution the poem can't give:

But a thought ran through her
Like a fire.
"Men don't tip their
Hats to me.
They pinch my arms
And they slap my thighs.
But when has a man
Tipped his hat to me?"

Queen of the blues!
Queen of the blues!
Strictly, strictly,
The queen of the blues!

Men are low down
Dirty and mean.
Why don't they tip
Their hats to a queen?[44]

In contrast to the organic consciousness and unifying voice of Hattie Jones, Brooks's "Queen of the Blues" deploys ironic slippage of voice and persona to foreground Mame's insults and injuries. Mame's fleeting "consciousness" of these injuries is interrupted by the intrusive but dislocated echo of the M.C. (now without quotation marks) as if to represent the drowning communal voice of a devouring crowd for whom her exterior performance is all. The breakdown of "call-and-response," real blues community, is implied by the disembodied reiteration of Mame's concerns in the last stanza. The problems and questions—"Why don't they tip / Their hats to a queen?—" are literally and figuratively rhetorical: call-and-response's *rhetorical inverse.* Neither Mame, the crowd, the M.C., the narrator of the poem, the authorial "persona," nor the reader of the poem can authoritatively lay claim to or responsibility for posing, or answering, Mame's lament.

Brooks's final and most obvious revision of the masculinist base of black and white protest poetry preceding her is "Ballad of Pearl May Lee." Few commentators have noted a significant fact of the poem: it is the only one in *A Street in Bronzeville* not located in the time and place of contemporary (early 1940s) Chicago. Instead, the poem is a return south, perhaps though not necessarily to an earlier era, from which Brooks rewrites and revises her generation's cornerstone moment of Black-Left affiliation: the Alabama Scottsboro Boys case. As noted earlier, the allegations by two white women against nine black boys for rape inaugurated perhaps the most impassioned collaboration in United States history between the organized Left, including the CP, and black writers and cultural workers. Party leaders and writers about the case, in both journalism and poetry, were predominantly male.[45] Not surprisingly, the case foregrounded the class and racial persecutions of black masculinity. Richard Wright's "Big Boy Leaves Home" and *Native Son* carried this theme literally from south to north, as did his powerfully influential essay "How Bigger Was Born," published in 1940. Extending nearly ten years of contemplation on the issue, Wright argued there that any and all acts of social resistance by black males had come to carry the accusation of rape. Wright wrote: "Any Negro who has lived in the North or in the South knows that times without number he has heard of some Negro boy being picked up on the streets and carted off to jail and charged with 'rape.' This thing happens so often that to my mind it had become a representative symbol of the Negro's uncertain position in America."[46]

The universal masculinizing of the "Negro" in Wright's account parallels his making generic and unspecific rape as a crime *against women*. Wright arguably displaces both rape itself and its white and black victims in ways many critics have argued Bigger himself dispatches both Mary and Bessie as emblems of his racialized masculinity in *Native Son*.[47] In "The Sundays of Satin-Legs Smith" Brooks hinted at a reconfiguration of this schema through the suggestive ellipsis of Smith's unresolved "appetite" for black women. In "Ballad of Pearl May Lee," Brooks quite openly reconfigures the tradition of Left masculinist evaluation of interracial sex, "rape," and black masculinity since Scottsboro by inscribing them from a black woman's point of view.

Brooks's challenge to the canonization of both victims and writers about black male lynchings begins with generic inversion. She retools the ballad genre, traditionally associated with black (or white) protest heroes, by using it to tell the story of a black woman outside of the public sphere of most lynching accounts. Pearl, not her black lover, is the heroic "victim" here. The generic inversion is paralleled by the wildly derisive irony of Pearl's response to what had become by 1945 a standard rallying point for black and white radicals:

Then off they took you, off to the jail,
A hundred hooting after.
And you should have heard me at my house.
I cut my lungs with my laughter,
    Laughter,
    Laughter.
I cut my lungs with my laughter.[48]*

Black women joining white lynch mob racists in "hooting" after a black man falsely accused of rape could hardly be considered a starting point for either interracial or cross-gender solidarity on the stage of the progressive Left of the 1930s or early 1940s. Yet Brooks's poem is essentially a complaint about the abandonment of black women's perspective or position on that stage. Instead, the language and imagery of the poem complicate monologic narratives of black male victimization (and white oppression) by refracting them through specific gender, sexual, class, and caste concerns of a black woman. The poem reveals that the narrator has been jilted by her one-time lover's uncritical and unconscious seduction by white beauty standards and concomitant black caste evaluations: at school "your girls were the bright little girls. / You couldn't abide dark meat. / Yellow was for to look at, / Black for the famished to eat."[49] As in "The Sundays of Satin-Legs Smith," Brooks configures sexual desire as both biological need and economic choice, here in order to imagine interracial sexuality as a masculine transaction or trade that backfires:

But you paid for your white arms, Sammy boy,
And you didn't pay with money.
You paid with your hide and my heart, Sammy boy,
For your taste of pink and white honey.[50]

Other images of lust and desire reiterate this logic: the woman in the poem "was white like milk . . . / And her breasts were cups of cream. / In the back of her Buick you drank your fill. / Then she roused you out of your dream."[51] In leaving his "black folks' bed" for the upward sexual mobility of a white woman's Buick, the lover exits the closed economy of black sexual exchange—the only one he can "profit" in—for another where he must be cashiered: "I'll tell every white man in this town. / I'll tell them all of my sorrow. / You got my body tonight, nigger boy. / I'll get your body tomorrow."[52] Sammy boy indeed pays for his "dinner": his "bill" is his life.

*See the appendix for the complete text of "Ballad of Pearl May Lee."

In the context of her earlier poems and the diction of this one, Brooks makes impossible a traditional "resistant" reading of lynching. Confounding the logic of the Left with its own dialectics, Brooks recreates Bigger Thomas not as tragic hero, existential victim, or race rebel but unlucky consumer. Indeed, the "rat" that lurks in the corner of Sammy's cell; the "fire" that winds within his breasts; the wink of the white girl that makes Sammy think "till you couldn't think" about the parameters of his desire mark him as an intertextual companion to his falsely accused brother from *Native Son*. Concurrently, Pearl's "lorner" status, her lovelorn "poor-me" blues, inspire comparison to Bigger's Bessie, with the latter now receiving something like a posthumous last laugh or death-wish on the man who done her wrong:

> You grew up with bright skins on the brain,
> And me in your black folks bed.
> Often and often you cut me cold,
> And often I wished you dead.
> Often and often you cut me cold.
> Often I wished you dead.[53]

Something of a conjure woman in Brooks's imagining, Pearl's "Laughin fit to kill" anticipates Sammy's being wrapped to a "cottonwood tree," where the lynch mob itself "laughed when they heard you wail." Her controlling consciousness, willfulness, malignant spite is all pervasive, incriminating, mystic. Her prophecy, "You had it coming surely" and its chantlike repetition—"Surely. / Surely. / You had it coming surely"—is not so much a blues lament by poem's end but a conjurer's curse. The word "surely" also resonates to the book's final section, where in "love note I: surely" a black soldier's imagination that his postwar black woman will "Surely" greet him with open arms—"Why, of course I love you, dear"—is mediated by his harrowing experiences defending the United States in war.[54] Indeed, the latter experience itself is imagined in "Negro Hero" as a black male courtship or seduction by a white woman, a protraction of the Scottsboro complex into the pit of World War II: "Their white-gowned democracy was my fair lady. / With her knife lying cold, straight, in the softness of / her sweet-flowing sleeve."[55]

Ultimately, this conflation in Brooks's poems of black masculinity destroyed and black womanhood betrayed by "interracial" coupling points to the larger catastrophe of black sexuality's interpellation by white, patriarchal, capitalist means and norms. Yet "Ballad of Pearl May Lee" is also a rebuke to the genre's traditional manipulation in the hands of white and black "folk" and "protest" poets for whom rape accusations and lynchings were occasions to *obscure* black women's significance in the discursive economy of miscegenation hysteria. Pearl is the embodied and articulate voice of Wright's Bessie redeemed from her status as forensic trial evidence of Bigger's crimes against white women; she fingers him, and the culture at large, for something quite different, unspoken, and in many ways unspeakable in the tradition of radical protest poetry both within and without the streets of Bronzeville.

Brooks's backward movement to earlier sites and sources of African-American protest and their suspicious feminist revision bears further contemplation as a metonymy for her ironic relationship to what I have been calling black cultural politics during the Negro People's Front period. The obstacles and omissions, rather than successes of the literary, political, and cultural work of the interracial Left dating at least to the early 1930s are foregrounded by Brooks's regressive chronology. Her formal and generic play, with the ballad, for example, also suggests a historical awareness of form's relationship to the struggle for a radical or resistant racial poetics. Part three of her collection, the famous sonnet sequence of war poems, may be viewed as the final word on that relationship.

Prior to her collection, no female African-American poet inside or outside of a protest tradition had made her mark with the sonnet form. Yet the question of the sonnet's place in both the black poetic and radical tradition had been raised by black men. Claude McKay's "If We Must Die," published in 1919 in *Liberator* to commemorate violent resistance by blacks during the "red summer" of that year, arguably jump-started not only the Leftmost political animus of the Harlem Renaissance but the radical revision by black poets and writers of their own relationship to political culture. McKay's appropriation of the sonnet for the elegiac celebration of black (and/or red?) warriors "pressed to the wall but fighting back" against white racist oppression united the nascent image of the white proletariat with the figure of a "new Negro" militant that McKay would formalize in theory and poetic practice through his association with white Leftists and proletarian literary movements in the 1920s.[56] McKay's subsequent forays in the sonnet during the early 1920s, many published in socialist periodicals like *Liberator,* revised the genre's formalism to include a call by black (and white) writers on the Left to batter down the doors of a racist, capitalist culture.

Yet as with Brown and Wright, McKay's political aesthetic largely ignored questions of black women's place in that revision. Too, its confidence in the possibility of a black male-led resistance marked it as part of a larger telos of gendered progressive radicalism that, in many respects, reached its culmination during the Negro People's Front. Yet as has been remarked throughout, Brooks's subversive power in *Bronzeville* was to upend or complicate master narratives of form, politics, gender, and class. Such a subversive power may also be said to inform her sonnet sequence. Put simply, Brooks's transgressive journey as a black female war poet speaking to and for black males abroad is also the lynchpin of her deconstruction, or uncoupling, of black masculinity (and by extension black American participation) with both racial and class revolution or the "mission" of global democracy. The formalism and precision of the sonnet sequence itself become ironic occasion for the emptying out or "designifying" of black militancy within both of these political traditions. Instead, black men and women are configured as caught in a fissure (or aporia) between resistance and oppression where they must "Wait" out the creation of a new, unnamed, and unnameable historical moment.

Cumulatively, the sonnet sequence reiterates modernist themes of alienation, dislocation, and disassociation as aspects of black experience of the war. What Ann Folwell Stanford calls the "Prufrockian" dilemma of black soldiers spiritually and physically disempowered by their participation in a segregated armed forces is the general theme of both "Negro Hero" and the sonnets "gay chaps at the bar," "still do I keep my look, my identity," "looking," "piano after war," "mentors," and the love note poems 1 and 2.[57] In addition, the sequence turns the war into what Stanford calls a "trope" for the civic arena of battle against racism at home. This conflation is evident in the "domestic" metaphors Brooks creates to describe black male anguish during war, meant to remind us of the concomitant suffering of black women at home. "I hold my honey and I store my bread / In little jars and cabinets of my will" says the narrator of "my dreams, my works, must wait till after hell."

> . . . I am incomplete.
> And none can tell when I may dine again.
> No man can give me any word but Wait,
> The puny light. I keep my eyes pointed in.[58]

As Folwell notes, "Wait," capitalized, was freighted with the portents of "go-slow" black and white reformers reminding a black population of the patience needed for attainment of social equality. The silent, almost Tomish response of "eyes pointed in" bespeaks the jeopardizing of black militancy on the home front once it has been utilized in the larger cause of saving the big house from obliteration.[59]

Indeed, Brooks's view of "war" as trope extends via her use of the sonnet to the very roots of the possibility of black rebellion or revolution. The difference between McKay's 1919 call for black arms in "If We Must Die" and 1944 is in part the exchange of black militant retribution for gradual entree into the larger popular "fronts" of American democracy: economic possibility at home, the fight for democracy abroad—the twin "fronts" of the mainstream Double V campaign. This is pointed to by Brooks's ascribing her only overtly "political" poetic title in the collection to the final poem in order to mock its deployment as a figure of optimistic consensus about black America:

"THE PROGRESS"

And still we wear our uniforms, follow
The cracked cry of the bugles, comb and brush
Our pride and prejudice, doctor the sallow
Initial ardor, wish to keep it fresh.
Still we applaud the President's voice and face.
Still we remark on patriotism, sing,
Salute the flag, thrill heavily, rejoice
For death of men who too saluted, sang.
But inward grows a soberness, an awe,
A fear, a deepening hollow through the cold.
For even if we come out standing up
How shall we smile, congratulate: and how
Settle in chairs? Listen, listen. The step
Of iron feet again. And again      wild.[60]

The reiteration of "Still" in a poem about the possibility of "advancing" the race freezes the dialectical tension between the permanence of racial, class, and gender oppression and the liquid myth of transformation of the social structure. The poem is also intentionally "retrospective" of the entire sonnet sequence, mocking its own poetic attempts at the valorization of black soldiers, the "death of men who too saluted, sang." Hence the sonnet form is not merely an explosion of confining traditions but an ironic comment on the smooth surface of Brooks's lashing critique: she, too, appears merely to "comb and brush / Our pride and prejudice." Clearly this is not the form, or message, of black liberation.

Hence Brooks offers up a cipher, a literal blank space in the poem's final line. It both forestalls the possibility of the poem's meeting or matching the requirements of a "real" sonnet (what meter, foot, and syllable count should that space be read in?) and precludes the reader from knowing what to make of her final, ominous "wild." About "gay chaps at the bar," Ann Folwell Stanford has written, "It is as if the poet asks, When one is invisible, unheard; when one's language and sense of self are obliterated by a more powerful and silencing entity (airplanes/racism), what is left? In both war and racism, the self is deconstructed (though not *destroyed*), language falls apart, and what is left is a harrowing poverty of history and culture that constitutes the many aspects of a self."[61] The derisive empty significance of Brooks's many ironic signifiers in "the progress"—bugles, presidents' voices, uniforms, flags—and the empty gesture of using a sonnet sequence to "protest" the myriad obstacles to black equality in America before, during, and after World War II may be the full meaning of Brooks's calculated blank space in the poem. The "iron feet" of oppression are heard approaching but there is no room, or time, or space for adequate response in fourteen measured lines. The book's liberating potential is preemptively "finished."

When *A Street in Bronzeville* was published in August 1945, the month of war's end, Brooks and the book were celebrated by friends and colleagues about whose lives and struggles she had just written. On Sunday, September 16, 1945, Brooks was feted at a South Side Community Art Center reception co-hosted by Alice Diffay and Brooks's publisher and friend Fern Gayden. Other members of Black Chicago's literary scene who were in attendance included Frank Marshall Davis, William L. Patterson, Alden Bland, author of the novel *Behold A Cry,* and an aging Claude McKay. Numerous other Chicago literary lights from the mainstream white commercial press and publishing world turned out to honor one of the first commercially and critically acclaimed books by an African-American woman poet.[62]

The conjunction of these divergent circles around Brooks, and the book itself, portended more than Brooks's future celebrity. *A Street in Bronzeville* was arguably a disturbing retrospective moment for African-American radicalism in Negro People's Front Chicago. Gwendolyn Brooks and her first book raised troubling uncertainty about the myriad dilemmas facing black American writers, activists, and cultural workers after the war. Brooks had also succeeded in fashioning a book of poems whose critical and commercial success owed in part to its ironic maskings and subversions that muted political disposition even as it interrogated virtually every question pressing on the minds and lives of black and white radicals in wartime Chicago. Such masking was, by 1945, of course, also becoming a prescient political strategy for black and white Leftists, who could already discern the "iron feet" not of fascism abroad, but of McCarthyism at home. Too, Brooks's feminist revisions raised the question and specter of the subversive potential of black women precisely at the moment the return of black and white male soldiers promised the return of prewar racial and gender hierarchies. Finally, the commercial appropriation of Brooks and her book as signs of black literary culture's new gentility—*Mademoiselle* magazine made her one of its ten "Women of the Year" in the wake of *Bronzeville*'s publication[63]—foretold the postwar conservative cultural and literary appropriations of her life and work she herself exploded in her 1960s leadership to the Black Arts Movement and New Black Aesthetic. Indeed, Brooks's resurgence as a figure of black nationalism may be read as one of a number of parables of the gradual elision and revision of Left politics in black Chicago beginning with the end of the war. My final chapter will undertake to describe how those changes and turns led to the dissolution of the Negro People's Front era in Chicago, and contributed to the construction of a more conservative era in black cultural history.

# 7 American Daughters, Fifth Columns, and Lonely Crusades: Purge, Emigration, and Exile in Chicago

> Life in Bronzeville is interesting, often exciting, and always
> "meaningful"—though usually not in terms or values Richard Wright
> would have respected or admired. . . . The mass culture provides a very
> wide range of satisfactions. Negro-sparked race riots or mass
> demonstrations; emigration to "Mother Africa," to the "Soviet
> Motherland" or to Mr. Mohammed's Utopia have no appeal, for they do
> not make sense in a Period of Prosperity and the Era of Integration. And
> the big questions, such as "What of the Bomb?" are seldom asked in
> Bronzeville.
> —St. Clair Drake and Horace R. Cayton, "Bronzeville, 1961"

> For black America, the "Scoundrel Time" was refracted through the prism
> of race, and was viewed in the light of their own particular class interests.
> —Manning Marable, Race, Reform, and Rebellion: The Second Reconstruc-
> tion in Black America, 1945–1982

In addition to the "official" Popular Front period itself, 1935–39, the end of World War II has provided anti-Communist historians and scholars ample material for jeremiads about the collapse of African-American relations to the organized Left. Books by Record, Cruse, and others cited in the introduction to this book, inspired by the cold war zealotry of their time, argued for the encroachment of a totalitarian model of Soviet Communism onto American soil as the liberatory final blow in the winnowing esteem with which black Americans regarded the possibility of an interracial radicalism with Communist support.[1] Thus far Manning Marable has provided the most challenging and provocative retort to these accounts. Marable argues generally that "The impact of the cold war, the anti-communist purges and near-totalitarian social environment, had a devastating effect upon the cause of black civil rights and civil liberties."[2] Yet he blames not only the Soviet Union, American CP, and McCarthyism but black leadership and institutions, particularly those from the middle class. By refusing to work with Marxists, organizations like the NAACP, writes Marable, "lost the most principled anti-racist organizers and activists."[3] In addition, he writes, "The black middle class's almost complete capitulation to anti-communism not only liquidated the moderately progressive impulse of the New Deal years and 1945–46; it made the Negroes unwitting accomplices of a cold war domestic policy which was, directly, both racist and politically reactionary."[4]

Marable's argument finds a relevant local opening to this study in the case of W. E. B. Du Bois. Du Bois's 1951 indictment as an "agent of a foreign principle" by the federal government after his open turn to Marxism was foretold and hastened by his columns for the *Chicago Defender,* which since 1945 had publicly marked the black leader's increasing radicalism. In a 1951 editorial in response to his arrest, his publisher recanted its affiliations entirely, noting the "supreme tragedy that he [Du Bois] should have become embroiled in activities that have been exposed as subversive in the twilight of his years."[5] The editorial marked a significant rightward shift in the political and cultural direction of the newspaper, and the city, that had been fermenting since at least the end of the war.

On August 18, 1945, for example, days after U.S. atomic bombs fell on Japan, the *Defender* prominently reported publication in the *Daily Worker* of the main resolution of the recently held Communist Party convention renouncing the Communist Political Association's "unwarranted illusion that the big bourgeoisie themselves would carry forward after V-E day the wartime gains of the Negro people."[6] The *Defender*'s designation of what it called the CP's "admitted soft-pedaling" on the Negro issue reflected both the paper's confidence of its own superior claims to progressive appeal among black Chicagoans (its circulation was at an all-time high, while party membership within Chicago remained low) and the seductions of democratic invitation heralded by the war's end. It also foreshadowed the *Defender*'s— and black America's—increasing devotion to a black species of cold war liberalism. One year later, NAACP Director Walter White's "People, Politics and Places" *Defender* column attacked a *New York Herald Tribune* headline describing "Leftist" participation in a September meeting of labor and liberal voters in Chicago.[7] Fearing that the head would "play directly into the hands of the Communist Party" by overemphasizing its influence and presence, White argued that "At a critical period in the world's history like this, it is imperative that we abandon the use of labels as far as is humanly possible lest unwittingly we build the very kind of Frankenstein monster which plagues our dreams."[8] One month later, in an editorial titled "The Defender Line," the newspaper reiterated White's cold war logic while attempting to define the paper and black leadership as the cart before the horse of progressive reformism. "Lest we be misinterpreted in the process," the paper wrote,

> we want it clearly understood we are not following any political line inspired by communistic interests or reactionary partisans. While we cannot help being followed by others who see in our policy a chance to hitch their wagons to our stars or those who from pure intellectual honesty follow our course of action, we feel that the time has come when the distinction should be made between those who are prostituting the cause of the Negro people for their own selfish gains and personal aggrandizement and those who are championing the rights of black humanity out of the sincere devotion to broad principles of righteousness.[9]

The paper's affirmation of its own "independent" protest voice, once a euphemism for black-Left interracial alliance, was now a spasmodic severance of Communist affiliation or influence deemed no longer necessary, or expedient, in an era of seeming black political ascent and encroaching McCarthyism. The *Defender* alone would defend Bronzeville. This severance also foreshadowed an increasing tendency among black intellectuals, artists, and cultural workers with roots in Chicago's Negro People's Front to disassociate themselves from the local milieu of interracial radicalism from which much of the city's black cultural "renaissance" had emerged. From the end of the war until the mid-1950s, these black artists and writers temporarily or permanently abandoned the city and their Leftist ties there: Willard Motley, Margaret Burroughs, Elizabeth Catlett, Charles White, Frank Marshall Davis, Horace Cayton, while Chester Himes and Richard Wright more famously sought exile in Paris. While various causes contributed to this sudden emigration, and while many also reconstructed Leftist ties in their new environments, Chicago's symbolic significance as an interchange and synthesis of Left-influenced black political and cultural work was never more apparent than in this sudden evacuation. Chicago's radical renaissance had created for each of these figures a crisis endemic to the Negro People's Front: each stood ready to reap the personal, including financial rewards of newly achieved professional successes at the very moment they were forced to choose between continued overt progressive or radical reform or compliance with an increasingly restrictive postwar political climate. One result of this was that differing degrees and kinds of individual support for the Communist and radical Left among black writers and artists were exacerbated into full-blown internecine debate over their role in postwar black culture. Division, rather than collegiality, began to rule the spirit and letters for those who had contributed to Chicago's Negro People's Front.

Correspondingly, the postwar period also saw increasing tensions between black middle-class political reformists, and middle-brow cultural ideals, and the militant grassroots ground of much of the South Side's vanguard cultural work. The writers, painters, and activists who had collaboratively revised and reformed Leftist interracial alliances found themselves isolated and alienated by the disappearance in the postwar period of progressive cultural (and financial) coalitions and new forms of racial and political repression. Chicago almost immediately became a site symbolic of the *impossibility* of sustained progressive or radical black cultural work, and a home to a new black bourgeosie endowed and entitled by postwar prosperity to makeover the streets in Bronzeville. The subsequent exodus and internal silencing of dissenting voices led to a diminishing of black radical intellectualism within Chicago parallel to that nationally. By the mid-1950s, the few remaining actors in Chicago's Negro People's Front drama constituted a threadbare but persistent memory of former times, struggling to maintain momentum threatened by political enemies without and within.

Gwendolyn Brooks's second book of poems *Annie Allen,* published in 1949, is in comparison to her first almost destitute of geography. *A Street in Bronzeville* offered in its title, names of individual poems ("the vacant lot," "southeast corner," "kitchenette building," "a song in the front yard"), and its thematic concerns a *locus classicus* for the interrogation of black social life. *Annie Allen* was about interiorities: of people, emotions, ideas. The notable exception is "Beverly Hills, Chicago," the collection's only poem ostensibly marked by place. The poem is narrated from the point of view of a passenger in a car driving with friends past an unnamed affluent neighborhood:

> Nobody is furious. Nobody hates these people.
> At least, nobody driving by in this car.
> It is only natural, however, that it should occur to us
> How much more fortunate they are than we are.[10]

The narrator does not clearly identify the neighborhood as either black or white, uptown or downtown. As the ambiguity and the title suggest, "Beverly Hills, Chicago" is any imagined place where poverty and political struggle can be superseded or escaped, and where neither haves nor have nots are overly exercised by the gulf between them.

"Beverly Hills, Chicago" serves as apt metaphor for the emergence of postwar black havens of refuge from the political and economic struggles of the Negro People's Front period. By the time of *Annie Allen*, for example, Richard Wright was the leader of a colony of expatriate black intellectuals and artists who had established Paris as their habitué. There, in a slap at American democratic pretensions, Wright had declared there to be "more freedom in one city block" than in all of the United States.[11] Wright's appropriately geographical metaphor bespoke his confidence in Paris as a place whose Western traditions in art, architecture, philosophy, and literature represented "an adequate relationship between the individual and his environment;"[12] the city was a literal rebuke—Wright called it his "sweet slum"[13]—to the political, commercial, and racial strictures of America's numerous Bronzevilles. Paris was thus also the perfect place for Wright to refit himself as what Fabre calls a "committed *Western* intellectual" rather than a representative of the black race, a mantle he had worn, ambivalently as noted in chapter 1, throughout the Popular Front period.[14] That refitting included yet another reconfiguration of his Marxism. Though his work appeared in left-wing magazines like *Les Temps Modernes* and he continued to identify with the Marxist writings of Aimee Cesaire, Wright's vehement anti-Stalinism, and his recurring insistence on a version of Western "humanism" as a guiding tenet of his work[15] made him a legitimate target for both the French and American Communist Parties, who saw in his exile an *embourgeoisement* of his (at least ten years removed by now) Third Period radicalism.

Ironically, Wright's alienation from his Marxist past, his lingering representative "racialism," and the pressures of the cold war were only reinforced as a result of his first, and final, return to Chicago after his emigration. After a 1949 trip there to scout out possible locations for the film version of *Native Son*, Wright was offered five hundred dollars by his friend Ben Burns to write an essay about the experience for *Ebony*, where Burns now worked as a full-time editor after being fired from the *Defender*. In his memoir, Burns describes his firing as a result of his "two-timing" practice of working as primary editor for John Johnson's new *Negro Digest* magazine, which debuted in 1943, while still working as city editor for the newspaper. The new position had marked the beginning of a rightward drift in Burns's career. As Burns himself noted, Johnson's editorial aim in creating *Negro Digest*, and later *Ebony* and *Jet*, "was to escape the 'radical' label that had been stamped on the Negro press because of its truculence in seeking immediate racial equality as the price of Negro support for the war effort."[16] Likewise, Burns came to seek and find refuge in the Johnson Publishing Company from his own Communist Party past affiliations. The merger of white radical and black capitalist, never an easy one according to Burns, had by the time of Wright's return altered the direction of black publishing. Burns routinely wrote articles and editorials of conciliation toward Johnson's growing black middle-class readership base, transmogrifying his former proletarian militancy into the rhetoric of black bourgeois race pride. Burns ghostwrote Johnson's famous editorial dictum for *Ebony*—"*Ebony* will try to mirror the happier side of Negro life—the positive, everyday accomplishments from Harlem to Hollywood"[17]—while using his experience at the *Defender* to help Johnson land blue-chip corporate advertising accounts by convincing advertisers that Johnson and his growing black readership constituted "the greatest barrier against communism."[18]

Burns's offer to his one-time comrade and friend Wright to describe his impressions of South Side Chicago during his return visit from Paris could thus be viewed as one of nostalgia for the moment of both Burns's, and Wright's, participation in the Chicago radical scene. Not surprisingly, the attempted rapprochement was a disaster. Wright's essay, originally titled "The Shame of Chicago" (later retitled "I Chose Exile") was a blast at the city's economic and racial divide reminiscent of his Marxian-inspired journalism and fiction of the 1930s. Its polemical force was also mediated by Wright's comparative personal liberty in Paris, whose political and economic largesse for blacks gave shape and dimension to Chicago's "shame." The city was now a black intellectual expatriate's nightmare. Both despite and for all of these reasons, *Ebony* rejected the piece. As Burns recalls, "For several years *Ebony* had been boasting about the new prosperity of black Americans, and here was Wright contradicting everything the magazine claimed—in effect, erasing at one stroke the glowing image that Johnson had sought to project."[19] On Johnson's order Burns wrote an editorial rationalizing the rejection of Wright's piece, "veering between candid confession and Chamber of Commerce flackery." The editorial pleaded with writers about black Chicago to "occasionally mix pride and self-esteem with discontent and belligerence."[20]

Wright's 1949 visit to Chicago signaled the end of his formal intellectual, political, and literary ties with the city. For Burns, the episode left him filled with "a sickening sense of dejection. Once again I agonized over my untenable position as editor of a magazine whose racial policies I so often differed with."[21] Becoming more and more an "echo" of Johnson's assimilationist editorial politics, Burns wrote, his "thoughts turned again to retreat and flight, to travel and escape."[22] During the 1950s Burns routinely traveled in and out of Paris. One trip provided material used as the basis for an attack on Wright's "hate school" of literature directed against U.S. racism.[23] His own previous radical political views suffocated and confused by cold war turbulence and a bitter falling out with the party, Burns effectively underwent internal political exile in Chicago. He remained a politically neuter editorial presence on Johnson's spin-off magazines of the 1950s, *Copper Romances, Tan Confessions,* and *Hue,* black imitations of sex and gossip white tabloids like *True Confession.* Like many other ex-Communists during the 1950s, Burns found refuge and disguise in the commercial world of pulp and mainstream journalism and literature.[24] His eventual firing by Johnson for putting too much emphasis on sensational issues like sex and mixed marriage—the very ones Johnson had hired him to promote—ironically reopened in his own mind the possible effect of his previous Leftist attachments: "Had the Red scare and McCarthyism finally caught up with me?"[25] Burns ends his appropriately entangled, unresolved, and tortured memoir with its most defining moment of self-imposed exile, driving across the Sahara and into black Africa in a Volkswagen camper considering, in Samuel Johnson's words, "instead of thinking how things may be, to see them as they are."[26]

Burns's and Wright's falling out as comrades through their vexed relationship to an increasingly hegemonic black middle-class culture underscores at least one of the ironic consequences sown by Negro People's Front Chicago. The postwar plights and collision of Chester Himes and Willard Motley provide a second example. Himes's status as a popular interpreter of racial radicalism in his *Negro Story* stories and first novel *If He Hollers Let Him Go* was undone by the bitter political endgame he described in his followup novel *Lonely Crusade* (1946). The personal and unsystematic digestion and interpretation of American Communism that had fueled the anti-white, prolabor invective of Himes's first novel—and made it a predictable success among both white and black radicals and liberals alike—turned phlegmatic in the postwar reconversion that included massive layoffs of black wartime workers.[27] The limited effectiveness of Communist organizers in Los Angeles to resolve black-white, male-female, and, increasingly, white-Mexican labor and social tensions as the war gave way to prewar racial and economic exclusions resulted in part in Himes's Brooks-like mockery of unfettered "progress" in the postwar period. Lee Gordon, protagonist of *Lonely Crusade,* is a black labor organizer caught in a web of race, gender, and class antagonisms Himes had made comic in early wartime stories like "Make With the Shape" now turned tragic by what he perceived as his own, the party's, and

the labor movement's inability to resolve them. The dark, satirical bent of
the novel is the most powerful clue to Himes's political disillusionment with
the Left's aspirations. Himes's novel adopted a post-Marxian perspective
resonant of Wright's newfound "Western humanism" that abandoned even
his homespun variety of radicalism. "I had attempted to be completely fair,"
he wrote in his autobiography. "I didn't believe in the sublimity of people,
black or white, any more than I believed in their depravity. . . . I believed that
people were capable of anything."[28] In another section, he added, "I had
written what I thought was a story of the fear that inhabits the minds of all
blacks who live in America, and the various impacts on this fear precipitated
by communism, industrialism, unionism, the war, white women, and marriage within the race."[29]

Himes's complex fatalism angered both Left readers, predictably disappointed by *Lonely Crusade*'s political skepticism, and the larger audience of
postwar liberals who might have banked on Himes as a black ally in the creation of a democratic postwar culture. As Himes recalls it, "Everyone hated
the book,"including the *New Masses,* whose three-page attack was headed by
a black silhouette captioned "Himes Carries the White Flag."[30] *Ebony* magazine, meanwhile, declared Lee Gordon and Himes "psychotic," while a young
James Baldwin's review for the socialist newspaper *New Leader* was headlined
"History as a Nightmare."[31]

Less famously, Himes's novel also provoked attack by Willard Motley.
Motley's own idiosyncratic version of American radicalism was itself put to
the test by the depths of Himes's political despair. Sounding more Marxian
than he ever had even in his own best-selling "radical" novel, Motley in effect accused Himes of bourgeois separatism and defeatism. His review of the
novel began by calling Himes's protagonist Gordon a racist, then added:

> We learn that unions will let innocent people suffer rather than lose the
> support of the Communist party; that unions will let an innocent man be
> executed if he can't swing an election for them. . . . But, one supposes, labor
> is not well thought of these days.
> We learn that Negroes shudder at the sight of every passing white person.
> But, one supposes, inter-racial and race relation groups are ineffective and
> no understanding and co-operation has come through such groups.[32]

Motley's review unintentionally underscored the aptness of Himes's bleak
prophecies even as it attempted to revert them back into the stream of a waning era of American radicalism and labor activism. Indeed, Motley's next

novel, *We Fished All Night*, published in 1952, was by the time of its publication a glaringly antiquated attempt to use the naturalistic novel to describe and protest the postwar black and labor experience. *We Fished All Night*'s cool critical and commercial reception marked this, and helped forecast Motley's own disappearance from the scene of both American literature and America. Like Himes, who followed Wright into Parisian exile in order to heal the wounds of *Lonely Crusade*'s rejection, Motley also fled Chicago after the tepid reaction to *Fished*, living in Mexico from 1955 to 1965, where, according to Jerome Klinkowitz, he "found a more hospitable culture" than cold war Chicago could provide.[33] Motley's departure and rejection by postwar black and white political culture might also have been prophesied by Himes, of whose final American novel the former wrote, "It is indeed a 'lonely crusade' for any man of any race or nationality if his life is to pivot on race or nationality and if through bitterness or pride he turns his back on the people as a whole."[34]

For his part Himes, once in Paris, vigorously denounced organized Communism and interracial work, adopting a version of Wright's "outsider" status by declaring himself a "man without a country."[35] In turn, Wright helped to champion *Lonely Crusade* upon its publication in France, where in 1952 it was chosen one of the five best books published in America. The remaining years of the Wright-Himes relationship, according to both Michel Fabre's biography of Wright and Himes's memoir, were uneasy rounds of friendly respect and rivalry and subtle class tensions, Himes playing the proletarian workaday detective writer to Wright's royal figure of international celebrity.[36] More so than the more notorious Wright-Baldwin rift of the 1950s, Wright's relationship to Himes during their years in Europe bears the marks of prewar black radical political culture's uneasy relationship to the postwar period. Both writers constructed a form of racialized humanism from the ashes of their anti-Communism, anticipating the postwar schisms of black nationalists and Communists that made both Wright and Himes reclaimable figures of the 1960s Black Arts Movement *absent* their Leftist pasts. Himes's "ambivalent triumph," meanwhile, as a protegé of the most famous exiled American black Marxist, a pattern Motley refigured in Mexico, ultimately bends back to Chicago's centrality as a site for measuring the mid-century migrations of black cultural and political radicalism.[37] Wright's influence and example for writers like Himes and Motley, both of whom outlived him as self-fashioned "radical" writers at home, was arguably most exerted not by the publication of *Native Son* in 1940, but when his exile offered them an example of life abroad as the best available plight for postwar black intellectuals.

Frank Marshall Davis's disappearance from prominence in postwar African-American letters also parallels the conservative ascent of the immediate postwar period. Davis first drew FBI attention when his work appeared in the League of American Writers booklet *Writers Take Sides.* During the war, he recalls FBI agents visiting the offices of the Associated Negro Press to inquire about the political associations of such benign black liberals as Mary McLeod Bethune and William Pickens, field secretary of the NAACP.[38] From 1944 to 1947, Davis served as vice chairman of the Chicago Civil Liberties Committee, formed in response to the 1943 urban riots in Detroit and Harlem. From 1947 to 1948 he was a member of the national board of the Civil Rights Congress, an organization that remained open refuge for black and white Communists and Leftists during the ascent of McCarthyism. Despite ideological rifts with the Chicago Communist Party that brought allegations of black nationalism, Davis remained a steadfast advocate of black-Left alliance, particularly for the black press. After Roosevelt's death in 1945, Davis wrote to Communist New York City Councilman Benjamin Davis recommending that "the party make a strong effort to maintain the huge reservoir of good will stored in the black press."[39] Noting that many black editors remained sympathetic to the Soviet Union, and that the postwar CP was showing renewed attention to black civil rights and anti-lynching legislation, Davis "suggested . . . that the national headquarters assign a capable liaison man whose exclusive duty would be traveling around the nation and becoming friends with all our editors."[40] According to Davis, Benjamin Davis responded affirmatively, but no action was taken. "And before long, Afro-American newspapers became almost as violently anti-Communist as the general press."[41] Despite his friendly relations with the more conservative Barnett,[42] Davis signed on as executive editor in 1946 of a new newspaper, the *Chicago Star,* born as a cooperative weekly financed by CIO and AFL unions. According to Davis, about a third of the paper's subscribers were black, and the paper avoided the red-baiting tendencies of the mainstream press.[43]

In the summer of 1948 Davis published his third volume of poetry, *47th Street: Poems,* which drew enthusiastic response from Langston Hughes. Yet it was Davis's last book of poetry until 1985, when a small collection of his jazz poems was published, *Jazz Interlude.* The closing of Patterson's Abraham Lincoln School, where Davis had lectured on jazz, had left him, with the exception of Margaret Burroughs, without his familiar network of cultural allies, and slowed progressive politics in Chicago.[44] Davis was also according to John Tidwell suffering from racial persecution directed at his interracial marriage to Helen Canfield Davis. Tidwell says that Davis was intrigued when Paul Robeson, returning from a concert tour in Hawaii to aid striking long-shoremen in their union effort, boasted of the comparative racial harmony there. In 1948, Davis left Chicago forever, resettling in Honolulu, where from 1949 to 1958 he wrote a column on labor and union workers' rights for the progressive *Honolulu Record*.[45] Like Ben Burns, the one-time radical journalist also resorted to commercial imperatives, surviving in part until his death by publishing pseudonymous soft-core pornography. Like Wright and Himes, Davis's reputation was temporarily resurrected during the 1960s Black Arts Movement, only to fade until the 1992 publication of his memoir *Livin' the Blues*. The book remains one of the best accounts of Chicago's wartime in-terracial radical renaissance and the anti-Communism that dogged Davis's own steps long after his exile from Chicago.

Davis's move to Hawaii also ended his association with the South Side Community Art Center, which in the immediate aftermath of the war was also undergoing a conservative reorientation. In October 1946, confronting moribund programming and flagging financial resources, the center board of directors named David Ross, a former *Defender* writer and exhibition di-rector with the Illinois Art Project, to replace Rex Gorleigh as director. Un-der Gorleigh's tenure the center had lost its base of established artists, many of whom began to exhibit nationally, and had come increasingly under the ideological sway of conservative socialites like Frankie Raye Singleton, the center's president. Although Margaret Taylor Goss Burroughs and Ishmael Flory remained on the center board as secretary and second vice president, respectively, the center's postwar agenda included insuring its political and commercial credibility by repressing dissenting Left voices. Postwar elections for center officers and its board were, according to Burroughs, routinely split between a "Progressive" and "Bourgeois" slate and were fraught with rumors of Communist affiliation.[46] Rumors intensified when Burroughs successfully persuaded Paul Robeson to visit the Art Center in 1952.

In 1953 Burroughs took a sabbatical leave from her position as art teacher at Chicago's DuSable High School. She used it to live and study under Leopold Mendez at the Insitute of Painting and Sculpture in Mexico City. By 1952 Mexico City had become a haven and refuge for African-American art-ists seeking an alternative to the repressive political atmosphere at home. In addition to Charles White and Elizabeth Catlett, discussed earlier, Hale Wood-ruff, John Wilson, and Lawrence Jones were among other artists who took up study at its Taller de Grafica Popular. Of the group of former Chicago artists who visited Mexico City, Catlett remained the most permanently committed to revolutionary international politics. She married the Mexican painter Franciso Mora in 1946 and later renounced her American citizenship, retaining full-time residence in Mexico. White, meanwhile, returned to the United States to remain a regular contributor of illustrations and graphics to *New Masses, The Worker,* and *Masses and Mainstream,* to which he was a contributing editor from 1951 to 1956.[47] In 1952 White contributed an article to *New World Review,* reprinted in the November 23, 1953, *Daily Worker,* describing his 1951 visit to the Soviet Union and a review of Soviet art. Throughout the 1950s, White's commitment to preservation of radical vanguardism was evident in his work and writing for the Left press. "My major concern," he wrote in "Path of a Negro Artist," published in a 1955 *Masses and Mainstream,* "is to get my work before common, ordinary people, for me to be accepted as a spokesman for my people, for my work to portray them better, and to be rich and meaningful to them. A work of art was meant to belong to people, not to be a single person's private possession. Art should take its place as one of the necessities of life, like good clothing and shelter."[48]

Burroughs, who would herself visit the Soviet Union with Dudley Randall in 1967, returned to Chicago in 1954 having assimilated many of the revolutionary principles of the Mexico school. Her 1950s prints and lithographs reflect this aesthetic shift, as well as her increasing interest in representations of black women. Upon her return to Chicago, she also sent in her membership renewal to the Art Center. According to Burroughs, the renewal elicited a visit from "A committee of the society ladies from the Center's Board," who returned her membership dues.[49] The implied rebuke to her radicalism temporarily severed Burroughs's connection with the center she had helped to found. She continued her private career as an artist and teacher, exhibiting nationally while remaining distant from the center. In 1961 Burroughs, in part in response to what she considered the continuing conservatism of the Art Center, co-founded the Ebony Museum, later the DuSable Museum of African-American History, Inc. Today she is director emeritus of that institution and a commissioner of the Chicago Park Board. In 1980 she was one of ten black artists honored by Jimmy Carter at a White House ceremony commemorating her lifetime contributions to the arts. The event came three years after the closing of her 450-page FBI file begun in the 1930s, which she obtained under the Freedom of Information Act. Burroughs, who was never by her own account a member of the Communist Party, is the city of Chicago's last and most important link to a history of cultural work conceived and implemented, with herself as a leading agent, during the Negro People's Front period. She remains today a supporter of the Art Center—the only WPA-sponsored Art Center still in operation.

Burroughs's example indicates another strand in the legacy of the city's Negro People's Front represented primarily by its female cultural workers. Fern Gayden, too, remained a member of the board of the South Side Community Art Center after the collapse of *Negro Story* magazine. In 1947 she became one of the founding members of the Free Religious Association, a self-described "liberal" religious body that in 1948 became officially known as the Free Religious Fellowship.[50] The church was founded as a progressive alternative to the more conservative Baptist and A.M.E. congregations on the South Side. In 1950 the fellowship moved its services to the Abraham Lincoln Center, former home of the All Souls Church and still refuge for some black Communists and radicals on Chicago's South Side. As a "Church History" published in 1986 reveals, the move, "for reasons not now known," was disapproved of by some members of the fellowship, who immediately withdrew.[51] When the Abraham Lincoln Center building was sold, the church moved and merged with the First Universalist Church at 83rd and Ingleside Streets. The church is today known as All Souls First Universalist Society.

Throughout the 1950s, according to Art Center histories, Gayden, along with friend and colleague Grace Leaming, nearly single-handedly kept the Art Center alive in times of dire financial crisis by paying heating and electric bills out of pocket.[52] Though her literary career formally ended with her severance from *Negro Story*, Gayden remained a close friend to prominent members of Chicago's 1930s and 1940s literary circles. At a May 18, 1975, tribute to Gayden at All Soul's Universalist Society, participants included Burroughs, the playwright Ted Ward, and Gwendolyn Brooks. Gayden wrote the Biographical Profile for the program for Ted Ward's own June 4, 1983, memorial service at the DuSable Museum of African-American History. In the 1970s, Gayden was a founding member and active participant in the Chicago Branch of the Women's International League for Peace and Freedom. Upon her own death on May 27, 1986, a *Chicago Defender* obituary described her as a "lifetime Black activist and confidante to many famous writers, poets and artists."[53] The memorial program at her own service described her as a longtime supporter of black activists like Paul Robeson, W. E. B. Du Bois, and William Patterson. Neither Gayden nor her surviving friends and colleagues ever testified to her membership in the Communist Party.

Alice Browning's post–Negro People's Front activities reiterated her entrepreneurial flair for capitalizing on black militancy. She returned to teaching at Forrestville School in Chicago after *Negro Story* expired, laboring throughout the 1950s and 1960s on short stories and an autobiography that was never published. In 1970, inspired by the Black Arts Movement and Black Nationalist movement headed in Chicago by Gwendolyn Brooks and Haki Madhubuti, she initiated her only other successful public literary venture, the International Black Writers Conference. Beginning in 1970, the IBWC annually hosted a three-day program in Chicago with workshops, speakers, and participation from both published and unpublished black writers. For Browning, the conference was a successor to the short-lived "Writers Guild" she had attempted to establish through *Negro Story* magazine. By her own revisionist accounts written during the 1970s, *Negro Story* was at the center of the second of four African-American "renaissances," the first in Harlem, the third the Black Arts Movement, the fourth her own International Black Writers Conference.[54] In conjunction with the latter, Browning initiated *The Black Writer,* a glossy magazine dedicated in the main to printing her own manifestoes as well as pictures and portraits of aspiring Chicago black writers. In 1972 Browning self-published from her same South Vincennes Avenue address from which issued *Negro Story, New Voices in Black Poetry,* an anthology of poems written by members of IBWC, few known outside of South Side Chicago. Before her death in 1986 Browning was profiled in *Essence* magazine and featured in passing in *Ebony.* At her own memorial service Haki Madhubuti commemorated Browning's life and work in a piece entitled "The Depth of Her." Gwendolyn Brooks paid tribute to one of the first editors to publish her work with a poem, "Alice Browning." The poem lovingly evoked Browning's cultural enterprises as protective spaces for black cultural work and herself as a beneficent facilitator providing access and entree for new black artists.[55]

Browning and Brooks's cyclical emergence as public figures of political activism during the two avowed periods of black cultural "renaissance" in Chicago also bespeaks their anxious relationship to a tradition of permanent interracial class struggle to which Burroughs, Gayden, White, Catlett, Frank Marshall Davis, and others remained essentially true despite the onerous oppression of McCarthyism. The example of Chicago's leading female cultural workers of the Negro People's Front "staying home" as it were well beyond the period of exile and migration by more prominent black males also underscores a final, gendered aspect of the politics of reputation in Chicago. Wright, Motley, and Horace Cayton had by 1947 established both local and national reputations by virtue of their singular contributions to black letters. Burroughs, Gayden, Browning, and to a much lesser extent Brooks, by comparison, were reserved more "local" celebrity indicative of the grassroots nature, and focus, of their cultural work in these years. As a result of their Negro People's Front experiences, however, each did, as did black women generally, in the words of Jacqueline Jones, "begin to test the limits of their own collective strength in ways that would reverberate into the future."[56] The role of black female political leaders and cultural workers in the "two revolutions"[57] of black civil rights and progressive reform between 1940 and 1955, the first during the Negro People's Front, the second during the civil rights period (cf. Rosa Parks, Fannie Lou Hamer, and others), were in spirit if not in fact anticipated by the noisy activism and entrepreneurship in the economic, political, civil, and cultural arenas by women like Burroughs, Gayden, Walker, Browning, and Brooks.

Likewise "reverberating into the future" out of Chicago's counter-migration of radicals were dimensions of the particular crisis if not of the "Negro" intellectual generally, at least of the black *male* intellectual in the postwar period. Pace Harold Cruse, that crisis was marked by a tortured self-assessment of individual relationship to the prewar and wartime Left that to varying degrees consumed Wright, Himes, Ellison, Davis, and Motley as well as numerous, lesser-known black male artists, including jazz musicians and painters.[58] While a detailed portrait of this larger crisis is the subject of another book, its features are thrown into dramatic relief by the postwar travails and reflections of Horace Cayton. Cayton's "talented tenth" upbringing as a descendant of America's first black senator, Revels Cayton; his easy assimilation and absorption by white society up to and including his entree into the University of Chicago; his friendly relationships to radicals like Wright and William Patterson; his celebrity within and outside Chicago after publication of *Black Metropolis* made him especially vulnerable to the polarizations within black political culture brought on by McCarthyism and his own relative postwar "affluence." Despite his close associations with Communists in Chicago, he was labeled a "Negro misleader" by the Communist Party after writing to denounce the CP for advising blacks to give blood to the Red Cross despite its practice of segregating samples, ending "any causal association I had with them on a United Front basis."[59] During the war, Cayton also discovered that he was being investigated by the FBI after publishing a column in the *Pittsburgh Courier* attacking the government for its superficial propaganda on the "Negro." Within Chicago during the war years, Cayton reluctantly accepted the mantle of "race leader," perhaps, he wrote, "in an ardent attempt to live down my past, to make up for having married white and for having so many white friends."[60] Self-divided by his own "fronting" strategies during the Negro People's Front, Cayton wrote in his memoir, "I had at last succeeded in becoming an important person among Negroes. But I had done so at great cost, for although outwardly I was established I had not really found my own identity. This search was to haunt my existence and provide an inner conflict which I would endure for the rest of my days."[61]

Cayton's crisis, reported as "The Crack-up" in his autobiography, not coincidentally coincided with the breakdown of Chicago's Negro People's Front and the end of the war: "I felt that the dynamic opportunity which the conflict had provided for dark peoples throughout the world had been dissipated. The armed forces were still for the most part segregated; with the closing down of defense industries employment for Negroes was at a low ebb; left-wing opposition to the status quo had largely disappeared; and the labor unions, with their treasures bursting, no longer were interested in Negro participation."[62]

Cayton left Chicago shortly after 1946. Some time in the 1950s he suffered a nervous breakdown in New York. The "long old road," the title of his memoir, from his "relatively high estate" to a shabby St. Marks' Place apartment was summed up by the author as a trajectory of alienation from Chicago's united front:

> Basement apartment, rent twenty-five dollars a month, toilet in the hall, and everything in disrepair. I had cracked up, I knew. The enemy world of race hatred had been mainly responsible. But there had been allies in my defeat, an internal fifth column that had aided my enemies: my own weakness and indecision and my failure to carry the fight to the enemy had helped betray me. But others had weathered such storms, why not I? . . .
>
> A feeling of shame at not knowing who I was swept over me, followed by an equally intense stab of fear. What did "they" do with a person who didn't know his name?[63]

Cayton's lament both echoes and rewrites the plight of the nameless protagonist of Ralph Ellison's 1952 novel *Invisible Man*. Ellison, who began writing the novel in 1946 in the midst of his own meandering break with the wartime Communist and interracial Left, seized the metaphor of "invisibility" to name, among other things, the condition of African Americans abandoned by (and abandoning) progressive paradigms for historical change and reform—from Garveyism to Communism. Ellison's cold war-era reappraisal of his own (and his comrade Richard Wright's) experiences of the radical Left likewise adopted the "failure to carry the fight to the enemy" as one of a number of symptoms plaguing the mid-twentieth-century black male intellectual and artist. The Invisible Man's extended period of "hibernation" portends an eventual coming up from underground to play a "socially responsible role" while asserting his temporary powerlessness in the face of a stultifying racial and political atmosphere. Likewise, Cayton's closing synopsis of a deeply felt political paralysis in the 1950s seemed a private riff on Ellison's final appeal in *Invisible Man* to both black and white readers—"Who knows but that, on the lower frequencies, I speak for you?":[64]

> I was sick and I knew it; I would need time to become well and whole again. But America was sick, too, and I wondered whether she was even aware of it. I at least knew the extent of my malady, but how long before America could face up to the true measure of hers? . . .
>
> Well, I thought suddenly, it's out of my hands now, and as I thought this I all at once realized how true it was. Nothing that I could do or say as an individual would either hinder or further the Negro's progress. Full, legal equality was as inevitable as if it had been written in the stars. And the longer white America put off the realization, the more awesome and terrifying it was likely to be when it arrived.[65]

Cayton's account ironically attributes to the era of civil rights achievement and promise a personal and political malaise. The passage is tacit complaint that the "fight" for equality is now an institutional one; that the battlefield has shifted from the streets of Black Metropolis to the courts and bureaucracy; that he himself is a spent warrior in this new terrain. Like Ellison's novel, which reclaimed prewar history as the ground for the struggle for black identity, Cayton's memoir implies that postwar black cultural politics and struggle for "the progress" were already becoming reified aspects of white and black debate. Cayton and Ellison's one-time fraternity with and support by American Communists, socialists, and other radicals made them, at best, ambivalent revolutionaries for a new generation, in limbo between their "underground" past and a more politically hegemonic black future. Both "memoirs" of *racial* identity crisis are fraught with the cold war anxiety experienced by a generation of more permanently committed black and white radicals and ex-radicals. As they had been for Leftists during the war, the "internal fifth column" of domestic fascism now in the guise of McCarthyism and resurgent racism (as well as the allure of bourgeois assimilation) lingered on as ghosts stalking the dreams of black intellectuals in the postwar period.

Horace Cayton's long road out of Chicago, and Chicago's own road to the post–Negro People's Front is contextualized and illuminated by one final important historical moment. In the spring of 1946 the University of Chicago Press, under the new direction of reactionary southern publisher William Couch,[66] published *American Daughter,* the autobiography of Era Bell Thompson. Thompson, born to the black middle class and raised in nearly all-white neighborhoods in Iowa and North Dakota, had arrived in Chicago in 1933 seeking employment and eager to discover her self-proclaimed racial identity. In 1946 she was employed with the U.S. Employment Service in Chicago, having worked her way up from a number of scattered, lesser jobs. Her autobiography was by and large a recounting of that successful trajectory. The book's appearance was, Ben Burns noted in his October 6, 1945, *Defender* book column, "publicized as an interesting contrast to Richard Wright's 'Native Son.'"[67] "Miss Thompson's autobiography is written 'with great wit and charm,'" noted Burns, citing University of Chicago promotional material; "'her story has none of the bitterness of Richard Wright's autobiography, yet it deals seriously with fundamental issues.'"[68] Indeed, the book echoed and limned almost the entirety of Wright's career to date: the title hearkened to *Native Son,* the autobiographical genre to *Black Boy,* Wright's just recently published memoir. The text itself mimicked at least in structure and theme Wright's classic "migration" texts, both *Twelve Million Black Voices* and *Black Boy,* describing Thompson's early years negotiating the white plains states until the cataclysmic break of chapter 15, titled, again after Wright, "Chicago, Here I Come!" Here, however, the breathless exclamatory tone captured Thompson's unsinkable good spirits in the face of new urban obstacles, and a resolute ambition to succeed in the big city. Even Thompson's layoff from the WPA in the late Depression, evoked with great good cheer, merely set the stage for the book's final chapter, "My America, Too," yet another signifying title, this one on Langston Hughes's "I, Too," one of the poet's militant assaults on exclusionary America. Famously, Hughes's speaker describes himself in the poem as the "darker brother" banished to the white folks' kitchen. His resentment only feeds his later reemergence at the table "when company comes" as a strong, laughing black singer of America whose beauty and resilience shame his hosts:

> Nobody'll dare
> Say to me,

"Eat in the kitchen,"
Then.[69]

As if an antidote to Hughes's and Wright's more radical mood, Thompson's final chapter was a triumphant account of surviving relief by attending journalism classes at night school, resuming work with the WPA, starting a small gossipy newspaper called *Giggle Sheet,* and saving enough money to visit New York, the Statue of Liberty, the Grand Canyon, and Niagara Falls, all described in sumptuous touristic detail. By 1941, Thompson is promising friends her writing career is about to take off. Undampened by Pearl Harbor or the outbreak of war, mentioned in passing, she exults in her newfound position as employment officer, relishing the fact that "Most of the applicants are good-natured, friendly people, eager to see the sunny side." The buoyant spirits of the wartime unemployed provide uplift and urgency to her closing words:

> Then I knew there is still good in the world, that, way down underneath, most Americans are fair; that my people and your people can work together and live together in peace and happiness if they but have the opportunity to know and understand each other.
> The chasm is growing narrower. When it closes, my feet shall be on a united America.[70]

Thompson's book about a black woman's relentless pursuit of success was unprecedented in Chicago's literature of itself and made her an instant celebrity on the club, sorority, and church speaking circuit. Her beneficent integrationism was also a tonic to that same world's increasing apprehensions, reflected in the *Defender* and elsewhere, about the possible jeopardy to black assimilation and prosperity in the postwar period. The book's appearance also upstaged Richard Wright's departure for Paris that same month in Chicago, an event unremarked upon by the *Defender* throughout 1946.

*American Daughter* and Era Bell Thompson's subsequent obscurity should not obscure their localized symbolism in the realignment of post–Negro People's Front Chicago. Thompson's work aptly forecast a general if incomplete shift from a proletarianized to a middle-class perspective in both black politics and literature; marked a shift in direction of American publishing less interested by 1946 in "protest" writings by black writers; legitimated black bourgeoisie postwar confidence in its new ascension; and marked the creation of an upwardly mobile black readership—Alice Browning's pet project—eager to create and consume images of itself. Finally, the book's resolution of black economic crisis through sunny entrepreneurship prophesied the role of postwar African-American mass culture, particularly as practiced by the Johnson Publishing Company, in shaping black cultural politics for both black and white Americans. It is to the dimensions of that postwar cultural politics, and the Negro People's Front legacy to it, that I will briefly turn in my postscript.

# Postscript: Bronzeville Today

*I've seen the Black and White future, and it works.*
—John P. Johnson

Era Bell Thompson's symbolic role in Chicago's Negro People's Front did not end with publication of *American Daughter.* Inspired by the book's success, *Ebony* publisher John P. Johnson offered Thompson a staff position on the magazine, at the time less than a year old. Though Johnson reports she told him she knew "nothing about Negroes," Thompson accepted and worked for the magazine for twenty-eight years, thirteen as co-managing editor.[1] In his autobiography *Succeeding against the Odds,* Johnson writes that in the late 1930s and early 1940s he "shunned" the Communist Party because "it wanted to destroy the system. I didn't want to destroy the system—I wanted to join it so I could change it and make it more responsive to poor people and Blacks."[2] Johnson's rebuff underscores the paradox most fundamental to the Negro People's Front and its legacy: as his revisionist turn on Lincoln Steffens's famous dictum makes clear, one legitimate version of African-American "radicalism"—beating white capitalism at its own game—has often historically been embedded within another—beating capitalism altogether. During the Negro People's Front Marxists and black capitalists undertook different paths toward the same goal: making the system "more responsive to poor people and Blacks." Hence their strategies, resources, and personnel invariably overlapped in the myriad ways documented in the preceding pages of this book.

The Negro People's Front also underscores two complementary truths about American radical cultural politics during the Popular Front period: that it was unthinkable without the presence of African Americans, who in many ways gave impetus, shape, and substance to its ecumenical "inclusivity," and that the presence of African Americans in turn permanently altered the nature of American radicalism. Laments about the dilution of vanguard proletariat-led Marxism during the Popular Front typically fail to take into account the general failure of that politics to create interracial, cross-class alliances brilliantly and routinely manufactured under black leadership during the Negro People's Front. What emerged from the postwar period in Chicago and other American cities, as many other critics have noted, were the outlines of the cultural politics of the 1950s and 1960s in which (white) big labor, the Communist Party, and the Old Left were challenged and in many ways superseded by civil rights coalitionism, insurgent black nationalism, and interracial alliances under black political leadership. In Chicago these events took the form of the increasing prominence of institutions like the NAACP and the real and symbolic severance of black political and cultural institutions, as well as the labor movement, from the Communist Left.[3] As Manning Marable has noted, this severance likely delayed by ten years the black "democratic upsurge" during the civil rights era.[4] With the exception of the 1954 *Brown vs. Board of Education* decision, much of the momentum in black civil rights legislation, including desegregation of the armed forces and elimination of restrictive convenants, was in place by 1948, fostered by race radicals in Chicago and elsewhere.

Many of the political and cultural strategies of the Negro People's Front era also survived its end. Its "Don't Shop Where You Can't Work" campaigns became the model for Jesse Jackson's economic withdrawal campaigns of the 1970s and 1980s. Jackson has since at least the 1960s marketed himself as the "united front" politician on Chicago's black cultural front. In 1969, in the wake of the assassination of Martin Luther King Jr., Jackson attempted to unify the West Side Chicago branch of the Black Panther Party and the South Side's Blackstone Rangers gang unit in support for his own Operation Breadbasket, the progenitor of Jackson's Operation Push and Rainbow Coalition.[5] The Panthers, adhering to the CP's forty-year-old "Black Belt Thesis," argued against encroaching "black capitalists" and "cultural nationalists" on the South Side, while the Rangers earned the support of the Chicago Democratic political machine, in part by rejecting the Panthers' Marxian/Maoist message.[6] Jackson's own 1984 and 1988 presidential campaigns were likewise reminiscent of the interracial class-based politics ascendant during the Negro People's Front. Nineteen sixties Chicago also saw the resurrection of Gwendolyn Brooks, Alice Browning, and Frank Marshall Davis, who discovered newfound popularity among a generation of black cultural nationalists inspired by the Black Arts Movement to reclaim the city's race rebels from an earlier era. In 1967 Brooks was an important supporter of the start-up of Chicago's Third World Press, the city's black nationalist publishing arm. The press became a dominant force in the establishment of a Chicago-based black literary renaissance. All of Brooks's books of poems, including *A Street in Bronzeville*, initially published by Harper and Row, became Third World Press titles. The press successfully reclaimed the race-first entrepreneurism of Negro People's Front ventures like *Negro Story* while articulating a distinctively anti-integrationist cultural politics.

Yet perhaps inevitably given its *own* ecumenical brand of "radicalism," the clearest legacy of Chicago's Negro People's Front to postwar Bronzeville was its *failure to adhere to and sustain a lasting cultural politics of class struggle.* As was the case for many white radicals of the era, Chicago's black radical renaissance afforded a too-easy consensus that prosperity, and racial equality, were just around the corner. The startling degree and kind of its local successes made Chicago's radicals naive or unwitting victims of the national assaults against race and class-based progressivism in the postwar period. Their exile and emigration was the most drastic sign of this, as if they had been ill-prepared for the calling to account by America at large for being both "black" and "red," or at least pink. Indeed, Chicago's radicals were nearly helpless not only in the face of McCarthyism but in the subsequent economic traumas that overtook Bronzeville as well as the rest of black urban America: the shift from goods-producing to service-producing industries, the increasing polarization of the labor market into low-wage and high-wage sectors, innovations in technology, the relocation of manufacturing industries out of central cities, and periodic recessions leading to increases in black joblessness.[7] Similarly, they were swept up in (or became part of) the radical change in class composition that overtook inner-city neighorhoods like Bronzeville. Between 1950 and 1980, South Side neighborhoods Washington Park lost 44 percent of its population, Grand Boulevard one-half, and Douglass 55 percent.[8] Many of these emigrés were middle-class and working-class families taking advantage of housing vacancies in changing city and suburban neighborhoods. These trends, exacerbated by periodic economic downturns and unemployment, transformed the job landscape of Bronzeville, particularly for black men: in 1950, in the Grand Boulevard and Washington Park areas of the South Side, there were seventy employed men for every one hundred women; by 1990, this proportion had dropped to twenty-six working men for every one hundred women inhabitants in Washington Park and twenty-one in Grand Boulevard. As William Julius Wilson puts it succinctly, "economic restructuring . . . broke the figurative back of the black working class."[9] Concomitantly the institutions that once provided the social "network" or glue described by Cayton and Drake in *Black Metropolis*—churches, block clubs, community groups—all lost members and effectivness. Summing up,

Wilson designates the move from *Black Metropolis* then to now as one from an "institutional ghetto"—in which the structure and activities of a larger society are duplicated—to a physical ghetto that lacks the capability to provide basic opportunities and resources.[10]

Wilson's own recommendations for federally based actions to reverse the conditions he has described—he has advocated improved academic standards for public schools, for example, and a WPA-style jobs program for the inner cities—has reopened new spaces in old debates also resonant of the Negro People's Front. Seeking workers' solutions to workers' problems, Robin D. G. Kelley has looked instead to contemporary Chicago movements like Black United Communities and the Black Independent Political Organization. The BUC and BIPO are supporters of the American Allied Workers Laborers International Union, a black independent Chicago union formed in 1955 to challenge racism in the building trades unions.[11] In 1996 the AAWLIU initiated training programs to help black workers get their journeymen cards, which Kelley notes might make it easier for them to find work throughout the country. The distance and difference between Wilson's neo "new dealism" and Kelley's cautious confidence in a multiracial workers' movement to ameliorate what both acknowledge as a crisis for contemporary black America suggests that the parameters of Chicago's Negro People's Front "cultural front" persist as dividing lines and boundaries in what we today more provocatively call the "culture wars."

Of course to lay blame or responsibility for modern-day Bronzeville's problems to the Old Left, CPUSA, Popular Front ideology, the *Chicago Defender,* the black bourgeoisie, or "new" black studies in the contemporary academy would be to miss the point. Indeed, the circumstances afflicting contemporary black Chicago confirm the power of laissez-faire democratic capitalism to construct black class and social structure in its own shape-shifting self-image. As it did during the Depression and 1940s, Chicago perhaps represents this truth better than any American city. So arguably do the products of its contemporary cultural front. The ongoing class struggle in the hometown of John Johnson's corporate headquarters—and many other black neighborhoods—has in turn amplified demand for his particularly American product. In creating and advocating what he calls "The New Negro Consumer" and the "Black Consumer Market," Johnson has fulfilled the dream-space within black America for the specter of a "classless" society and permanent upward mobility. The power and durability of this image is told in its scope and duration. *Ebony*'s readership has risen from 125,000 in 1945 to nine million in 1990.[12] Meanwhile even Johnson's own corporate strategies also reflect the economic predicament of Chicago's South Side: Johnson Publishing Company itself long ago "outwardly" migrated from its former South Side address at 1820 South Michigan avenue to the business loop in Chicago.

Yet Johnson's and Johnson Publishing Company's achievements are still prominently celebrated in the Black Metropolis Convention and Tourism Council web site commemorating its campaign to save and restore the geographic district known as Bronzeville that is ongoing as I write. In the late 1980s a group of young Chicago black entreprenuers created the council in cooperation with the Mid-South Planning and Development Commission and the Chicago Office of Tourism. Its self-described mission is to preserve and restore Bronzeville's historical sites—including the original *Chicago Defender* building—as the "Premiere African American Heritage Tourism District." The BMCTC advertises its efforts as aimed not only at preserving and restoring Chicago's South Side as a historical landmark but to allow black Chicagoans to achieve "community economic empowerment for the 21st Century." In its web site Johnson is described as "The Boy Who Conquered Bronzeville." The Tourism Council will occupy the restored Liberty Life/ Supreme Life Insurance Co. Building at 3501 S. King Drive, home to the first African-American owned and operated insurance company in the North and where Johnson got his business start in 1936.[13]

As the BMCTC project confirms, Johnson Publishing Company and its legacy of black capitalist entrepreneurship is the most lasting contribution to America—and black America—of the Negro People's Front "cultural front." Other sites in contemporary Chicago arguably adjacent to that front are Oprah Winfrey's television show, book club, and HARPO Productions, Inc., and the singular black economy that is Michael Jordan. It is perhaps worth noting that the social and economic gulf between these sites and the "poor people and blacks" they often appeal to or claim to represent is considerably broader than could have been realized (or even dreaded) by Negro People's Front Chicago's radicals and entrepreneurs.

Yet the ideals and ambitions of its most visionary flank also live on in the real—not virtual—streets of present-day Bronzeville. On August 9, 1997, for example, the *Chicago Defender's* annual "Bud Billiken Parade" down King Drive on Chicago's South Side featured interracial protests by Refuse and Resist!, the independent Left coalition movement, against the continued imprisonment of accused Philadelphia death row inmate Mumia Abu-Jamal. One of the "vehicles" in the parade was a 13-foot black obelisk on wheels with names of more than three hundred Americans murdered by police. The obelisk was sponsored by the Stolen Lives Project, another interracial independent left agency targeting police brutality. In its reporting of the event, as had the Cayton-Warner researcher in 1938, the RCP's *Revolutionary Worker* correspondent tried to summon up and imagine the significance of both the parade and the response of the largely African-American crowd:

> Many were intrigued that *this* contingent was so multinational—white, Black, Latino, Asian marching together for all the people.
>
> All along the route the crowd shouted its encouragement and love. They pumped their fists in the air. One guy came running, waving his "New Black Panther Party" T-shirt and shouting, "I'm with you!" ...
>
> Even *after* the parade, as participants were walking down nearby streets with the two huge brown fists and rolled banners, older people yelled from their porches "All Power to the People!" One girl rode by on her bicycle and said "I think you were the goodest ones in the parade." And she wasn't alone: there was soon a report in the *Chicago Defender* that this contingent won a top "vehicle award" for the 13-foot Stolen Lives monument on wheels.[14]

The eerie déjà vu of this moment from Chicago's radical present should not merely connote uncritical nostalgia for its radical past. Rather, it is a reminder of the prescience and continuing usefulness of Chicago's Negro People's Front's best features: its class-based insurgency, interracial radicalism, anti-racism, and the continuing appeal of the American Left to a broad multiracial constituency. This final parade account should remind us that for all of its inevitable incompleteness, frustrations, and imperfect legacies, the Negro People's Front's improvisatory activism remains an inspired model for other continuing struggles in our time.

# Appendix

"QUEEN OF THE BLUES"

Mame was singing
At the Midnight Club.
And the place was red
With blues.
She could shake her body
Across the floor.
For what did she have
To lose?

She put her mama
Under the ground
Two years ago.
(Was it three?)
She covered that grave
With roses and tears.
(A handsome thing
To see.)

She didn't have any
Legal pa
To glare at her,
To shame
Her off the floor
Of the Midnight Club.
Poor Mame.

She didn't have any
Big brother
To shout
"No sister of mine ! . ."
She didn't have any
Small brother
To think she was everything
Fine.

She didn't have any
Baby girl
With velvet
Pop-open eyes.
She didn't have any
Sonny boy
To tell sweet
Sonny boy lies.

"Show me a man
What will love me
Till I die.
Now show me a man
What will love me
Till I die.
Can't find no such a man
No matter how hard
You try.
Go 'long baby.
Ain't a true man left
In Chi.

"I loved my daddy.
But what did my daddy
Do?
I loved my daddy.
But what did my daddy
Do?
Found him a brown-skin chicken
What's gonna be
Black and blue.

"I was good to my daddy.
Gave him all my dough.
I say, I was good to my daddy.
I gave him all of my dough.
Scrubbed hard in them white folks'
Kitchens
Till my knees was rusty
And so'."

The M.C. hollered,
"Queen of the blues!
Folks, this is strictly
The queen of the blues!"
She snapped her fingers.
She rolled her hips.
What did she have
To lose?

But a thought ran through her
Like a fire.
"Men don't tip their
Hats to me.
They pinch my arms
And they slap my thighs.
But when has a man
Tipped his hat to me?"

Queen of the blues!
Queen of the blues!
Strictly, strictly,
The queen of the blues!

Men are low down
Dirty and mean.
Why don't they tip
Their hats to a queen?

Then off they took you, off to the jail,
A hundred hooting after.
And you should have heard me at my house.
I cut my lungs with my laughter,
    Laughter,
    Laughter.
I cut my lungs with my laughter.

They dragged you into a dusty cell.
And a rat was in the corner.
And what was I doing? Laughing still.
Though never was a poor gal lorner,
    Lorner,
    Lorner.
Though never was a poor gal lorner.

The sheriff, he peeped in through the bars,
And (the red old thing) he told you,
"You son of a bitch, you're going to hell!"
'Cause you wanted white arms to enfold you,
    Enfold you,
    Enfold you.
'Cause you wanted white arms to enfold you.

But you paid for your white arms, Sammy boy,
And you didn't pay with money.
You paid with your hide and my heart, Sammy boy,
For your taste of pink and white honey,
    Honey,
    Honey.
For your taste of pink and white honey.

Oh, dig me out of my don't-despair.
Pull me out of my poor-me.
Get me a garment of red to wear.
You had it coming surely,
    Surely,
    Surely.
You had it coming surely.

At school, your girls were the bright little girls.
You couldn't abide dark meat.
Yellow was for to look at,
Black for the famished to eat.
Yellow was for to look at,
Black for the famished to eat.

You grew up with bright skins on the brain,
And me in your black folks' bed.
Often and often you cut me cold,
And often I wished you dead.
Often and often you cut me cold.
Often I wished you dead.

Then a white girl passed you by one day,
And, the vixen, she gave you the wink.
And your stomach got sick and your legs liquefied.
And you thought till you couldn't think.
    You thought,
    You thought,
You thought till you couldn't think.

I fancy you out on the fringe of town,
The moon an owl's eye minding;
The sweet and thick of the cricket-belled dark,
The fire within you winding . . .
    Winding,
    Winding . . .
The fire within you winding.

Say, she was white like milk, though, wasn't she?
And her breasts were cups of cream.
In the back of her Buick you drank your fill.
Then she roused you out of your dream.
In the back of her Buick you drank your fill.
Then she roused you out of your dream.

"You raped me, nigger," she softly said.
(The shame was threading through.)
"You raped me, nigger, and what the hell
Do you think I'm going to do?
    What the hell,
    What the hell
Do you think I'm going to do?

"I'll tell every white man in this town.
I'll tell them all of my sorrow.
You got my body tonight, nigger boy.
I'll get your body tomorrow.
        Tomorrow.
        Tomorrow.
I'll get your body tomorrow."

And my glory but Sammy she did! She did!
And they stole you out of the jail.
They wrapped you around a cottonwood tree.
And they laughed when they heard you wail.
        Laughed,
        Laughed.
They laughed when they heard you wail.

And I was laughing, down at my house.
Laughing fit to kill.
You got what you wanted for dinner,
But brother you paid the bill.
        Brother,
        Brother.
Brother you paid the bill.

You paid for your dinner, Sammy boy,
And you didn't pay with money.
You paid with your hide and my heart, Sammy boy,
For your taste of pink and white honey,
        Honey,
        Honey.
For your taste of pink and white honey.

Oh, dig me out of my don't-despair.
Oh, pull me out of my poor-me.
Oh, get me a garment of red to wear.
You had it coming surely.
        Surely,
        Surely.
You had it coming surely.

# Notes

INTRODUCTION

1. *Chicago Defender,* Sept. 12, 1942.

2. Michael Denning, *The Cultural Front: The Laboring of American Culture in the Twentieth Century* (London: Verso, 1996), xix.

3. Ibid. *The Cultural Front* is an exhaustive account of the development and use of the idea of a "cultural front" by American artists, laborers, and cultural workers between the early 1930s and the mid-1950s.

4. Lawrence Schwartz, *Marxism and Culture: The CPUSA and Aesthetics in the 1930s* (Port Washington, N.Y.: Kennikat Press, 1980), 10.

5. Earl Browder, "Writers and the Communist Party," *The People's Front* (New York: International Publishers, 1938), 281.

6. James W. Ford, *The Democratic Front* (New York: International Publishers, 1938), 74; William Z. Foster, *History of the Communist Party* (New York: International Publishers, 1952), 309; Harvey Klehr, *The Heyday of American Communism* (New York: Basic Books, 1984), 346–47.

7. Ford, *Democratic Front,* 74.

8. Ibid., 87.

9. Ibid., 193.

10. Mark Naison, *Communists in Harlem during the Depression* (Urbana: University of Illinois Press, 1983; rpt., New York: Grove Press, 1985), 199; James W. Ford, "Uniting the Negro People in the People's Front," *Communist* 16 (Aug. 1937): 727.

11. See Irving Howe and Lewis Coser, *The American Communist Party: A Critical History, 1919–1957* (Boston: Beacon Press, 1957); Harold Cruse, *The Crisis of the Negro Intellectual* (New York: William Morrow, 1967); Wilson Record, *The Negro and the Communist Party* (Chapel Hill: University of North Carolina Press, 1951), and *Race and Radicalism* (Ithaca: Cornell University Press, 1964).

12. Naison, *Communists;* Denning, *Cultural Front;* Robin D. G. Kelley, *Hammer and Hoe: Alabama Communists during the Great Depression* (Chapel Hill: University of North Carolina Press, 1990). Though not directly about the Popular Front, other works that recognize the special appeal of the CP and radicalism to black activists and cultural workers in this period include Kelley, *Race Rebels: Culture, Politics, and the Black Working Class* (New

York: Free Press, 1994), especially "'This Ain't Ethiopia, But It'll Do': African Americans and the Spanish Civil War," 123–58; Maurice Isserman, *Which Side Were You On?: The American Communist Party during the Second World War* (Middletown: Wesleyan University Press, 1982; rpt., Urbana: University of Illinois Press, 1993); George Lipsitz, *Rainbow at Midnight: Labor and Culture in the 1940s* (Urbana: University of Illinois Press, 1994); Gerald Horne, *Black and Red: W. E. B. Du Bois and the Afro-American Response to the Cold War, 1944–1963* (Albany: State University of New York Press, 1983). In general I am indebted to all of these works for their creative and meticulous readings of black-Left alliance and black revision of leftist thought and practice.

13. See Warren Susman, ed., *Culture and Commitment, 1929–1945* (New York: George Braziller, 1973); Robert Warshow, *The Immediate Experience* (New York: Doubleday and Co., 1962); Howe and Coser, *American Communist Party.*

14. Naison, *Communists,* 298.

15. Robert Bone, "Richard Wright and the Chicago Renaissance," *Callaloo* 9.3 (1986): 446–68; Carla Cappetti, *Writing Chicago: Modernism, Ethnography, and the Novel* (New York: Columbia University Press, 1993); Craig Hansen Werner, *Playing the Changes: From Afro-Modernism to the Jazz Impulse* (Urbana: University of Illinois Press, 1994). See also Robert Bone, *The Negro Novel in America* (New Haven: Yale University Press, 1958).

16. Robert Bone is primarily responsible for the term "renaissance" in application to Chicago's cultural scene during this time. It is also used, with different inflection, by Cappetti and Werner.

17. Harvey Klehr, *The Heyday of American Communism* (New York: Basic Books, 1984), 333.

18. Harry Haywood, *Black Bolshevik: Autobiography of an Afro-American Communist* (Chicago: Liberator Press, 1978), 209.

19. St. Clair Drake and Horace R. Cayton, *Black Metropolis: A Study of Negro Life in a Northern City* (Chicago: University of Chicago Press, 1993), 743.

20. Kelley, *Race Rebels,* 107.

21. Klehr, *Heyday,* 327.

22. Ibid., 343.

23. Lizabeth Cohen, *Making a New Deal: Industrial Workers in Chicago, 1919–1939* (Cambridge: Cambridge University Press, 1990), 263.

24. Ibid., 266.

25. Ibid., 262; Klehr, *Heyday,* 331.

26. Cohen, *Making a New Deal,* 261.

27. Ibid., 262.

28. Harold Lasswell and Dorothy Blumenstock, *World Revolutionary Propaganda: A Chicago Study* (New York: Knopf, 1939), 77.

29. Klehr, *Heyday,* 336.

30. Drake and Cayton, *Black Metropolis,* 736.

31. Kelley, *Hammer and Hoe,* 137. See especially chapter 6, "The Road to Legality: The Popular Front in Birmingham, 1935–1937," 119–37, and chapter 9, "The Popular Front in Rural Alabama," 159–95.

32. Drake and Cayton, *Black Metropolis,* 8.

33. Klehr, *Heyday,* 346.

34. Drake and Cayton, *Black Metropolis,* 507, 522.

35. Ford, *Democratic Front*, 75; Klehr, *Heyday*, 346.

36. See, e.g., Robert Bone, "Richard Wright and the Chicago Renaissance"; see also "God's Country: The Negro Comes to Illinois," both in Writers' Program of the Works Projects Administration, Vivian C. Harsh Collection, Carter Woodson Library; Douglas Wixson, *Worker-Writer in America: Jack Conroy and the Tradition of Midwestern Literary Radicalism, 1898–1990* (Urbana: University of Illinois Press, 1994).

37. Frank Marshall Davis, *Livin' the Blues: Memoirs of a Black Journalist and Poet* (Madison: University of Wisconsin Press, 1992), 279.

38. Ibid., 281.

39. This notion can be traced to Howe and Coser's *American Communist Party,* where the authors decry Popular Front art as a dumbing down of "proletarian" vanguard aesthetics, an end to high modernism, and a general cheapening of American mass culture. The argument is made elsewhere with variations by Walter Rideout, Susman, and Warshow. Prior to this study, Michael Denning's *The Cultural Front* made the most ambitious and broadscale retort to this claim. Denning argues in part, as I do, that artists of color—what he calls "ethnic" artists—engaged in political and aesthetic experiment inspired by Popular Front inclusivity that undermined critical clichés or generalizations about what "popular front" art was.

40. Drake and Cayton, *Black Metropolis,* 434.

41. Ibid., 215, 219.

42. Ibid., 701.

43. Ibid., 387–89.

44. Ibid., 518.

45. Davis, *Livin' the Blues,* 182.

46. See Robert A. Hill, ed., *The FBI's RACON: Racial Conditions in the United States during World War II* (Boston: Northeastern University Press, 1995); Patrick S. Washburn, *A Question of Sedition: The Federal Government's Investigation of the Black Press during World War II* (New York: Oxford University Press, 1986).

CHAPTER 1: CHICAGO AND THE POLITICS OF REPUTATION

1. Richard Wright, *American Hunger* (New York: Harper and Row, 1977), 133.

2. St. Clair Drake and Horace R. Cayton, *Black Metropolis: A Study of Negro Life in a Northern City* (Chicago: University of Chicago Press, 1993), 737.

3. See in particular Irving Howe and Lewis Coser, *The American Communist Party: A Critical History, 1919–1957* (Boston: Beacon Press, 1957); Harold Cruse, *The Crisis of the Negro Intellectual* (New York: William Morrow, 1967); Wilson Record, *The Negro and the Communist Party* (Chapel Hill: University of North Carolina Press, 1951).

4. Drake and Cayton, *Black Metropolis,* 739.

5. Craig Hansen Werner, *Playing the Changes: From Afro-Modernism to the Jazz Impulse* (Urbana: University of Illinois Press, 1994), 187.

6. Ibid.

7. Robert Bone, "Richard Wright and the Chicago Renaissance," *Callaloo* 9.3 (1986): 446–68; *The Negro Novel in America* (New Haven: Yale University Press, 1958), 156.

8. Carla Cappetti, *Writing Chicago: Modernism, Ethnography, and the Novel* (New York: Columbia University Press, 1993); Margaret Walker, "Richard Wright," in *How I Wrote*

Jubilee *and Other Essays on Life and Literature* (New York: Feminist Press, 1990), 33–49, and *Richard Wright: Daemonic Genius* (New York: Warner, 1988).

9. Addison Gayle, *Richard Wright: Ordeal of a Native Son* (New York: Anchor Press/ Doubleday, 1980), 97.

10. Ibid., 167.

11. Michel Fabre, *The Unfinished Quest of Richard Wright*, 2d ed. (Urbana: University of Illinois Press, 1993), 137.

12. Ibid.

13. Gayle, *Richard Wright*, 161.

14. Bone, "Renaissance," 449.

15. Bone, *Negro Novel*, 156.

16. Ibid.

17. Barbara Foley, "The Politics of Poetics: Ideology and Narrative Form in *An American Tragedy* and *Native Son*," in *Narrative Poetics: Innovations, Limits, Challenges*, ed. James Phelan (Columbus: Ohio State University Press, 1987), 63.

18. "Call for an American Writers' Congress," *New Masses* 14.4 (Jan. 22, 1935): 20.

19. Wright, *American Hunger*, 113.

20. Ibid., 114.

21. Ibid.

22. Ibid., 115.

23. Ibid.

24. Richard Wright, "Blueprint for Negro Writing," in *Within the Circle: An Anthology of African American Literary Criticism from the Harlem Renaissance to the Present*, ed. Angelyn Mitchell (Durham: Duke University Press, 1994), 98.

25. Ibid., 99.

26. Ibid., 106.

27. Wright had attended its first meeting in February 1936 in Chicago, and his favorable report on the congress meeting, entitled "Two Million Black Voices," appeared in the February 1936 *New Masses*. See Richard Wright, "Two Million Black Voices," *New Masses* 18.9 (Feb. 25, 1936): 15.

28. Drake and Cayton, *Black Metropolis*, 738.

29. Ibid.

30. Ibid.

31. "White Fog," *Time* 31 (Mar. 28, 1938): 63–64, reprinted in *Richard Wright: The Critical Reception*, ed. John M. Reilly (New York: Burt Franklin and Co., 1978), 4.

32. Granville Hicks, "Richard Wright's Prize Novel," *New Masses* 27 (Mar. 29, 1938): 23, reprinted in Reilly, ed., *Richard Wright*, 7.

33. Zora Neale Hurston, "Stories of Conflict," *Saturday Review of Literature* 17 (Apr. 2, 1938): 32, reprinted in Reilly, ed., *Richard Wright*, 9.

34. Ibid., 10.

35. See Drake and Cayton, *Black Metropolis*, 392, 394–95, 751.

36. *Chicago Defender*, Mar. 30, 1940, 6.

37. See, e.g., Ross Pudaloff, "Celebrity as Identity: Richard Wright, *Native Son*, and Mass Culture," *Studies in American Fiction* 11 (1983): 3–18.

38. Reilly, ed., *Richard Wright*, xiv.

39. "Bad Nigger," *Time*, Mar. 4, 1940, 72.

40. C. L. R. James, "Native Son and Revolution: A Review of *Native Son* by Richard Wright," in *C. L. R. James and Revolutionary Marxism: Selected Writings of C. L. R. James, 1939–1949*, ed. Scott McLemee and Paul LeBlanc (Ashland Heights, N.J.: Humanities Press, 1994), 88.

41. *Chicago Defender*, May 25, 1940, 7.

42. Ibid., June 15, 1940, 9.

43. Ibid., Apr. 6, 1940, 1.

44. Ibid., Apr. 27, 1940, 1.

45. Drake and Cayton, *Black Metropolis*, 415.

46. See, e.g., Lucius Harper, "Every Black Man a Communist, But Doesn't Know It," *Chicago Defender*, May 4, 1940, 1. Harper's column was indicative of other moments of muted support for the CP in the *Defender* during the war. For example, the July 12, 1941, "National Grapevine" column addressed to "Comrades" reported that "The Communists, in spite of the hell they are catching, are, according to Organizer Pat Toohey, concerned because their work among the Negro masses is 'sagging.'" The column reported on joint efforts of the party and blacks against defense discrimination, and gave a plug for a Communist camp in upper New York state. It also praised the *Daily Worker* for constantly berating "publications, industrialists and everybody and thing contributing to defense employment race discrimination" (15).

47. As quoted in Fabre, *Unfinished Quest*, 259.

48. *Chicago Defender*, Nov. 15, 1941, 12.

49. Ibid., Sept. 25, 1943, 11.

50. Ibid., Sept. 6, 1941, 14.

51. Ibid.

52. Ben Burns, "Off the Book Shelf," *Chicago Defender*, Sept. 30, 1944.

53. As quoted in Fabre, *Unfinished Quest*, 325.

54. Arnold Rampersad, "Chronology," *Uncle Tom's Children* (New York: HarperPerennial, 1993), 281.

55. Richard Wright, "Introduction," in St. Clair Drake and Horace R. Cayton, *Black Metropolis* (New York: Harcourt Brace and Co., 1945), xviii.

56. Cappetti, *Writing Chicago*, 210.

57. Earl Conrad, *Jim Crow America* (New York: Duell, Sloan and Pearce, 1947), 51.

58. *Chicago Defender*, Sept. 25, 1943, 17.

59. Ibid., Feb. 3, 1945.

60. Ibid., Jan. 27, 1945.

61. Ibid., Mar. 3, 1945, 15.

62. Ibid.

63. Isidor Schneider, "One Apart," *New Masses* 54 (Apr. 3, 1945): 23–24, reprinted in Reilly, ed., *Richard Wright*, 150.

64. Wright, "Introduction," xvii.

65. Cappetti, *Writing Chicago*, 209.

66. Werner, *Playing the Changes*, 243.

67. John Edgar Tidwell, "Introduction," in Frank Marshall Davis, *Livin' the Blues: Memoirs of a Black Journalist and Poet*, ed. John Edgar Tidwell (Madison: University of Wisconsin Press, 1992), xxv.

68. Davis, *Livin' the Blues*, 244.

69. Ibid., 244

70. Ibid.

71. Tidwell, "Introduction," xiv.

## CHAPTER 2: TURNING WHITE SPACE INTO BLACK SPACE

1. Roi Ottley, *The Lonely Warrior: The Life and Times of Robert S. Abbott* (Chicago: Henry Regnery, 1955), 11.

2. Martin Jackson Terrell, *A Study of the* Chicago Defender's *"Great Migration Drive"* (M.A. thesis, Ohio University, 1991), 25.

3. Ibid., 80.

4. Enoch P. Waters, *American Diary: A Personal History of the Black Press* (Chicago: Path Press, 1987), 137.

5. Terrell, Chicago Defender's *"Great Migration Drive,"* 63.

6. Ottley, *Lonely Warrior*, 141.

7. Terrell, Chicago Defender's *"Great Migration Drive,"* 60.

8. According to Horace R. Cayton and St. Clair Drake, the term "race man" referred to "any person who has a reputation as an uncompromising fighter against attempts to subordinate Negroes," but was also used "in a derogatory sense to refer to people who pay loud lip-service to 'race pride.'" Abbott much more likely drew the first meaning of the term to himself. See St. Clair Drake and Horace R. Cayton, *Black Metropolis: A Study of Negro Life in a Northern City* (Chicago: University of Chicago Press, 1993), 392, 394n.

9. Ottley, *Lonely Warrior*, 11.

10. Lee Finkle, *Forum for Protest: The Black Press during World War II* (Rutherford: Fairleigh Dickinson University Press, 1975). See also Patrick S. Washburn, *A Question of Sedition: The Federal Government's Investigation of the Black Press during World War II* (New York: Oxford University Press, 1986).

11. Finkle, *Forum for Protest*, 223.

12. Letter from John Sengstacke to Claude Barnett, Jan. 6, 1940, Claude Barnett Papers, Chicago Historical Society.

13. Terrell, Chicago Defender's *"Great Migration Drive,"* 59.

14. Linda Evans, "Claude A. Barnett and the Associated Negro Press," *Chicago History: The Magazine of the Chicago Historical Society* 12.1 (Spring 1983): 52.

15. Ibid.

16. Finkle, *Forum for Protest*, 53.

17. Gunnar Myrdal, *An American Dilemma: The Negro Problem and Modern Democracy*, vol. 2 (New York: Harper and Row, 1969), 923.

18. "Program of 1940 National Conference of Negro Publishers," Claude Barnett Papers, Chicago Historical Society.

19. Ibid.

20. Letter from Owen L. Heggs to Associated Negro Press, June 20, 1940, Claude Barnett Papers, Chicago Historical Society.

21. Myrdal, *An American Dilemma*, vol. 2, 912.

22. *Chicago Defender*, Mar. 23, 1940, 14.

23. Ibid., July 6, 1940.

24. James W. Ford, *The Negro and the Democratic Front* (New York: International Publishers, 1938). Ford's collected speeches demonstrate both the party's fluid definitions of the "democratic front" as an attempt to get "the widest section of the masses into the struggle" and the National Negro Congress's prominent role in formulating and dispersing party policy on black life in America (74).

25. Ibid., 187.

26. Waters, *American Diary,* 368.

27. Letter from Ben Burns to the author, July 1, 1996; Ben Burns, "Nitty-Gritty: A White Editor in Black Journalism," unabridged ms., Vivian C. Harsh Collection, 24. This is an unabridged manuscript version of Burns's 1996 published memoir *Nitty-Gritty: A White Editor in Black Journalism* (Jackson: University Press of Mississippi, 1996).

28. Burns, *Nitty-Gritty,* 16.

29. Ibid., 64.

30. Burns, "Race: None," 1954, ms., Vivian C. Harsh Collection, 87.

31. Letter from Ben Burns to the author, June 22, 1996.

32. Burns to the author, July 1, 1996.

33. Ibid.

34. Burns to the author, June 22, 1996.

35. Drake and Cayton, *Black Metropolis,* 737.

36. *Chicago Defender,* Mar. 21, 1942, 11.

37. Washburn, *Question of Sedition,* 8, 82.

38. *Chicago Defender,* May 23, 1942.

39. Ibid.

40. Ibid., Apr. 11, 1942.

41. Ibid., Sept. 28, 1940, 1.

42. Ibid.

43. Michael Denning, *The Cultural Front* (New York: Verso, 1997), 107, 363, 365, 381–84, 391. In general, Denning makes a persuasive case for "War of the Worlds" and most all of Welles's Mercury Theater and Hollywood film projects as emblems of the cultural politics of the Popular Front.

44. In *The Cultural Front,* Denning uses "proletarian grotesques" to describe the harrowing representations of working-class life in the Popular Front period. The term might also apply to the *Defender* illustration of its mock-blitz. Denning, *Cultural Front,* 122–23, 149–50.

45. *Chicago Defender,* Sept. 28, 1940, 1.

46. Cary Nelson, *Repression and Recovery: Modern American Poetry and the Politics of Cultural Memory* (Madison: University of Wisconsin Press, 1989), and "Poetry Chorus: Dialogic Politics in 1930s Poetry," in *Radical Revisions: Rereading 1930s Culture,* ed. Bill Mullen and Sherry Linkon (Urbana: University of Illinois Press, 1996), 29–59. Nelson's argument in both instances is that Bakhtin's model of a "dialogic" politics is represented by Left poets of the early twentieth century whose overlapping themes, techniques, subjects, and publication in small journals and newspapers helped to create a communal or "choral" moment in American poetry in which writing, reading, and political activism were simultaneously engaged.

47. *Chicago Defender,* Feb. 14, 1942, 1.

48. Ibid.

49. Ibid. Trent's poem urged readers to "Heave against that gate, San Quentin's gate! / Put your vast, united strength against it—."

50. Claude Barnett Papers, Chicago Historical Society.

51. See Christopher C. De Santis, ed., *Langston Hughes and the* Chicago Defender: *Essays on Race, Politics, and Culture, 1942–62* (Urbana: University of Illinois Press, 1995). De Santis collects many of Hughes's *Defender* columns and provides a compelling and insightful introduction. The columns reveal Hughes's persistent commitment to a radical agenda well into the 1950s.

52. Lawrence H. Schwartz, *Marxism and Culture: The CPUSA and Aesthetics in the 1930s* (Port Washington, N.Y.: Kennikat Press, 1980), 60.

53. Irving Howe and Lewis Coser, *A History of the Communist Party* (Boston: Beacon Press, 1957), 425.

54. *Chicago Defender,* July 11, 1942, 1.

55. Ibid., Aug. 1, 1942, 1.

56. Ibid.

57. Ibid., July 3, 1943.

58. Ibid., Sept. 4, 1943.

59. See Manning Marable, *Race, Reform, and Rebellion: The Second Reconstruction in Black America* (Jackson: University of Mississippi Press, 1984). Marable makes a compelling case for the disappearance of working-class and left interests from a postwar consensual black politics dominated by the black middle class and middle-class institutions like the NAACP and the Urban League.

60. *Chicago Defender,* Oct. 28, 1944, 3.

61. Ibid., Oct. 7, 1944.

62. Ibid., May 19, 1945.

63. Finkle, *Forum for Protest,* 223.

64. Washburn, *Question of Sedition,* 202.

65. Ibid., 199.

66. Ibid., 133.

67. *Chicago Defender,* Feb. 26, 1944, 1.

68. Washburn, *Question of Sedition,* 59.

69. Ibid., 8.

70. For the most complete published survey and excerpts from these documents, see Robert A. Hill, ed., *The FBI's RACON: Racial Conditions in the United States during World War II* (Boston: Northeastern University Press, 1995).

71. Washburn, *Question of Sedition,* 86.

72. Ibid., 108.

73. Burns, "Nitty-Gritty," 87. According to Burns, Mrs. Edna Abbott, Abbott's widow, was so fair-skinned that she had to claim in probate court that she was black in order to stake a claim to the newspaper after Abbott's death. Sengstacke, according to Burns, claimed Mrs. Abbott was white and should have no control over a black newspaper. Sengstacke won control of the paper.

74. *Chicago Defender,* May 26, 1945.

## Chapter 3: Artists in Uniform

1. Alain Locke, *The American Negro Exposition's Showing of the Works of Negro Artists* (catalog for the 1940 exhibition "The Art of the American Negro, 1851–1940").

2. Alain Locke, "Resume of Talk and Discussion: Alain Locke Sunday Afternoon Session: National Negro Congress," *Official Proceedings Second National Negro Congress* (Oct. 15–17, 1937).

3. Margaret Taylor Goss Burroughs, "Saga of Chicago's South Side Community Art Center (1938–1943)," in *The South Side Community Art Center 50th Anniversary, 1941–1991* (1991), 1.

4. Ibid.

5. Quoted in Patricia Hills, *Social Concern and Urban Realism: American Painting of the 1930s* (Boston: Boston University Press, 1983), 32.

6. George J. Mavigliano and Richard A. Lawson, *The Federal Art Project in Illinois, 1935–1943* (Carbondale: Southern Illinois University Press, 1990), 17.

7. Michael Denning, *The Cultural Front: The Laboring of American Culture in the Twentieth Century* (New York: Verso, 1997), 122–23, 249–50.

8. Hills, *Social Concern and Urban Realism,* 41.

9. Frank Marshall Davis, *Livin' the Blues: Memoirs of a Black Journalist and Poet,* ed. John Edgar Tidwell (Madison: University of Wisconsin Press, 1992), 265.

10. See *The South Side Community Art Center 50th Anniversary, 1941–1991,* an anniversary program published by the Art Center staff, and *South Side Community Art Center,* a study of the Art Center's history by the Commission on Chicago Landmarks, published by the Chicago Department of Planning and Development.

11. James Graff, "The South Side Community Art Center," in *The South Side Community Art Center 50th Anniversary, 1941–1991* (1991).

12. Burroughs, "Saga," 2.

13. Graff, "South Side Community Art Center."

14. See Burroughs, "Saga," 1–6; Graff, "South Side Community Art Center."

15. Burroughs, "Saga," 3.

16. Ibid.

17. *Chicago Defender,* Dec. 21, 1940, 11.

18. *Exhibition of Negro Artists of Chicago.* Exhibition catalog, Howard University Gallery of Art, Feb. 1–25, 1941.

19. Alain Locke, "Foreword," *The Negro in Art: A Pictorial Record of the Negro Artist and of the Negro Theme in Art* (Washington, D.C.: Associates in Negro Folk Education, 1940), 3.

20. Ibid., 9.

21. Ibid., 10.

22. Ibid.

23. Burroughs, "Saga," 5.

24. Ibid., 8.

25. Franklin Folsom, *Days of Anger, Days of Hope: A Memoir of the League of American Writers* (Niwot: University Press of Colorado, 1994), 75.

26. Margaret G. Burroughs, "He Will Always Be a Chicago Artist to Me," *Freedomways* 20.3 (1980): 153.

27. *Chicago Defender,* Aug. 31, 1940, 24.

28. Horace R. Cayton, *Long Old Road* (New York: Trident Press, 1965), 176.

29. Leslie King-Hammond, "Black Printmakers and the W.P.A." *Alone in a Crowd: Prints of the 1930s–40s by African-American Artists* (exhibition catalog), 13.

30. Mavigliano and Lawson, *Federal Art Project in Illinois,* 30.

31. John Walley, "Artists' Union of Chicago 1935–1943," ms., John Walley Papers, Special Collections, College of Architecture and Art, University of Illinois at Chicago, 2.

32. Mavigliano and Lawson, *Federal Art Project in Illinois,* 69.

33. Letter from Margaret Burroughs to the author, Aug. 23, 1996.

34. Gordon Parks, *A Choice of Weapons* (New York: Harper and Row, 1965), 194.

35. Ibid., 215.

36. *Chicago Defender,* June 14, 1941, 18.

37. Ibid., Nov. 1, 1941, 24.

38. Samella Lewis, *The Art of Elizabeth Catlett* (Claremont, Calif.: Hancraft Studios, 1984), 8–13.

39. Catlett's Mexico period is described in Lewis, *Art of Elizabeth Catlett,* 21–23.

40. After her Chicago visits Catlett taught at the George Washington Carver School in Harlem, a community-based school serving the poor and working class. The school was later accused of being a Communist front. See ibid., 19–20.

41. Gwendolyn Brooks, *Report from Part One* (Detroit: Broadside Press, 1972), 68.

42. Ibid., 69.

43. Cunard was a white modernist poet and Afrophile who in 1934 published *Negro,* an anthology of black writing. Her role as mediator between European modernism and black culture and black radicalism is reminiscent of Starks's role at the South Side Community Art Center.

44. Peter Pollack, "What the Art Center Can Do in '42: Director's Report," Report of Works Projects Administration District 3 for 1942, 5–6.

45. Ibid., 4.

46. *Chicago Defender,* Apr. 18, 1942.

47. William Patterson, *The Man Who Cried Genocide: An Autobiography* (New York: International Publishers, 1971), 149.

48. *Chicago Defender,* Apr. 8, 1944, 15.

49. Ibid., May 27, 1944, 3.

50. Ibid., Nov. 11, 1944, 19.

51. Letter from Margaret Burroughs to the author, n.d., 1.

52. Ibid., 3.

53. Mauson later married Sidney Bernstein. The two befriended Lorraine Hansberry in New York. They may have been two of the people who inspired Hansberry's play "The View from Sidney Brustein's Window."

54. Burroughs to the author, n.d., 8–9; *Chicago Defender,* Nov. 11, 1944, 19.

55. Burroughs to the author, n.d., 9.

56. *Chicago Defender,* Oct. 14, 1944, 5.

57. Ibid., May 12, 1945, 13.

58. Denning, *Cultural Front,* 9, 115–18, 128, 135, 159.

59. Sterling Stuckey, *Going through the Storm: The Influence of African-American Art in History* (New York: Oxford University Press, 1994), 223.

CHAPTER 4: WORKER-WRITERS IN BRONZEVILLE

1. Frank Marshall Davis, *Livin' the Blues: Memoirs of a Black Journalist and Poet,* ed. John Edgar Tidwell (Madison: University of Wisconsin Press, 1992), 241.

2. Fern Gayden, unpublished interview with Horace Cayton, Vivian C. Harsh Collection, Carter Woodson Library.

3. *Chicago Defender,* Mar. 26, 1938, 13; ibid., Apr. 2, 1938, 19.

4. The South Side Writers' Group contributed "Blueprint for Negro Writing" to *New Challenge,* a single-issue reincarnation of Dorothy West's 1934 start-up publication *Challenge* published in November 1937. Richard Wright and Marian Minus took the lead in editing, though Wright made most of the editorial decisions. The lone issue also included poetry by Frank Marshall Davis and Robert Hayden. While there is no record of Gayden's direct editorial involvement with the magazine, its example is easily viewable as a precursor to *Negro Story.* See Michel Fabre, *The Unfinished Quest of Richard Wright* (Urbana: University of Illinois Press, 1993), 145–46.

5. *Negro Story* 1.1 (Aug.–Sept. 1945): 1.

6. Ibid.

7. Patrick S. Washburn, *A Question of Sedition: The Federal Government's Investigation of the Black Press during World War II* (New York: Oxford University Press, 1986), viii, 8, 9.

8. Ibid., 130.

9. Lee Finkle, *Forum for Protest: The Black Press during World War II* (Rutherford: Fairleigh Dickinson University Press, 1975), 121.

10. Roi Ottley, *New World A-Coming: Inside Black America* (New York: Arno Press, 1968), 265.

11. Christopher C. De Santis, ed., *Langston Hughes and the* Chicago Defender: *Essays on Race, Politics, and Culture, 1942–62* (Urbana: University of Illinois Press, 1995), 7.

12. *Negro Story* 1.3 (Oct.–Nov. 1944): 55.

13. See, e.g., Jacqueline Jones, *Labor of Love, Labor of Sorrow: Black Women, Work, and the Family from Slavery to the Present* (New York: Basic Books, 1985), 232–38; Trudier Harris, *From Mammies to Militants: Domestics in Black American Literature* (Philadelphia: Temple University Press, 1982), 24.

14. *Negro Story* 1.2 (July–Aug. 1944): 59.

15. Ibid. 1.3 (Oct.–Nov. 1944): 63–64.

16. Ibid. 1.2 (July–Aug. 1944): 11.

17. Ibid. 2.1 (Aug.–Sept. 1945): 50.

18. Finkle, *Forum for Protest,* 170; Florence Murray, *The Negro Handbook, 1946–47* (New York: Current Books, 1947), 370.

19. *Negro Story* 1.4 (Dec. 1944–Jan. 1945): 59.

20. Ibid., 60.

21. Ibid., 59.

22. Ibid.

23. Ibid. 1.5 (Mar.–Apr. 1945): 60–61.

24. Ibid. 1.2 (July–Aug. 1944): 27.

25. George Lipsitz, *Rainbow at Midnight: Labor and Culture in the 1940s* (Urbana: University of Illinois Press, 1994), 33–41.

26. *Negro Story* 1.2 (July–Aug. 1944): 5–9.

27. Chester Himes, "Democracy Is for the Unafraid," in *Primer for White Folks*, ed. Bucklin Moon (Garden City, N.Y.: Doubleday, 1945), 480.

28. See Doxey Wilkerson, "Freedom—Through Victory in War and Peace," in *What the Negro Wants*, ed. Rayford W. Logan (Chapel Hill: University of North Carolina Press, 1944), 193–216. Wilkerson, who joined the Communist Party on June 15, 1943, after eight years on the faculty at Howard University, became its educational director for Maryland and the District of Columbia. In 1944, while serving as a member of the National Committee of the newly organized Communist Political Association, Wilkerson published "Freedom—Through Victory in War and Peace." The essay is important for insisting on the party's commitment to linking black civil and political rights to victory in the war effort and for echoing Communist Party Chairman Earl Browder's formulation that World War II was "A People's War for National Liberation" (see Browder, *Victory—and After* [New York: International Publishers, 1942]). The essay's insistence that the party was dedicated to wiping out "every law, custom, and habit of thought" that discriminates against blacks was a calculated response to A. Philip Randolph's claim that the CPUSA and Communist Political Association had "dropped" Negro rights from their agendas. The essay's plea that the "Negro freedom movement must forge the closest possible unity among the Negro people themselves, and between the Negro people and their natural allies in the progressive white population and the organized labor movement" (213) also complements the interracial political sensibility evinced in *Negro Story*'s coalition of progressive and radical black and white writers and labor supporters.

29. A. Philip Randolph, "March on Washington Movement Presents Program for the Negro," in *What the Negro Wants*, ed. Rayford W. Logan (Chapel Hill: University of North Carolina Press, 1944), 135.

30. Edward Braithwaite, "Introduction," in Roger Mais, *Brother Man* (London: Heinemann, 1974), 7.

31. *Negro Story* 1.2 (July–Aug. 1944): 4.

32. Ottley, *New World A-Coming*, 347; Finkle, *Forum for Protest*, 211. Finkle also notes that Adam Clayton Powell's *People's Voice* newspaper used the term "people's war."

33. *Chicago Defender*, Apr. 28, 1945, 4.

34. Earl Conrad on several occasions made this claim for the magazine's circulation; documenting its accuracy is impossible.

35. *Chicago Defender*, Feb. 24, 1945, 13.

36. *Negro Story* 2.2 (Dec. 1945–Jan. 1946): 63.

37. Ibid., 64.

38. *Chicago Defender*, July 14, 1945, 2. Browning did bring out at least one issue of *Child Play*.

39. Ibid., Aug. 11, 1945.

40. Jones, *Labor of Love*, 270.

41. Ben Burns, *Nitty-Gritty: A White Editor in Black Journalism* (Jackson: University Press of Mississippi, 1996), 32.

42. Ibid., 114.

43. Ibid., 39, 88.

44. *Negro Story* 2.2 (Dec. 1945–Jan. 1946): 62.

45. Ibid. 2.3 (Apr.–May 1946): 65.

46. Robert Bone, "Richard Wright and the Chicago Renaissance," *Callaloo* 9.3 (1986): 466.

47. Earl Conrad, *Jim Crow America* (New York: Duell, Sloan and Pearce, 1947), 59–60. Conrad had first used the coinage "blues school" in a *Chicago Defender* interview and profile of Chester Himes. See *Chicago Defender,* Dec. 22, 1945, 9.

CHAPTER 5: GENRE POLITICS/CULTURAL POLITICS

1. Carla Cappetti, *Writing Chicago: Modernism, Ethnography, and the Novel* (New York: Columbia University Press, 1993), 14.

2. Craig Hansen Werner, *Playing the Changes: From Afro-Modernism to the Jazz Impulse* (Urbana: University of Illinois Press, 1994).

3. Robert Bone, "Richard Wright and the Chicago Renaissance," *Callaloo* 9.3 (1986): 446–68.

4. Cary Nelson, "Poetry Chorus: Dialogic Politics in 1930s Poetry," in *Radical Revisions: Rereading 1930s Culture,* ed. Bill Mullen and Sherry Linkon (Urbana: University of Illinois Press, 1996), 31–33; see also Cary Nelson, *Repression and Recovery: Modern American Poetry and the Politics of Cultural Memory, 1910–1945* (Madison: University of Wisconsin Press, 1989).

5. Nelson, "Poetry Chorus," 39.

6. Ibid.

7. Ibid.

8. For a brief history of the short story's role in the history of black women's writing, see Bill Mullen, "Introduction," *Revolutionary Tales: African-American Women's Short Stories from the First Story to the Present,* ed. Bill Mullen (New York: Dell/Laurel, 1995), xxi–xxxi.

9. Bonner moved to Chicago in 1930. Between 1930 and 1941 she wrote many stories about the imaginary mixed ethnic Chicago neighborhood Frye Street, including "Corner Store" and "A Possible Triad on Black Notes." As Joyce Flynn notes, the stories do "not present the middle-class element of black Chicago as a source of hope for the black working class." See Joyce Flynn, "Introduction," *Frye Street and Environs: The Collected Works of Marita Bonner,* ed. Joyce Flynn and Joyce Occomy Stricklin (Boston: Beacon Press, 1987), xi–xxvii.

10. Nick Aaron Ford and H. L. Faggett, "Introduction," *Best Short Stories by Afro-American Writers, 1925–1950* (Boston: Meador Publishing Co., 1950; rpt., Kraus Reprint Co., 1969), 10–11.

11. Ibid., 6.

12. Hans Ostrom, *Langston Hughes: A Study of the Short Fiction* (New York: Twayne Publishers, 1993), 5.

13. Ibid., 6.

14. Arnold Rampersad as quoted in ibid. See Arnold Rampersad, *The Life of Langston Hughes,* vol. 1: *1902–1941* (New York: Oxford University Press, 1986), 269.

15. Michael Denning, *The Cultural Front: The Laboring of American Culture in the Twentieth Century* (London: Verso, 1996), 218.

16. Hughes was pictured with Reynolds in the May 25, 1940, *Chicago Defender* under the heading "2 Noted Writers Together." The caption claimed that Hughes, while in town

"gathering material for a story about Chicago," had "praised Reynolds for his fine work" (5). The item was meant to commemorate Reynolds's fifty-second consecutive story in the *Defender.*

17. Denning, *Cultural Front,* 218. Hughes's "Simple" sketches ran in the newspaper from 1943 until 1965.

18. Edward J. O'Brien, "Introduction," *Best American Short Stories, 1938* (Boston: Houghton Mifflin, 1938), xii.

19. Ibid., xiii, xiv.

20. Two exceptions to this, both collected in *Best American Short Stories, 1934,* were Langston Hughes's "Cora Unashamed," originally published in the *American Mercury,* and Rudolph Fisher's "Miss Cynthie," originally published in *Story.*

21. Elma Godchaux, "Wild Nigger," *Best American Short Stories, 1935, and the Yearbook of the American Short Story,* ed. Edward J. O'Brien (Boston: Houghton Mifflin, 1935), 168.

22. Richard Paulett Creyke, "Niggers Are Such Liars," in *Best American Short Stories, 1938,* ed. Edward J. O'Brien (Boston: Houghton Mifflin, 1938), 48.

23. Eric Lott, *Love and Theft: Blackface Minstrelsy and the American Working Class* (New York: Oxford University Press, 1993), 15–37.

24. David L. Cohn, "Black Troubadour," *The Best American Short Stories, 1939,* ed. Edward J. O'Brien (Boston: Houghton Mifflin, 1939), 61.

25. *Negro Story* 1.2 (July–Aug. 1944): 1.

26. The short story's role in the creation of a proletarian literature of the 1930s was perhaps first noted by Arnold Shukotoff in "Proletarian Short Stories," *New Masses* 30.2 (Jan. 3, 1939): 28. The essay notes the success in the genre of Albert Maltz, Richard Wright, and Pietro di Donato, occasioned in part by Maltz's winning first prize for "The Happiest Man on Earth" in the 1938 O. Henry Memorial Award competition. See Lawrence Schwartz, *Marxism and Culture: The CPUSA and Aesthetics in the 1930s* (Port Washington, N.Y.: Kennikat Press, 1980), 89. Michael Denning also notes the importance of short stories in 1930s Left "mushroom mags," in *Cultural Front,* 216–21.

27. Walter Rideout, *The Radical Novel in the United States* (New York: Hill and Wang, 1956), 288.

28. Jerome Klinkowitz, "Introduction," *The Diaries of Willard Motley,* ed. Jerome Klinkowitz (Ames: Iowa State University Press, 1979), xv.

29. Ibid.

30. Robert E. Fleming, *Willard Motley* (Boston: Twayne Publishers, 1978), 18.

31. Klinkowitz, *Diaries,* xvii.

32. Fleming, *Willard Motley,* 20–21.

33. Ibid., 24.

34. Ibid., 22, 24.

35. Ibid., 26.

36. Ibid.

37. Meridel Le Sueur, "The Fetish of Being Outside," in *Writing Red: An Anthology of American Women Writers, 1930–1940,* ed. Charlotte Nekola and Paula Rabinowitz (New York: Feminist Press, 1987), 299–303.

38. Fleming, *Willard Motley,* 29.

39. Ibid., 31. Douglas Wixson reports in his biography of Conroy that the latter accepted Motley's story but that *New Anvil* "ceased publication before it could appear." Conroy

did consider Motley a talent and a friend, making suggestions for revisions on *Knock on Any Door.* Yet Motley's work was often a target of ridicule by other Chicago writers. For example, Nelson Algren, after reading a manuscript of Motley's "Let Noon Be Fair," written in the 1950s, remarked that Motley had "moved backward since *Knock on Any Door,* 'from the derivative to the imitative.'" See Douglas Wixson, *Worker-Writer in America: Jack Conroy and the Tradition of Midwestern Literary Radicalism, 1898–1990* (Urbana: University of Illinois Press, 1994), 451, 477.

40. Philip Oakes, "The Man Who Goes Too Fast," in *Conversations with Chester Himes,* ed. Michel Fabre and Robert E. Skinner (Jackson: University Press of Mississippi, 1995), 20; originally published in *The Sunday Times Magazine,* Nov. 9, 1969, 69, 71.

41. Earl Conrad, "Blues School of Literature," *Chicago Defender,* Dec. 22, 1945, 9.

42. Ibid.

43. Chester Himes, *The Quality of Hurt: The Autobiography of Chester Himes,* vol. 1 (New York: Doubleday and Co., 1972), 72.

44. Ibid., 73–74.

45. Chester Himes, *Black on Black; Baby Sister and Selected Writings* (Garden City, N.Y.: Doubleday, 1973), 230.

46. Ibid., 231.

47. Ibid.

48. Ibid., 223.

49. See "Warning to Zoot Suiters (An Editorial)," *Chicago Defender,* June 12, 1943, 1; "Zoot Suit Disorders Sweep across Nation," ibid., June 19, 1943, 15. *The Defender* had, at best, mixed reactions to the riots, noting that while beatings of black zoot-suiters were unjustified, a "minority" of wearers were giving the race a "bad name" and urging them to "put the zoot suits in moth balls . . . at least for the duration" (ibid., 1).

50. *Negro Story* 2.1 (Aug.–Sept. 1945): 4.

51. Ibid.

52. Ibid.

53. Himes, *Quality of Hurt,* 75.

54. Ibid.

55. *Negro Story* 1.6 (May–June 1945): 3–9.

56. Barbara Foley, "The Rhetoric of Anticommunism in *Invisible Man,*" *College English* 59.5 (Sept. 1997): 26–43. Though anything but a party-liner during the Popular Front, Ellison, Foley notes, praised the John Reed Clubs and the League of American Writers for enabling the "revolution" in black writing during the 1930s in his essay "Recent Negro Fiction," published in *New Masses* 40 (Aug. 5, 1941): 12–13. Foley's essay argues that Ellison kept his disagreements with the CPUSA under wraps until the postwar period and especially publication of *Invisible Man,* with its scathing allegorical portrayal of the Communist Party as "The Brotherhood."

57. Frank Marshall Davis, *Livin' the Blues: Memoirs of a Black Journalist and Poet* (Madison: University of Wisconsin Press, 1992); Wixson, *Worker-Writer in America,* 138, 441, 446. Conroy had published Yerby's short story "The Thunder of God" in an early issue of *New Anvil.*

58. Frank Yerby, "The Health Card," *Harper's* 188.1128 (May 1944): 553.

59. Ben Burns, *Chicago Defender,* Sept. 30, 1944.

60. H. J. Kaplan, "The Mohammedans," in *Best American Short Stories of 1944,* ed. Martha Foley (Boston: Houghton Mifflin, 1944), 189.

61. Burns, *Chicago Defender*, Sept. 30, 1944.

62. Ibid., July 1, 1944.

63. *The Negro Handbook, 1946–1947*, ed. Florence Murray (New York: Current Books, 1947), 258.

CHAPTER 6: ENGENDERING THE CULTURAL FRONT

1. Darlene Clark Hine, *HineSight: Black Women and the Re-Construction of American History* (Brooklyn: Carlson Publishing Co., 1994), 97, 94.

2. St. Clair Drake and Horace R. Cayton, *Black Metropolis: A Study of Negro Life in a Northern City* (Chicago: University of Chicago Press, 1993), 389, 662.

3. Ibid., 389, 658–63.

4. Hine, *HineSight*, 97, 98; Drake and Cayton, *Black Metropolis*, 389.

5. *Chicago Defender*, May 29, 1943, 23. The *Aframerican Woman's Journal* reported on women, information on family planning, "plans for world peace," and black women's role in "art, professions, government, defense plants, unions and the home front."

6. Robert Bone, "Richard Wright and the Chicago Renaissance," *Callaloo* 9.3 (1986): 446–68. Bone makes passing reference to Brooks's poetry and connections to *Negro Story* magazine, yet none to her politics in his essay. Craig Hansen Werner, in *Playing the Changes: From Afro-Modernism to the Jazz Impulse* (Urbana: University of Illinois Press, 1994), devotes a chapter to Brooks's appropriations of black blues aesthetic but again gives no attention to her politics during this period. Much of the other Brooks criticism, including that by George Kent, "Portrait, in Part, of the Artist as a Young Girl and Apprentice Writer," *Callaloo* 2.3 (Oct. 1979): 74–83, and Harry B. Shaw, *Gwendolyn Brooks* (Boston: G. K. Hall, 1980), acknowledges Brooks's Left cultural milieu but ascribes nonpolitical motives to her work. Shaw, for example, writes that "During the 1940s and 1950s she believed innocently in the basic goodness of man and of Christianity, that integration was the solution to the black man's [*sic*] problems, and that whites would eventually stop discriminating against blacks" (31). In contrast, Ann Folwell Stanford's "Dialectics of Desire: War and the Resistive Voice in Gwendolyn Brooks's 'Negro Hero' and 'Gay Chaps at the Bar,'" *African-American Review* 26.2 (Summer 1992): 197–211, and James Smethurst's chapter on Brooks in "The New Red Negro: African American Poetry of the 1930s and 1940s" (Ph.D. diss., Harvard University) attempt to relocate Brooks as a figure much influenced by the Left cultural and political milieu of the Popular Front and Negro People's Front.

7. Gwendolyn Brooks, *Report from Part One* (Detroit: Broadside Press, 1972), 38.

8. Ibid.

9. Gwendolyn Brooks, *Maud Martha* (New York: AMS Press, 1953), 77.

10. Ibid., 56.

11. In *Report from Part One*, Brooks excludes, for example, any reference to her participation in the League of American Writers. Similarly, in an undated response to a letter from the author, Brooks rejects Margaret Burroughs's claim that the two took part as early as 1933 in anti-lynching marches, claiming she first met Burroughs in 1937 when she joined the NAACP Youth Council. In the same response Brooks also discounts the influence of Leftists and fellow travelers in her milieu on her first book of poems, though writing that politics "mattered immensely" during this period in her life. Ambiguities like these have

led to the accusations by critics like Shaw that Brooks was politically "naive" or conservative during this period, a notion her personal history and her own writings at the very least complicate.

12. Maria K. Mootry, "'The Step of Iron Feet': Creative Practice in the War Sonnets of Melvin B. Tolson and Gwendolyn Brooks," *Obsidian II* 2.3 (1987): 81.

13. Barbara Johnson, *A World of Difference* (Baltimore: Johns Hopkins University Press, 1987), 191.

14. Gwendolyn Brooks, *Blacks* (Chicago: Third World Press, 1994), 19.

15. Ibid., 20.

16. Margaret Walker, *This Is My Century: New and Collected Poems* (Athens: University of Georgia Press, 1989), 7.

17. Brooks, *Blacks,* 26.

18. Ibid., 34.

19. Ibid., 24.

20. Ibid., 45.

21. See Drake and Cayton, *Black Metropolis,* 456; see also their table 19, "The Ten Most Numerous Types of Negro-Owned Businesses in Chicago: 1938," 438.

22. Brooks, *Blacks,* 23.

23. Ibid., 29.

24. James Smethurst, "The New Red Negro: African American Poetry of the 1930s and 1940s," Ph.D. diss., Harvard University, 7. Smethurst's is a brilliant interpretation of the role and influence of mass culture in Brooks's work and its relationship to poetic "form" in the African-American tradition.

25. Michel Fabre, ed. *Richard Wright: Books and Writers* (Jackson: University Press of Mississippi, 1990), 186.

26. Brooks, *Blacks,* 42–47.

27. Karl Marx and Frederick Engels, *The Marx-Engels Reader,* ed. Robert C. Tucker (New York: Norton, 1978), 475–76.

28. Smethurst, throughout his chapter on Brooks, stresses her attention to mass cultural markers and connects her to Wright via this theme.

29. Richard Wright, *Native Son* (New York: HarperCollins, 1993), 153.

30. Ibid., 520.

31. Stanford, "Dialectics of Desire," 197–211.

32. For more on the condition of black women workers, particularly domestics, during World War II, see Jacqueline Jones, *Labor of Love, Labor of Sorrow: Black Women, Work, and the Family from Slavery to the Present* (New York: Basic Books, 1985), 232–60; Karen Tucker Anderson, "Last Hired, First Fired: Black Women Workers during World War II," *Journal of American History* 69.1 (June 1982): 82–97. Margaret Burroughs's "A Negro Mother Looks at War," published in the 1941 *Defender* and discussed earlier, was a black woman's revision of an earlier Left line on the "double burden" of black women. With the outbreak of war, as Burroughs's article noted, black women's work and economic position shifted in potentially destructive ways: many became single mothers owing to enlistment and the draft; many others were preliminarily hired into industry at low-paid and unskilled positions, where they faced frequent harassment and marginalization by both white males and white females hired above them. In addition, while wartime industrialization allowed many black women to escape domestic servitude and laundress work

for the first time, many others were forced into these same positions when white women abandoned them for industrial work.

These traumas resulted in a variety of conflicting and decidedly short-term alterations in black women's labor and economic status. For example, during wartime, as Jacqueline Jones has noted, black women working as "kitchen mechanics" found they could command a higher wage from white housewives in regions like Baltimore and Chicago, where alternative forms of employment (steel, packing, social work, teaching) kept the supply of domestics low (237). "The Whip Changes Hands" reported one Baltimore newspaper in response to this phenomenon. In the South, rumors of "Eleanor Clubs" (named for the progressive first lady) were reported wherein black women were said to be colluding to withhold their labor from the job market in order to demand unprecedented wage concessions. Yet by 1944 and 1945, the black press and women's groups were also already documenting the emerging postwar trend of black women as "last hired, first fired" and the concomitant return of black women to domestic, unskilled, nonunion labor or domesticity after the war.

For a consideration of the treatment of the black domestic in American literature, see Trudier Harris, *From Mammies to Militants: Domestics in Black American Literature* (Philadelphia: Temple University Press, 1982).

33. Brooks, *Blacks,* 51.

34. As Smethurst notes, Brooks may have been influenced by Hughes's poems, or his by hers. George Kent reports that Hughes may have heard Brooks read the "Hattie Scott" poems, which Brooks wrote for Inez Cunningham Stark's poetry workshop at the South Side Community Art Center (George Kent, *A Life of Gwendolyn Brooks* [Lexington: University Press of Kentucky, 1994], 59–60). Hughes's "Madam, To You" poems were written in 1942 and began publication in 1943. See Smethurst, "New Red Negro."

35. Brooks, *Blacks,* 52.

36. Ibid.

37. Ibid., 54.

38. See, e.g., Richard Wright, "Blueprint for Negro Writing," in *Within the Circle: An Anthology of African American Literary Criticism from the Harlem Renaissance to the Present,* ed. Angelyn Mitchell (Durham: Duke University Press, 1994), 97–106, and Wright's introduction to *Black Metropolis: A Study of Negro Life in a Northern City,* ed. St. Clair Drake and Horace R. Cayton (New York: Harcourt Brace and Co., 1945), xvii–xxxiv. See all of Brown's early poems and collections of poems, especially *Southern Road* and "Ma Rainey" in, among other places, *The Jazz Poetry Anthology,* ed. Sascha Feinstein and Yusef Komunyakaa (Bloomington: Indiana University Press, 1991), 24–25.

39. Brooks, *Blacks,* 56.

40. Ibid., 57.

41. Ibid., 58.

42. Ibid.

43. Ibid.

44. Ibid., 58–59.

45. See, e.g., Langston Hughes's one-act play *Scottsboro Limited* and Countee Cullen, "Scottsboro, Too, Is Worth Its Song."

46. Wright, *Native Son,* 532.

47. See, e.g., Sherley Anne Williams, "Papa Dick and Sister-Woman: Reflections on

Women in the Fiction of Richard Wright," in *American Novelists Revisited: Essays in Feminist Criticism* (Boston: G. K. Hall, 1982), 394–415. Though she doesn't address *Native Son* explicitly, Williams's examination of women in *Uncle Tom's Children* and *Black Boy* provides a critical context for Bigger's relationship to both black and white women in that novel. See also Maria K. Mootry, "Bitches, Whores, and Woman Haters: Archetypes and Typologies in the Art of Richard Wright," in *Richard Wright: A Collection of Critical Essays,* ed. Richard Macksey and Frank E. Moorers (Englewood Cliffs, N.J.: Prentice-Hall, 1984), 117–27.

48. Brooks, *Blacks,* 60.

49. Ibid., 61.

50. Ibid., 60.

51. Ibid., 62.

52. Ibid.

53. Ibid., 61.

54. Ibid., 73.

55. Ibid., 49.

56. See William J. Maxwell, "The Proletarian as New Negro: Mike Gold's Harlem Renaissance," in *Radical Revisions: Rereading 1930s Culture,* ed. Bill Mullen and Sherry Linkon (Urbana: University of Illinois Press, 1996), 91–119; see also James A. Miller, "African-American Writing of the 1930s: A Prologue," in *Radical Revisions,* 78–90.

57. Stanford, "Dialectics," 202–3.

58. Brooks, *Blacks,* 66.

59. Ibid., 207.

60. Brooks, *Blacks,* 75.

61. Stanford, "Dialectics," 205.

62. *Chicago Defender,* Sept. 15, 1945, 3.

63. Ibid., Dec. 29, 1945, 13.

## CHAPTER 7: AMERICAN DAUGHTERS, FIFTH COLUMNS, AND LONELY CRUSADES

1. See especially Harold Cruse, *The Crisis of the Negro Intellectual* (New York: Morrow, 1967), and Wilson Record, *Race and Radicalism: The NAACP and the Communist Party in Conflict* (Ithaca: Cornell University Press, 1964).

2. Manning Marable, *Race, Reform, and Rebellion: The Second Reconstruction in Black America, 1945–1982* (Jackson: University Press of Mississippi, 1984), 18.

3. Ibid., 27.

4. Ibid., 33.

5. Ibid., 29.

6. *Chicago Defender,* Aug. 18, 1945, 5.

7. Ibid., Sept. 28, 1946.

8. Ibid.

9. Ibid., Oct. 12, 1946.

10. Gwendolyn Brooks, *Blacks* (Chicago: Third World Press, 1994), 129.

11. Michel Fabre, *From Harlem to Paris: Black American Writers in France, 1840–1980* (Urbana: University of Illinois Press, 1991), 176.

12. Ibid.

13. Ibid., 187.

14. Ibid., 178.

15. Ibid., 182.

16. Ben Burns, *Nitty-Gritty: A White Editor in Black Journalism* (Jackson: University Press of Mississippi, 1996), 34.

17. Ibid., 88.

18. Ibid., 123.

19. Ibid., 169.

20. Ibid., 170.

21. Ibid.

22. Ibid., 170–77.

23. Quoted in Fabre, *From Harlem to Paris,* 187. See Ben Burns, "They're Not Uncle Tom's Children," *Reporter,* Mar. 8, 1956, 22. The remarks appeared in Burns's "Cafe Society" column for the periodical.

24. See, e.g., Alan Wald, "The 1930s Left in U.S. Literature Reconsidered," in *Radical Revisions: Rereading 1930s Culture,* ed. Bill Mullen and Sherry Linkon (Urbana: University of Illinois Press, 1996), 13–28.

25. Burns, *Nitty-Gritty,* 190.

26. Ibid., 217.

27. *The Defender* began reporting on black layoffs as early as 1943 and editorialized militantly for the permanent establishment of the Fair Employment Practices Commission to prevent postwar discrimination. During the war, black union membership, particularly in the CIO, rose precipitously, as did black worker self-activity in industries like the automotive. The beginnings of black labor solidarity combined with postwar layoffs contributed to white "hate strikes" against black workers during the war and to the upsurge of interracial wildcat strikes in the immediate postwar period. See George Lipsitz, *Rainbow at Midnight: Labor and Culture in the 1940s* (Urbana: University of Illinois Press, 1994), 69–95; Richard Dalfiume "The 'Forgotten Years' of the Negro Revolution," in *The Negro in Depression and War,* ed. Bernard Sternsher (Chicago: Quadrangle Books, 1969), 298–316; Joe William Trotter Jr., *Black Milwaukee: The Making of an Industrial Proletariat, 1915–45* (Urbana: University of Illinois Press, 1985); Robin D. G. Kelley, *Race Rebels: Culture, Politics, and the Black Working Class* (New York: Free Press, 1994), especially "The Riddle of the Zoot: Malcolm Little and Black Cultural Politics during World War II," 161–82; Karen Tucker Anderson, "Last Hired, First Fired: Black Women Workers during World War II," *Journal of American History* 69.1 (June 1982): 82–97; Jacqueline Jones, *Labor of Love, Labor of Sorrow: Black Women, Work, and the Family from Slavery to the Present* (New York: Basic Books, 1985), especially "The Roots of Two Revolutions, 1940–1955," 232–60; Harry Haywood, *Black Bolshevik: Autobiography of an Afro-American Communist* (Chicago: Liberator Press, 1978), 516–98; Marable, *Race, Reform, and Rebellion;* Michael Denning, *The Cultural Front: The Laboring of American Culture in the Twentieth Century* (London: Verso, 1996), especially "The Age of the CIO," 21–37. See also Charles Denby, *Indignant Heart: A Black Worker's Journal* (Detroit: Wayne State University Press, 1978), 69–179. Denby's experiences with the CP and CIO make interesting companion readings to Himes's fictional accounts of Los Angeles industry in *If He Hollers Let Him Go* and *Lonely Crusade.* Finally, for insights on labor and the CP's postwar role in labor and race prob-

lems in the labor movement see all of the above, especially Marable, and Lipsitz, *Rainbow at Midnight*, 335–47.

28. Chester Himes, *The Quality of Hurt: The Autobiography of Chester Himes*, vol. 1 (New York: Doubleday and Co., 1972), 93.

29. Ibid., 100.

30. Ibid.

31. Ibid.

32. Quoted in Robert E. Fleming, *Willard Motley* (Boston: Twayne Publishers, 1978), 65.

33. Jerome Klinkowitz, ed., *The Diaries of Willard Motley* (Ames: Iowa State University Press, 1979), xix.

34. Fleming, *Willard Motley*, 65.

35. Himes, *Quality of Hurt*, 103.

36. See Chester Himes, *My Life of Absurdity: The Autobiography of Chester Himes*, vol. 2 (New York: Thunder's Mouth Press, 1976); Michel Fabre, *The Unfinished Quest of Richard Wright* (Urbana: University of Illinois Press, 1993); Michel Fabre, *From Harlem to Paris*.

37. I take the phrase from Michel Fabre. See "Chester Himes' Ambivalent Triumph," *From Harlem to Paris*. Himes remained an admirer of Wright for helping to make the commercial success of black literature possible, though petty jealousies and real conflicts about their literary roles in Paris helped to sever their friendship after 1957. See Himes, *My Life of Absurdity*, 158, 214, 217.

38. Frank Marshall Davis, *Livin' the Blues: Memoirs of a Black Journalist and Poet* (Madison: University of Wisconsin Press, 1992), 262.

39. Ibid., 282.

40. Ibid.

41. Ibid.

42. In *Livin' the Blues*, Davis writes: "I looked upon Claude Barnett's and my activities as complementing each other. Each of us was working in his own way for an end to white supremacy. Claude sincerely felt he could get farther by joining with those men of means willing to spend money to better our conditions without really drastic change in the establishment. I felt that together we covered both sides of the street" (283). See also Linda J. Evans, "Claude A. Barnett and the Associated Negro Press," *Chicago History* 12.1 (Spring 1983): 44–56, and Claude A. Barnett Papers, Chicago Historical Society.

43. Davis, *Livin' the Blues*, 298.

44. Davis writes of Burroughs that "her special value to me was her ability to turn me on poetically" (*Livin' the Blues*, 278).

45. Ibid., xv, xix.

46. Letter from Margaret Burroughs to the author, Aug. 23, 1996.

47. *Freedomways* 20.3 (Third Quarter 1980): 216–27.

48. Charles White, "Path of a Negro Artist," *Masses and Mainstream* 8.4 (April 1955): 36.

49. Burroughs to the author, Aug. 23, 1996.

50. "One Hundred and Fiftieth Anniversary All Souls First Universalist Church," 1986.

51. Ibid.

52. *The South Side Community Art Center 50th Anniversary, 1941–1991* (1991).

53. *Chicago Defender*, May 31, 1986, 18.

54. *The Black Writer Souvenir Book of the International Black Writers' Conference* (International Black Writers' Conference), June 1980.

55. Gwendolyn Brooks, unpublished poem provided to the author by Barbara Browning Cordell.

56. Jones, *Labor of Love*, 235.

57. See ibid., 232–60.

58. In addition to Fabre, *Unfinished Quest of Richard Wright;* Himes, *The Quality of Hurt* and *My Life of Absurdity;* and Fabre, *From Harlem to Paris;* see also William Gardner Smith, *Return to Black America* (Englewood Cliffs, N.J.: Prentice-Hall, 1970). Smith, a columnist for the *Pittsburgh Courier* and ally to the Left, also identifies McCarthyism as one reason for his own exile to Paris. See also Horace Cayton, *Long Old Road* (Seattle: University of Washington Press, 1963).

59. Horace Cayton, *Long Old Road* (rpt., New York: Trident Press, 1965), 253.

60. Ibid., 2-0.

61. Ibid., 254.

62. Ibid., 309. Cayton's first book, with George S. Mitchell, *Black Workers and the New Unions,* had been published in 1939.

63. Cayton, *Long Old Road* (1965), 342.

64. Ralph Ellison, *Invisible Man* (New York: Vintage Books, 1972), 568.

65. Cayton, *Long Old Road* (1965), 401.

66. Couch had become a target of derision after he invited fourteen black writers to contribute to the volume *What the Negro Wants,* edited by Rayford Logan and published in 1944 by the University of North Carolina Press, his prior employer. After reading the essays, which included liberal to radical statements by the likes of A. Philip Randolph and Doxey Wilkerson, Couch wrote an introduction to the volume that, à la *The Bell Curve,* raised "fate" and black natural inferiority as reasons for anti-black prejudice. When he arrived at the University of Chicago Press, the *Defender* referred to him in its coverage as an "educated Bilbo," after the notoriously racist southern politician.

67. *Chicago Defender,* Oct. 6, 1945, 4.

68. Ibid.

69. Langston Hughes, *Selected Poems of Langston Hughes* (New York: Alfred A. Knopf, 1979), 275.

70. Era Bell Thompson, *American Daughter* (Chicago: University of Chicago Press, 1946), 301.

## POSTSCRIPT

1. John Johnson with Lerone Bennett Jr., *Succeeding against the Odds* (New York: Warner Books, 1989), 192.

2. Ibid., 77.

3. St. Clair Drake and Horace R. Cayton, "Bronzeville 1961," in *Black Metropolis: A Study of Negro Life in a Northern City* (Chicago: University of Chicago Press, 1993), 793–807.

4. Manning Marable, *Race, Reform, and Rebellion: The Second Reconstruction in Black America, 1945–1982* (Jackson: University Press of Mississippi, 1984), 17.

5. Drake and Cayton, "Appendix, 1969," in *Black Metropolis,* 834–35.

6. Ibid., 835.

7. William Julius Wilson, "Foreword to the 1993 Edition," in St. Clair Drake and Horace

R. Cayton, *Black Metropolis: A Study of Negro Life in a Northern City* (Chicago: University of Chicago Press, 1993), xlix.

8. Ibid., l.

9. Ibid.

10. Ibid., li. In addition, see William Julius Wilson, *The Declining Significance of Race: Blacks and Changing American Institutions* (Chicago: University of Chicago Press, 1978). Wilson's controversial book argued that class stratification within the black community, ironically wrought by many successful liberal reforms of the 1960s, had superseded race as a dominant factor for individual achievement for most African Americans.

11. Robin D. G. Kelley, *Yo' Mama's Disfunktional!: Fighting the Culture Wars in Urban America* (Boston: Beacon Press, 1997), 117. For a biting left analysis of contemporary attempts to describe the urban ghetto, see Kelley, "Looking for the 'Real' Nigga: Social Scientists Construct the Ghetto," ibid., 15–42.

12. Johnson, *Succeeding against the Odds*, 162.

13. See the Black Metropolis Convention and Tourism Council's Web site at http://www.interman.net/bronzeville.

14. *Revolutionary Worker* 19.17 (Aug. 24, 1997): 13.

# Index

Abbott, Robert, 13, 20, 44; founding of *Chicago Defender*, 44; as symbol of racial equality, 73

*Abbott's Monthly Magazine*, 130

Abraham Lincoln Center, 100, 107

Abraham Lincoln School, 55, 73, 100, 102, 117, 121, 190

Abu-Jamal, Mumia, 205

Addams, Jane, 136

*Aframerican Woman's Journal*, 149

African Blood Brotherhood, 6

Algren, Nelson, 25, 33; *Somebody in Boots*, 66

American Artists' Congress, 65, 80

*American Daughter* (Thompson), 198–200, 201

*American Dilemma* (Myrdal), 11, 37

*American Hunger* (Wright), 26, 36, 41

American Labor Party, 53

American Negro Exposition, 75, 80

American Negro Labor Congress, 6

American Writers' Congress, 3; role of short story at 1935 meeting, 130

American Youth for Democracy, 11

anti-communism (black), 13, 17, 181–82

Art Exhibition of the Negro Exposition, 75

Art Institute of Chicago, 83

Artists' Union of Chicago, 91

Associated Negro Press, 10, 58, 120

Attaway, William, 120

Bakhtin, Mikhail, 16, 61; "dialogic" politics, 127

*Baltimore Afro-American*, 32, 50, 125

Bardner, Benjamin Franklin, 61

Barnett, Claude, 10, 19; advertising innovations, 49, 63

Barthe, Richmond, 99

Bass, Charlotta, 110; and *California Eagle*, 110

Bennett, Gwendolyn, 66, 85, 128

Benton, Thomas Hart, 90

*Best American Short Stories*, 131–33; racist tendencies, 132–33, 145

Bibb, Joseph, 6

*Birth of a Nation*, 2

*Black and White*, 130

Black Arts Movement, 180, 189

Black Belt Thesis, 7, 202

*Black Boy* (Wright), 39, 41, 121

*Black Man's Verse* (Davis), 10

*Black Metropolis*, 1, 10, 11, 20, 37, 41, 148. See also Cayton, Horace; Drake, St. Clair

Black Panther Party, 202

"Blitz Over Georgia," 58

Bone, Robert, 5; and "Chicago Renaissance," 22, 23; on *Negro Story*, 124, 126

Bonner, Marita, 128; *Frye Street Stories*, 128

Bontemps, Arna, 9, 10, 22, 75, 86, 117; *They Seek a City*, 117

Britton, Edgar, 77, 79

"Bronzeville, 1961," 181

Brooks, Gwendolyn, 10, 14, 15, 16, 17, 86, 89; *Annie Allen*, 184; and Black Arts Movement, 180; black women's work, 167–72; engendering left ideology, 166–67, 176–79; migration experiences, 150; participation in Interracial Conference on the Arts, 101; *Report from Part One*, 96, 150; revision of black blues aesthetic, 170; re-